Praise for Allan Ferguson and *Golf in Scotland*

"Allan Ferguson has paved the way . . . . Take an iron or two out of your bag and carry this book instead."—**Michael Bamberger**, *Sports Illustrated;* author of *To the Linksland*

"*Golf in Scotland* is an excellent guide to the Scottish links, their inns, and many other amenities of the Scottish game."— **Michael Murphy**, author of *Golf in the Kingdom* and *The Kingdom of Shivas Irons*

"If you're inclined to travel to . . . Scottish courses, your best guide is Allan McAllister Ferguson's *Golf in Scotland.*"—**Lorne Rubenstein**, Toronto *Globe and Mail*, author of *A Season in Dornoch*

"Laced with history and local lore as well as the nitty-gritty of modern golf travel, *Golf in Scotland* may prove an indispensable guide for the wise golf traveler."—**James Dodson**, author of *The Dewsweepers, Final Rounds*, and *A Golfer's Life*

"Valuable insider information . . . the book gives the skinny on planning a trip to the Auld Sod."—*Golf Magazine*

"The best inside track on how to do golf in Scotland." —**Michael Tobert**, author of *Pilgrims in the Rough: St. Andrews Beyond the 19th Hole*

"Two essentials for your golf holiday in Scotland—a knockdown shot into the wind and Allan Ferguson's book, *Golf in Scotland*. The best and most comprehensive guide available." —**Graeme Lennie**, *Head Professional, Crail Golf Society, Fife, Scotland*

"Allan Ferguson fulfills his guarantee of taking high cost out of Scottish golf. It's not so difficult to do it yourself and Allan comprehensively shows you how."—**Willie Wallace**, *Celtic Legend Travel, Edinburgh, Scotland*

"A must for those headed for the old country."
—**Tom Kensler**, The Denver *Post*

"Allan McAllister Ferguson won't make many friends in the tour guide industry . . . but he'll compensate for that with a big boost in popularity with the individual traveler."—**Jeff Barr**, *Golfweek*

GOLF IN SCOTLAND:

A Travel-Planning Guide

with

Profiles of 60 Great Courses

by

Allan McAllister Ferguson

www.fergusongolf.com

Ferguson Golf

Ferguson Golf, a division of WF Enterprises, Inc.
Denver • Colorado

First edition June 2001
Second printing February 2002
Second edition April 2003

Published by:

WF Enterprises, Inc.
1743 S. Marion St.
Denver CO 80210 USA
303-722-3441; 800-835-6692 (toll free in USA)
fax: 303-722-3441
Email: aferguson@fergusongolf.com
Web: http://www.fergusongolf.com

Cover photograph by Allan Ferguson
Cover design by Mike Jenson, Jenson Advertising
Graphics by Rust Graphics
Line art by Carol McKellar from photographs by Allan Ferguson
Index by Lisa Probasco
Printed on recycled paper in the USA by United Graphics, Mattoon, Illinois

ISBN 0-9710-326-1-0

Dedications, Acknowledgements, Disclaimers, and Apologies

This updated edition of *Golf in Scotland* is still dedicated to the warm and wonderful people of Scotland—especially those in the travel trade and at the golf clubs who work so hard to make visitors to Scotland feel welcome and appreciated.

Special thanks and appreciation go to Ruth Wimmer, my partner in life and business. As one among those never to have touched a pitching wedge or putter, Ruth has learned to love Scotland on her own terms. Thanks also to my father-in-law, Harold Wimmer, who reintroduced me to the life-altering possibilities of golf after my clubs had collected dust for some twenty years between adolescence and semi-responsible adult life.

Writing a book is hard work. You hope you get most of it right. Inevitably, errors of fact creep in. For these I am entirely responsible and offer an apology with a promise to correct those errors brought to my attention. Unless they're enclosed by quotation marks, all the opinions expressed in this book are mine too, and, since I'm a pretty opinionated guy, some will disagree with my assessments. That's ok. That's what makes the world go 'round. My opinions are only that and, through persuasive argument or experience, I reserve the right to change them! Stay tuned for the next edition of *Golf in Scotland*. Travel writing, by definition, is writing about a moving target.

Allan McAllister Ferguson
Denver CO USA
March 2003

TABLE OF CONTENTS

Preface to the Revised Edition, Update 2003

Since the publication of *Golf in Scotland* in 2001, I have found little reason to make wholesale changes in the essential message or organization of this book. Therefore, readers of the edition published in 2001 will find only minor changes in tone, text, and interpretation.

On the other hand, the updating is substantial and important. A critical eye has been cast upon every jot and tittle. All tour examples have been refreshed. All prices are now current to 2003 and the weakness of the dollar has been recognized in upward price adjustments to reflect £1 = $1.55 (one could make a good case for £1 = $1.60, but I'm an optimist). Web sites have been checked and updated and many new ones have been added. Several dozen lodging recommendations have been added; others have been dropped for one reason or another—usually because they are no longer in business. Other improvements include revamped maps, expanded travel tips, new bibliographic entries, and additional appendices.

Though new courses have opened in Scotland during the past two years—notably at St. Andrews Bay in Fife and Southern Gailes in Ayrshire—I have resisted the temptation to expand the Directory of Courses and have maintained my reluctance to open the subject of golf in Glasgow and Edinburgh proper. After years of working with golf tourists to Scotland, I just haven't observed enough consumer interest in the subject to warrant its inclusion here.

In short, for its currency and refinement, this is a more valuable book than its predecessor—but with the same goal as before: I want you to have a trip that is *more fun, more rewarding,* and *less expensive* than anything offered in a pre-packaged tour.

Allan McAllister Ferguson
Denver CO USA
March 2003

INTRODUCTION

This book stems from my work as a travel planner. I help people make golf trips to Scotland. Some of my clients have said something like, "Allan, you ought to put all your knowledge between the covers of a book. A lot of people would buy it." Well, I don't know if a lot of people will buy this book, but that's what I've done and here it is.

It's not that there aren't a lot of books out there about Scottish golf. There are. But no single book does what I've done here. This is not just a book about Scottish golf. It's a book about *smart traveling* and, specifically, how to plan a trip on your own and thus avoid the overpriced package tours pedaled by tour operators and commissioned travel agencies. It's a book about how to get comfortable with the idea of doing it on your own and, consequently, not only saving a lot of money, but having a superior trip as well.

Organization of the book

Planning your own golf trip to Scotland requires a certain amount of motivation. A prime motivator for most people is *MONEY*. That's why, in Part I, Chapter One, I analyze actual tours offered circa 2003 by mercifully unnamed tour operators. Here you can explore, in detail, the most important piece of information in this book: *most tour operators work on a profit margin of fifty to one hundred percent!*

In contrast, Chapter Two presents itineraries followed by some of my clients. This chapter will give you some ideas regarding routes that work and give you benchmarks for estimating the cost of your own trip. And, should you decide to use a travel operator, you'll at least know how they "operate," so that you can negotiate with them. Forearmed is forewarned in this business.

Part II is the general planning part of the book. Here I offer answers to several fundamental questions: First, "What's the best time to go?". Next, "Where should I go?". This is a critical chapter where major golf destinations in Scotland are defined and a system for building itineraries is suggested. Part II, Chapter Three is devoted to

St. Andrews and the Old Course simply because, "Everyone Wants to Go—and Why Not?". In Chapter Four, I address the four elements common to every golf trip: *air travel, ground transportation, tee times,* and *lodging.*

In Part III we come to the critical detail—the main course, if you will, or rather *sixty courses,* fully described and profiled so that any golfer can write, make a call, send a fax, or email to get a tee time. Everything you need to know is here: *addresses - phone numbers - web sites - key contacts - visitor restrictions - prices and deposit requirements.* Along with objective data, you'll find my subjective evaluations of the courses and their locales. This is where I try to answer the question, "Why should I want to play this course?". This is also where you'll find many inside tips, lodging suggestions, and nongolf ideas to make your trip to the Home of Golf something special.

Appendices include a list of useful internet sites and an annotated bibliography. Together, these can help you learn more about Scotland and Scottish golf—a rewarding journey for all who love golf and the land of its origin.

The premise of this book is simple: *Most first-time golf travelers to Scotland need a helping hand; they don't need to have their hand held.* If you picked up this book because the title intrigued you, you're already half way toward booking your trip directly and saving hundreds, even thousands, of dollars. With this book you truly can *do it yourself without doing it alone.*

Even with all the information between these covers, if you still think you'd like to engage a travel planner, you can learn more about how I work by visiting my web site *www.fergusongolf.com.* Whether through this book or in person, I want you to experience a golf trip to Scotland that is *more fun, more rewarding,* and *less expensive* than anything offered in a pre-packaged tour.

Yours for great golf (and travel) in Scotland,

Allan McAllister Ferguson
President, Ferguson Golf
Denver CO USA
March 2003

Telephone/Fax Calling Procedures

All UK telephone and fax numbers in this book are formatted like this: 01334-466-666 (main telephone number for the St. Andrews Links Trust). To call that number, do this:

From the United States: Dial 011 (international long distance), then 44 (country code), then the number in Scotland without the leading "0" (i.e., 011-44-1334-466-666).

In Scotland: Use the leading "0" and dial the rest of the number from anywhere in the country (i.e., 01334-466-666). For a local call, use only the last six digits.

Prices and Exchange Rate

All prices are current to 2003. Throughout, I have used an exchange rate of £1 = $1.55. This is a good median. In recent years, the exchange rate sometimes has been more favorable to American travelers. Sometimes it has been less favorable.

PART I

AVOID THE TOURS!

CHAPTER ONE

How Tour Operators Pick Your Pocket

I'd really like for you to read this book from cover to cover. But, in case you don't, I'm putting the most important sentence in the first paragraph of the first chapter. Here it is: *Tour operators typically mark up their "product" by fifty to one hundred percent.*

What does this mean? Simply put, it means if a pre-packaged tour is offered at $2,200, you can bet the *real cost* of that trip—the price you *could* pay—is somewhere between $1,100 and $1,600. If you are considering a luxury trip to the "Home of Golf" with a round on St. Andrews' Old Course for, say, $4,000 per person, the real cost of that trip is about $2,000 to $3,000. In other words, whatever the price, you could do the same trip yourself—with a little help from this book—for about *half to two-thirds the advertised price.*

In the St. Andrews example above, four golfers making this $4,000-per-person trip (not uncommon at all) could either do the trip themselves for a total of about $8,000 to $10,000 or they could pay a tour operator about $16,000—a savings or profit (depending upon your point of view) of $6,000 to $8,000!! I don't know about you, but that sounds like real money to me—money worth saving.

A fifty to one-hundred-percent markup wouldn't be so bad if tour operators were buying at wholesale and selling at retail the way most businesses do. But that's not what is happening. With few exceptions, tour operators are buying services at retail and re-selling them to travelers for *two times retail.* With their colorful brochures and romantic language, tour operators are good at implying that you're getting a retail package at a wholesale price. But here's the truth: (1) golf courses in Scotland don't give discounts to anyone;

3

(2) rental car agencies in Scotland don't give serious discounts to anyone; (3) only a few hotels (e.g., Turnberry) pay commissions.

The "Trip of a Lifetime" Syndrome

Every day I work with highly-educated people—teachers, business executives, CPAs, attorneys, doctors, et. al. In their professional and family lives, these are people who are knowledgeable and careful about financial matters. Thus, it never ceases to amaze me how so many of them will turn over their expensive travel decisions to a tour operator without doing the homework necessary to know whether the product they are buying is reasonably priced. Most of the time these are people who have done a considerable amount of golf travel on their own, at least in the United States. And, yet, when it comes to making a golf trip to Scotland, they somehow lose confidence and think they have to hire an "expert."

At the same time, I understand the process. I know what happens when people start considering a golf trip to Scotland. So often these are "bonding" experiences—among old friends and/or current golf partners; between father and son; between husband and wife. This is what I call the "Trip of a Lifetime" syndrome. With growing anticipation, the trip to Scotland starts to take on an aura of glamour and undue importance. You can't afford to let it fail; you can't afford to screw up the *trip of a lifetime*.

Now the search for an expert begins. You browse the internet. You go to the back of major golf magazines to find advertisements for the various companies that offer tours. Or you call your favorite travel agent who has brochures from those same companies. You send off for some brochures or use the internet to download information. Maybe you talk to a few buddies who have made a trip to Scotland.

At some point, you get around to making a decision. All the trips seem expensive. But, of course, this is your *trip of a lifetime*. It may be the one and only trip you'll ever make to the Home of Golf. So you don't want any mistakes. You've heard so many stories about how difficult it is to get on Scottish courses. You've heard the hotels and food are awful. All of sudden you feel like you need help.

I know. I've "been there, done that." The first time I went to Scotland, I used an operator. With three friends from high school days,

4

I had a great time. The agency did a good job for us. I asked for a tour a bit off the beaten path and they gave it to us. No complaints.

But here's the problem with this scenario (and every other operator-planned trip): When you get to Scotland you will see the room rates at your hotel posted in a public place. When you go to the golf course you'll see the green fees posted. And you know from previous experience the approximate cost of a rental vehicle. When you start adding up these numbers, you don't have to be a CPA to figure out who just made a very nice profit on your *trip of a lifetime*. You know what you paid (an "all-inclusive" package price). Now you know what you *could* have paid. Subtract the latter from the former and you have operator profit.

Was it worth the money? Only the buyer can answer that question. But I think most people who go through this experience end up feeling like they've been "taken to the cleaners." On that trip with my high-school friends, I fell in love with Scotland, but I did not fall in love with the game most tour operators play with the golf public.

And, what's the root of the decision-making problem? As usual, the answer is a lack of information. Even though information is available and increasingly easy to get, most people don't have the time or inclination to do the necessary research. And, even if they do, the accumulated research can be pretty confusing. Consequently, many intelligent people end up buying overpriced golf trips to Scotland. They simply give up and turn their travel decisions over to an expert.

I want to change that situation. I want to make *you* the expert. Ideally, I'd like to see you take the approach that you are going to make *two trips for the same price most people pay for one trip*. I guarantee, when you adopt that attitude, you'll feel the pressure coming off. You'll no longer feel like you have to "do it all" in one trip. All those rota courses may not seem quite so important. And the Old Course may even assume its proper perspective—one of many great courses to be played on more than one trip.

Getting There is Half the Fun

Apart from the dollars-and-cents side of travel, there's something more important—and that's what you gain from the *process* of creating a trip. When you really dig in and create a trip, or at least participate in the creation of a trip, it becomes an educational, learning experience. And, with an interesting and culturally-rich country like Scotland to study, you can only become wiser and better for having made the effort. Sure, it takes an investment of time and energy. But the result is worth it. That's why the first three items I send to my clients are (1) a detailed map of Scotland; (2) a questionnaire designed to elicit their thoughts about travel in Scotland; and (3) a copy of this book. I want my clients to be involved in their trip because I know the more deeply they are involved the more the trip will become *their* trip rather than the trip I designed for them. Anticipation of the event is just as important as the event. Or, as one of my clients reported, "Reading all this material is like foreplay. We just can't wait to go." Remember: getting there is, indeed, half the fun.

Knowledge is Power

After reading this book, even if a person chooses to engage a tour operator, I hope that he or she at least will have enough information to take a *bargaining* approach with an operator. Knowledge is power. And if you know how to determine the real cost of a trip, you will have a powerful bargaining chip in your hand. You don't need to accept the "list price" of an operator's tour. Treat it just as you would treat the list price of a piece of real estate or a new car. If an operator wants your business, you'll be able to negotiate a discount from the list price.

Distinguishing Between Travel Agents and Tour Operators

Travel agents sell the products of tour operators. In other words, tour operators (or organizers) assemble attractive "package tours," then sell them directly to the buyer or sell them through travel agents. Travel agents get a sales commission of ten to fifteen percent.

My quarrel is not with travel agents. They are just conduits for the tour operators. They are information brokers. My quarrel is with the tour operators who sell the romance of golf in Scotland without regard for fair profit or for the democratic spirit of the game. This targeted and clever selling of Scottish golf to affluent consumers has had many unfortunate effects. Primary among them is that some of the finest golf courses in the world have been turned into ghettos for the rich—overpriced, overplayed, and now off limits to most visitors (including Scots) of average income. What's more—and I'll name names here—places like Gleneagles, Kingsbarns, Royal Troon, and

Turnberry, with their exorbitant green fees, have ensured that most visitors, if they choose to play those courses at all, will play only once and never come back. For most golfers, these truly will be once-in-a-lifetime experiences, and that is unfortunate for the clubs, the hotels, and the golfers alike. It's a lose-lose-lose proposition.

Where this business of price increases will stop no one knows. Scottish courses can only raise prices so far before they push people away to other, more affordable locations. One could argue that has already happened. Golf tourism to Scotland has declined precipitously since 2000. Evidence indicates that some have begun to understand the connection between price and demand. Management committees at top-drawer clubs like Carnoustie, Cruden Bay, Nairn, North Berwick, and Royal Dornoch have held the line on prices in recent years and now are relatively good bargains compared to the other major courses mentioned in the preceding paragraph.

Benchmark Costs for Your Trip

Following are benchmark costs *per-person* circa 2003 for a group of four golfers on a fairly typical, moderately-priced, seven-day/six-course itinerary. This is meant to give you a measuring stick for quickly sizing up trips offered by tour operators. For longer trips, take the daily average and multiply times the appropriate number of days.

Transportation - If you rent a vehicle from the right place (see *Part II, Chapter 4*), you will pay **$155** (£1 = $1.55) for a fully insured VW Caravelle minibus with automatic transmission. A minivan is less ($135), but minivans are not adequate for most groups of four golfers.

Lodging - Just about everywhere in Scotland, £35 to £45 ($54 to $70) will buy you a good night's sleep and breakfast at a three-star hotel OR a four-star bed and breakfast. In St. Andrews you'll pay a little more for a hotel but not necessarily for a B & B. Assuming the upper end of this range, budget **$490** for lodging ($70 x 7 nights).

Golf - Assume a mix of expensive and moderately-priced courses: *Prestwick* and *Western Gailes* in Ayrshire; *North Berwick* and *Gullane #1* in East Lothian; and *St. Andrews New Course* and *Kingsbarns* in Fife. Cost: **$736**

TOTAL = $1,379 divided by 7 days = $197 per day

If you see a trip similar to this priced between $1,800 and $2,200 (and you will), you will know that the margin built into the trip is about $400 to $800 *per golfer*—or a total of $1,600 to $3,200 for making ten reservations and having a guy in a green coat meet you at the Glasgow airport. You'll get a road map and a bag tag too. It's no wonder there's such a glut of competition in the business! That kind of profit for that amount of service is hard to resist.

Tour Analysis

With that much introduction, following are three *actual* self-drive tours offered by tour operators in 2003. In every example I've included the names of hotels on the package tours, so that if you want to check up on *me* you can do so. The green fees are all in the directory portion of this book, and my discussion of rental car rates in *Part II, Chapter Four*, explains how I arrive at the rates used in my analysis of real costs. All examples use the exchange rate £1 = **$1.55**. In recent years, the rate has sometimes been more favorable; sometimes it has been less favorable. This is a good average. *All costs are stated per person.*

EXAMPLE #1 - A Premium for the Old Course. The centerpiece of this trip is St. Andrews' Old Course. The markup is breathtaking—the price one pays for a "guaranteed" tee time on the Old Course. The lesson: plan ahead or enter the daily lottery (see *Part II, Chapter 3)* and cut your cost nearly in half.

Trip Elements
1. Five rounds at the following courses: *Carnoustie, St. Andrews New Course, Old Course, Gullane #1,* and *North Berwick*
2. Seven nights lodging, double occupancy, at *(a) The Dunvegan Hotel* in St. Andrews; *(b) Carnoustie Golf Hotel; (c) Apex International* in Edinburgh
3. Rental vehicle: four golfers in a minivan

TOUR PRICE: $2,497 golfer   (no price for nongolfer)

Notes: This is a good example of the industry's "bait and switch" tactic, with the Old Course being the bait. What if the Old Course is not available when you want to go? Or the Old Course time is not really guaranteed (they don't say)? All that aside, if you were to make the arrangements yourself, here's how the costs break down:

Cost Analysis

1. $538 Green fees at the five courses cited

2. $639 Accommodations - doubles at the hotels cited

3. $135 Rental Vehicle: four people in a minivan for 7 days

ACTUAL COST: $1,312

Thus: $2,497 Tour Price

- 1,312 Actual Cost

$1,185 GOLFER SAVINGS *(Operator markup: 90%)*

EXAMPLE #2 – East/West "Budget" Tour. This tour was cooked up by a company whose name, in golf parlance, means, "Watch out!". How appropriate.

Trip Elements

1. Five rounds of golf at the following courses: *Prestwick, Western Gailes, Carnoustie, St. Andrews' Old Course* and *New Course*

2. Nine nights lodging, double occupancy, at (a) the *Anchorage Hotel* in Troon and (b) the *Ardgowan Hotel* in St. Andrews

3. Rental vehicle: four golfers in a minivan

TOUR PRICE: $2,290 golfer *(no nongolfer price)*

Notes: Four free days on this tour make it a good one for nongolfers but, strangely, the nongolfer price is available only upon request. Once again the Old Course acts as a "come on." The hotels are modest three-star experiences—nothing special here except the price tag.

Cost Analysis

The following assumes these hotels' "rack rate" for five and four-night stays. No doubt a multinight discount could be negotiated.

1. $646   Green fees at the five courses cited above
2. $550   Nine nights lodging - double occupancy
3. $175   Rental Vehicle - minivan for nine days

ACTUAL COST: $1,371

Thus: $2,290 Tour Price
   - 1,371 Actual Cost
   ──────────

    $ 919   GOLFER SAVINGS *(Operator markup: 67%)*

──────────

EXAMPLE #3 - How about making that "Under $1300"?:
Here's one from a company that advertises "18 Links Golf Vacations Under $2,000." The appeal is enticing but, upon closer examination, the prices are less than sterling.

Trip Elements

1. Five rounds of golf at the following courses: *Royal Dornoch, Tain, Cruden Bay, Carnoustie, Kingsbarns*
2. Six nights at (a) *Morangie House* in Tain; (b) *Udny Arms* in Newburgh (north of Aberdeen); and (c) *Carnoustie Golf Course Hotel* in Carnoustie
3. Rental vehicle: four people in a VW Caravelle

TOUR PRICE: $1,900 golfer $1,100 nongolfer

Cost Analysis

1. $575   Green fees at the five courses cited above
2. $507   Six nights lodging - doubles at the hotels cited
3. $155   Rental Vehicle – VW Caravelle for seven days

ACTUAL COST: $1,237 golfer $662 nongolfer

Thus: $1,900 *Tour Price - golfer*
   - 1,237 *Actual Cost*
   ――――
   $663 GOLFER SAVINGS *(Operator markup: 54%)*

   $1,100 *Tour Price - nongolfer*
   -   662 *Actual Cost*
   ――――
   $448 NONGOLFER SAVINGS *(Operator markup: 68%)*

Comment: This is a good example of how even the most average, budget-oriented trip can be vastly overpriced. Imagine how much markup is involved with the "deluxe" or "five-star" trips sold by these operators! Incidentally, the operators love nongolfers. In this case, they are asking a nongolfer to pay nearly $1,000 for hotels that you could book yourself for about $500.

――――――

EXAMPLE #4 - In the 2001 edition of this book, I reported the following offer as an example of the most outlandish kind of profiteering indulged in by tour operators. This one was posted on the "Special Offers" page of a leading company's web site in the fall of 2000 for sale during the winter months, *December through March.* It's so priceless, I must repeat it here.

Assuming someone might want to play winter golf in Scotland, here was their pitch: the company said, "through a very special arrangement with the St. Andrews Links Management," for $1,995 they could offer air fare, seven nights lodging at the four-star Rusacks Hotel, and five rounds of golf on St. Andrews' *Old, New,* and *Jubilee; Crail Balcomie Links;* and *Kingsbarns.* "Wow, what a deal!"—that would be the unsuspecting traveler's normal reaction at first blush.

Here's what the company failed to mention: (1) air fares to the UK are rock bottom all winter except at Christmas break; (2) the St. Andrews Links Management doesn't make special arrangements of this sort—not even "very special" arrangements; the same package of St. Andrews courses is available to *all* golfers and *all* lodgings in St. Andrews; (3) all the major hotels in St. Andrews cut their prices in half after about October 15 and certainly by November 1; (4) Kingsbarns Golf Links was *closed* from November 2000 through March 2001; and, here's the kicker, from November through March, to prevent damage to the hallowed fairways of the Old Course, golfers must play from astroturf mats!! Do you think this tour operator would have sold any of his "exceptional values" if the truth were told? Souvenir astroturf anyone?!!

Well, that's the way it goes with tour operators. It's *caveat emptor* ("buyer beware"). If you don't have information, you can't fight them. They're not all bad guys. Some present their services accurately; most do not. Not one of them will tell you their cost basis; it's all obscured in a "package price." You have to dig up the details yourself. Once you've done that, you'll be in a position to bargain effectively with the tour operators. More likely, once you've done that you'll be in a position to do it yourself and, in the process, create a trip that is *more fun, more rewarding,* and *less expensive* than anything offered by a tour operator.

CHAPTER TWO

How to Keep the Money in *Your* Pocket

You can keep the money in *your* pocket—and out of the pocket of a tour operator—in one of three ways: (1) plan the trip yourself; (2) hire a fee-based trip planner like Ferguson Golf to do the legwork; or (3) learn enough about your actual costs to bargain effectively with a tour operator for a pre-packaged trip below "list price."

In the previous chapter, you learned by example about the gap between tour prices and actual costs—the "mark up" or gross profit margin typical of package tours. In this chapter we'll look at seven trips taken by clients of Ferguson Golf during 2002 and 2003. Typically, my gross profit margin works out to fifteen percent or less, depending upon how many people are traveling. Subtract my fee in the examples and you'll have the per-person cost of trips you can take when you book yourself. Again, figures reflect an exchange rate of £1 = $1.55. Thus, actual expenditures might have been slightly higher or lower depending upon the rate of exchange when the trip was taken. Because the rate was more favorable during the tourist season in 2002 most of the clients represented here spent less than the indicated totals. All totals are *per person* with vehicle costs apportioned to the number of people traveling.

Apart from all the intangible benefits of planning your own trip, when you book yourself directly you gain two highly-tangible benefits:

✓ All costs are spelled out. Nothing is hidden in a package price, so you're not buying a "pig in a poke."

✓ Bills aren't paid until they're due. Since you are not buying a 100% prepaid package deal, you make only the minimum deposits and/or prepayments required by golf courses and hotels. This simultaneously reduces your exposure to financial loss and increases your range of travel options.

The following itinerary summaries are designed to generate ideas for planning your own trip and give you clear examples of *real* travel costs. The costs of these Ferguson Golf trips stand in stark contrast to the operator itineraries analyzed in the previous chapter.

Trip #1 - Historic Homes of Golf: This trip approximated Itinerary #2 described in Part II, Chapter Two. It was tightly-focused around Edinburgh and St.Andrews, but without a sidetrip to Carnoustie. Did these folks play the Old Course?—of course they did. It's not nearly so hard to get a time as rumor has it.

Travelers: 1 male golfer; 1 female golfer
8 nights, 4 rounds of golf (3 booked, Old Course by ballot)

- $486 Golf *(North Berwick West Links, St. Andrews Old Course, Crail, Lundin Links)*
- $540 Accommodations *(Glebe House -* North Berwick; *Jill Hardie B & B -* St. Andrews)
- $140 Rental Vehicle *(manual mid-size sedan)*
- $175 Ferguson Golf (2002)

$1,341 TOTAL

Notes: This young couple was at least as interested in a romantic break from kids and cooking as they were in a golf-intensive week. Combining easy access to Edinburgh with classy B & B lodging in North Berwick and St. Andrews, they enjoyed a first-class trip at a reasonable price. Subtract my planning fee and you have a great land package including play on the Old Course for under $1,200.

———————

Trip #2 - Fathers and Sons: Some of my favorite trips involve fathers and sons making the "grand tour" of Scotland. This golf marathon started in Ayrshire, went north to Dornoch, and finished at St. Andrews with success in the Old Course ballot. Imagine the thrill!

Travelers: 1 adult male golfer, 1 junior male golfer
11 nights, 11 rounds of golf (10 booked, Old Course by ballot)

$853 Golf *(Prestwick, Western Gailes, Brora, Tain, Royal
Dornoch 2x, Boat of Garten, Pitlochry, Carnoustie,
St. Andrews Old Course, New Course)*
$473 Accommodations *(Glenside Hotel* - Troon; *Mallin Hotel* -
Dornoch; *Dunmurray Lodge* - Pitlochry; *Jill Hardie B &
B* - St. Andrews; *Travel Inn* - Glasgow)
$209 Rental Vehicle *(automatic Vauxhall Astra)*
$175 Ferguson Golf (2002)

$1,710 TOTAL (less $83 savings in jr. fees at some courses)

Notes: This trip holds two useful lessons. First, if a golfer is eighteen
years of age or under, be sure to ask about junior rates. Many Scottish
courses encourage junior golf by discounting green fees by fifty
percent or more. Among these are Brora, Carnoustie, North Berwick,
and Royal Dornoch. Second, remember *it's never too late to go to
Scotland!* I was booking this trip in early June for travel in early July.
Especially for singles and duos, the idea that top-drawer courses have
to be booked a year in advance is simply a myth.

Trip #3 - Running the Table on Scotland's "Rota" Courses: *For
many, this is the ideal golf trip to Scotland (Itinerary #1 in Part II,
Chapter Two)—again, not so hard to do when you can plan ahead
and you know what to do and when to do it.*

Travelers: 4 male golfers
9 nights - single occupancy, 9 rounds of golf

$1,305 Golf *(Turnberry Ailsa, Prestwick, Royal Troon Old &
Portland, Kingsbarns, Carnoustie, St. Andrews New, St.
Andrews Old, Muirfield)*
$ 880 Accommodations *(Turnberry Hotel, Marine Hotel* -
Troon; *Jill Hardie B & B* - St. Andrews; *Golf Inn* -
Gullane; *Holiday Inn Express* - Glasgow airport)

$ 201 Rental Vehicle *(automatic VW Caravelle minibus)*
$ 150 Ferguson Golf (2003 early bird discount)

$2,536 TOTAL

Notes: Perhaps because they read this book in 2001 or 2002, in 2003 many clients of Ferguson Golf got to the front of the advance-reservation queue for both Muirfield and St. Andrews' Old Course. Once successful there, booking the rest of Scotland's historic and current venues for the British Open was easy. Throw in Royal Troon's Portland, Kingsbarns, and St. Andrews' New Course and you have a dream trip that tour operators typically sell for $3,000 to $5,000. This was *not* a budget trip. It featured single-occupancy lodging everywhere but Turnberry. But it demonstrates the real cost of a trip sold by the industry as a super high-end experience. How do you "run the table" on the rota courses?—two *Travel Tips:* (1) apply to St. Andrews twelve to eighteen months in advance of intended date of play (for more information see *Part II, Chapter Three)*; and (2) apply to Muirfield beginning May 1 in the year preceding the year of intended date of play (for more information see *Part III, The Directory of Courses).*

---

*Trip #4 – **Midlands to Highlands and Back:** Three days in St. Andrews, followed by two days each in Aberdeen, Nairn/Dornoch, and Ayrshire—a popular route for the ambitious.*

Travelers: 4 male golfers
9 nights, 8 rounds of golf (7 booked, Old Course by ballot)

$1,000 Golf *(St. Andrews Old Course, Kingsbarns, Royal Aberdeen, Cruden Bay, Nairn, Royal Dornoch, Western Gailes, Turnberry Ailsa)*
$ 929 Accommodations *(The Scores Hotel* - St. Andrews; *Red House Hotel* - Cruden Bay; *Links Hotel* - Nairn; *Glenside Hotel* - Troon; *Turnberry Hotel)*
$ 199 Rental Vehicle *(automatic VW Caravelle minibus)*
$ 124 Ferguson Golf (2002)

$2,252 TOTAL

Notes: This group of guys came to me after receiving a quote on a similar trip from an agency that, in militaristic metaphor, turns every golf trip into a "Scottish Golfing Expedition." The golfers are "Expeditionary Forces" led by a "Group Captain" (no kidding). Their quote for seven nights and seven courses: $3,491. This itinerary is a little too ambitious for my taste but, on the other hand, it offers a great selection of courses and hotels and it's an effective way to get an overview of the country in anticipation of a more focused return visit. This group canceled a low-deposit (£10) pre-booked time at Lundin Links to accommodate success in their first attempt at the Old Course ballot. When it was all over, the "Group Captain" wrote in his post-trip evaluation: "I was skeptical of your price estimate at first, but the trip was perfect and the $1,400 per man we saved with Ferguson Golf paid for our airfare plus most of the caddies."

---

*Trip #5 – **Roads Less Traveled:** Two days in Perthshire with play at Gleneagles before starting a southward loop leading to the famous courses of Ayrshire.*

Travelers: 2 male golfers
11 nights - single occupancy, 10 rounds of golf

$1,047 Golf *(Gleneagles - Kings, Peebles, Southerness, Stranraer, Turnberry Ailsa, Royal Troon Old & Portland, Western Gailes, Prestwick, Southern Gailes)*
$ 886 Accommodations *(Gavelbeg B & B* - Crieff; *Hazeldean House* - Dumfries; *Glenotter Guest House* - Stranraer; *Turnberry Hotel; Glenside Hotel - Troon)*
$ 280 Rental Vehicle *(automatic mid-size wagon)*
$ 200 Ferguson Golf (2003)

$2,413 TOTAL

Notes: One of my favorites of 2003. On a previous trip these golfers had played the great links courses along the east coast and in the Highlands. They were ready to get off the beaten path, so I routed them for several days through the gorgeous, green countryside of Scotland's "Southern Uplands" where few North Americans tread.

After a splurge at Turnberry ($475 golf and lodging), they still spent less than $2,500. *Travel tip:* Single occupancy in B & Bs costs no more than double occupancy at most hotels. On same-sex golf trips, why double up when you can have your own room? It's another reason to sleep at B & Bs while wining and dining at the hotels and pubs.

Trip #6 - A Graduation Celebration—Golf, Golf, and More Golf: *Four days in St. Andrews followed by Carnoustie, North Berwick, and Troon on the trail of Scotland's historic links courses.*

Travelers: 4 male golfers
11 nights, 11 rounds golf (10 booked, Old Course by ballot)

$1,232 Golf *(St. Andrews Old Course, Elie, Crail, Carnoustie*
        Championship and Burnside, Dunbar, North Berwick
        West Links, Royal Troon & Portland, Western Gailes,
        Turnberry Ailsa)
$ 479 Accommodations *(Annandale Guest House* - St.
        Andrews; *Lochlorian Hotel* - Carnoustie; *Belhaven*
        Hotel - North Berwick; *Glenside Hotel* - Troon)
$ 221 Rental Vehicle *(automatic VW Caravelle minibus)*
$ 124 Ferguson Golf (2002)
$2,056 TOTAL

Notes: Four graduates of the Wharton School of Business decided to celebrate with a trip to the Home of Golf. Again, look at how much you can do for $2,000 when you avoid the tours! This trip compares to seven nights and five or six courses typically offered by the operators. What's the secret?—two *Travel Tips:* (1) Remember that great advertising slogan, "Spend a night, not a fortune." Put your emphasis on golf rather than on expensive lodging. I've stayed at all these small guest houses and inns and can attest to their quality. The average cost per night on this trip: $44 including breakfast. (2) To book Turnberry without staying at the hotel, call for a time two weeks before intended date of play. Nine times out of ten you'll be successful.

Trip #7 – A Walk on the Wild Side: Four days on Kintyre and Islay before heading north to Dornoch on the A82 and back to Glasgow through the center of the country on the A9.

Travelers: 1 male golfer, 1 female golfer
9 nights, 10 rounds of golf

- $535 Golf *(Machrihanish 2x, Machrie 2x, Royal Dornoch 3x, Boat of Garten, Blairgowrie Rosemount, Pitlochry)*
- $439 Accommodations *(Ardell House* - Machrihanish; *Glenmachrie B & B* - Islay; *Eagle Hotel* - Dornoch; *Moulin Hotel* - Pitlochry)
- $292 Transportation *(automatic Vauxhall Astra; ferry)*
- $175 Ferguson Golf (2002)

$1,441 TOTAL

Notes: My absolute favorite of 2002. This adventurous couple, on their first trip to Scotland, turned their backs on the meccas of Scottish golf in favor of roads less traveled and multiple rounds at Machrihanish, Machrie, and Dornoch. *Travel Tip:* The most common refrain after a round on a great course is, "I wish I could play that course more than once." This is particularly true at places like Machrihanish and Machrie where blind shots abound. Consider leaving time and space for multiple rounds. You'll be glad you did.

People ask me, "How can you do trips like these for so little?". The answer has two parts: first, I work at home and do very little advertising—thus, my overhead is low; second, I'm not greedy. But the important point is that, with a little investment of time, YOU can do the same thing. In any case, you deserve to know the *real cost* of golf in Scotland—information you'll never get from a tour operator. If you decide to use a tour operator, at the very least I hope the information in these sample itineraries will put you in a position to *bargain* with the seller. Better yet, keep reading . . . because in the next section, I'll walk you through the process of putting together your own trip. Off we go to Scotland!

PART II

HOW TO PLAN A GOLF TRIP TO SCOTLAND: STEP-BY-STEP INSTRUCTIONS

CHAPTER ONE

When To Go

The most frequently-asked question I get is, "What's the best time to go to Scotland?" One answer is, "Whenever you can." Scotland can accommodate any time of year. You might be surprised to learn that some golf courses in the "micro-climates" around St. Andrews and North Berwick are open throughout the winter. What that means, of course, is that while it may be cold there's not much snow.

As a practical matter, most people want to be as warm as possible and enjoy the longest days of the year. This means going sometime during the five months from May through September. Family, school, and job considerations often limit travel options to the summer months of June, July, and August. Now we move toward a definition of high season for Scottish golf tourism. To be most precise, the busiest months of the year are: (1) August, particularly the first half; (2) June and July; (3) May and September about equal; (4) April and October about equal. Most innkeepers consider May through September the high season. Thus, good lodging bargains abound during the "shoulder months" of April and October. Many B & Bs and guest houses close their doors for five months from November 1 to March 31.

Generalizations About the Weather

Implicit in the question, "What's the best time to go to Scotland?" is another question: "What can I expect from the weather?". The only remotely intelligent answer to that question is, "You can expect the weather to be *unpredictable*." I've been so cold in Scotland in June that I had to go shopping for a wool sweater. On the other hand, I've played golf in seventy-degree weather in May and October. In the early 1990s Scotland suffered a severe summer drought that turned the golf courses to hardened, brown runways; the winter of 2000-01 brought heavy rains and flooding to many parts of the UK.

So, if unpredictability is the key word, what generalizations can one make? For golfers, three generalizations are important:

✓ *The west coast is wetter than the east coast.* For example, though no more than sixty miles apart, Glasgow gets almost twice as much rain as Edinburgh during September and October. The ratio narrows during other months.

✓ *The west coast is warmer than the east coast.* All along Scotland's west coast, from south to north, you'll find semi-tropical plants growing in open air gardens during the summer. To my knowledge, nothing like that exists on Scotland's east coast. Why? Because the gulf stream waters wash the west coast. On the east coast, despite justifiable pride in their "micro-climates," they can get brutally cold winds off the North Sea at any time of year—and no one, not even the Scottish tourist board, can deny it.

✓ A typical Scottish day may bring sunshine, clouds, mist, rain, wind, and calm. This is the reason you are advised by all who have been there to *dress in layers.* Don't be surprised if, during a round of golf, you go from short-sleeved golf shirt to sweater to rain jacket to full rain suit before returning to sweater and short-sleeved golf shirt.

Temperature

The chart on the next page shows average high and low Fahrenheit temperatures in Edinburgh for twelve months. As a measure, Edinburgh is as good as any. Temperatures don't vary much from north to south. For example, the average high temperature during January is precisely the same in the Orkney Islands and Inverness as it is in Edinburgh. East (Edinburgh) to west (Glasgow), on average, the west coast might be a degree or two colder in winter and a degree or two warmer in summer.

This chart illustrates a fundamental point: *extremes are rare*—it doesn't get very cold and it doesn't get very hot. During the peak tourist season, May through September, daily high temperatures typically range between 55° and 75°. For golfers, this is wonderful weather—soft, cool air and no oppressive, humid heat to beat you down and sap your strength (as in many parts of the United States and, for that matter, the rest of the world). The United Kingdom, indeed, is blessed with a climate congenial to golf. Here are the details:

Edinburgh - High and Low Temperatures - Monthly Averages

Jan	43	May	58	Sept	61
	34		43		49
Feb	43	June	63	Oct	54
	34		49		45
Mar	47	July	65	Nov	49
	36		52		40
Apr	52	Aug	65	Dec	45
	40		52		36

Rainfall

You must bring good rain gear to Scotland. On the west coast from Oban on up, from August through April, it's wet a lot of the time—from six to ten inches a month. Fortunately, there aren't many golf courses in that part of the country.

For golfers, the driest part of Scotland is around Edinburgh (Fife and the Lothians). What does that mean? It means, on average, about two to three inches of rain during each of the summer months. That's not bad, especially when it comes in the form of a soft Scottish mist that hangs about all day and doesn't really get in the way of play. On the other hand, it can come in sheets and buckets and stay all day. Fortunately, those days are relatively rare and there's always a castle or museum or pub nearby where one can seek shelter. Most often, the sky will be intermittently cloudy and, out of the clouds, you might get a quick burst of showers followed by warm sunshine. Who knows? Take everything said here (and everywhere else) with a grain of salt and remember this little Scots limerick I learned from Florence McAndie at the Annandale Guest House in St. Andrews:

> Whether it rains or whether it shines,
> Whether it's chilly or hot,

You must weather the weather,
Whatever the weather,
Whether you like it or not.

The point is, there's *no* point in being concerned about the weather. No one needs another chart on rainfall. Just go on your trip and take what comes. And be prepared!

While all commentary about weather in Scotland may begin and end with the word, "unpredictable," the basic truth is that you should expect rain. That's what makes Scotland blossom into a breathtaking land of green and yellow and lavender. That's what creates her mountain rivulets and trickling burns and flowing rivers. Warm rains are the stuff of elephantine leaves and semi-tropical plants on the west coast, of heather on the hills in the Highlands, and of springy turf and silky-smooth greens in all parts of the country. Whatever the weather, you'll enjoy Scotland for what it is—wet and wild!

Daylight Hours

Related to weather, remember that Scotland is one of the northernmost countries in the world. Scotland is on latitude with Hudson Bay in Canada, Norway, and the southern reaches of Siberia. Consequently, in the months around the summer solstice (mid-June) the nights are short and the days are long. In May, June, and July you can play golf until 9 or 10 p.m. Twilight is long and lovely. This subject arises when my clients say, "I want to play early in the morning," and I say, "You can't get on that golf course early in the morning. The only available time is after lunch—and, by the way, you can play until ten o'clock at night." And they say, "Oh, yeah, I hadn't thought about that."

The tradeoff for the long days of May, June, and July are the short days of early spring and late fall. The Earth's time machine moves more rapidly in these northern climes. Here's what I mean: starting September 1, daylight hours shrink at a rate of about forty-five minutes every two weeks. Thus, sunset in Glasgow on September 1 is at 7:11 p.m.; by October 15 it's at 5:17 p.m.; by the end of October sunset is at 4:40 p.m. At the winter solstice you had better be done with your round of golf by about 3:15 p.m. (For more information, see *Appendix D*.)

26

The Case for April and October

If your heart's desire is to play the Old Course and you want to get the best rates at hotels, the best months to be in Scotland are April and October. One case in point: the four-star Old Manor Country House Hotel overlooking the golf course at Lundin Links routinely cuts its prices in half after the first week in October. That is typical of hotels throughout Scotland—many starting in September. In St. Andrews, most of the major hotels offer attractive package deals after play for the Dunhill Cup concludes in late September. And the golf courses can be surprisingly free of traffic. Personal testimony: On a Wednesday in late April 2002, I was one of *three* singles playing on world-famous Cruden Bay. The same story at Brora—just me, the sheep, and few other lone wolves.

A special attraction of spring and fall travel is the beauty of the countryside. In spring, daffodils line many of the highways and byways offering up a dazzling yellow display of welcome to the earth's new year. In the fall, an equally appealing palette of autumnal browns and golds spreads throughout the countryside in field upon field of newly-mown and gathered hay.

But tradeoffs are part of the bargain. In the spring, putting greens are not likely to be in "top nick." Course maintenance is conducted at that time, just as it is at most golf courses. In the fall, the heather is past its prime, gardens have lost their luster, and most nongolf attractions have either closed or adopted drastically shortened hours. And, in both spring and fall, daylight hours are shorter and one must risk the possibility of enduringly cold, nasty weather. For all the benefits, I think it's a good gamble and, if pressed on the point, I would choose April over October.

Calendar Highlights

By month, following are additional factors that might influence your decision on when to go.

May-June

✓ Late May and June are visually stunning. Spring has sprung and bright yellow flowers on the gorse (or whins) are in full bloom. The gorse will cost you strokes on the golf course, but at least you'll enjoy the view. In May you'll be a bit ahead of the summer tourist curve.

July

✓ Late in the month, if the British Open is in Scotland, you'll have to plan well ahead—that is, plan ahead to make your reservations near the Open venue or to be at the opposite end of the country to find accommodations and available golf courses. Here's where the Open will be held over the next few years: 2003 - Royal St. George's (England); 2004 - Royal Troon; 2005 - St. Andrews.

August

✓ Like May, August is a visual stunner with heather in bloom, casting its lavender glow over the countryside. The Highlands are especially beautiful.

✓ August is the busiest month because (a) that's when UK families take their traditional summer holiday; and (b) the Edinburgh International Festival draws thousands of tourists from around the world. In other words, you are fighting for space not only with other tourists from North America but with the Brits and every other nationality within striking distance of Scotland. Reservations must be made well in advance to lodge in Edinburgh and are recommended for most parts of the Highlands.

✓ Plan to arrive around the third week of the month when UK schools resume. You'll see a discernible drop in the level of tourist activity, particularly in the Highlands.

September

✓ Don't assume this is a relatively quieter month. It's the most popular month for "empty nesters."

The Old Course and Your Travel Plans

For many golfers, playing the Old Course at St. Andrews is the "bottom line," the *sine quo non*, of a trip to Scotland. Whether applying for an advance reservation or angling for your best shot in the daily ballot, *you can't play the Old Course if it's not open to the public.* Therefore, travel dates must be picked carefully. You will want to avoid or plan around:

✓ *May - first or second full week:* Spring meeting of the Royal and Ancient Golf Club; other events during the month impinge on Fridays and Saturdays.

✓ *June - second and third week:* Rotary International Week; graduation at St. Andrews University. The town is "full up."

✓ *All of July every fifth year* (2005, 2010, etc.) when the Old Course hosts the British Open.

✓ *September - second, third, and fourth weeks:* Queen Victoria Jubilee Vase Tournament; Bing Crosby Tournament; Royal and Ancient autumn meeting; Dunhill Cup.

✓ *Mid-November through March:* you will be issued a piece of astroturf for playing shots from the fairways. Fairway mats are also issued at Carnoustie. This, of course, is to preserve the turf at those hallowed links during the harsh winter months. Check with the courses for the exact dates. Most visiting golfers are not interested in playing Carnoustie and St. Andrews from mats, in effect eliminating four months from consideration.

The above notes on Old Course closings are for general guidance only. Normally the calendar is fixed by late November for the ensuing year. *For a complete calendar of events, check with the St. Andrews Management or visit their web site* ***www.standrews.org.uk***. For a wider discussion of the Old Course in your travel plans, see Chapter Three in this section.

Now that you have some ideas about when to go, let's turn to the next important issue: *where* to go.

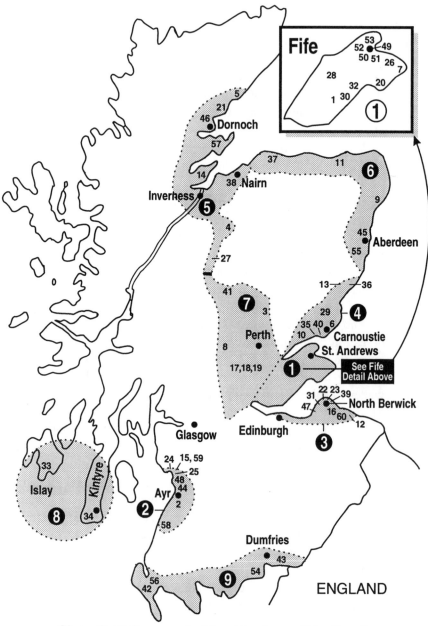

Fife

52 53 49
50 51 26 7
28 20
1 30 32
①

5
21
46 Dornoch
57
37 11 ⑥
14
38 Nairn 9
Inverness ⑤
45
4 55 Aberdeen
27
13 36
41
⑦ 29
3 35 40 6
Perth 10 ④
8 Carnoustie
St. Andrews
17,18,19 ① See Fife
Detail Above
22 23 39
31 North Berwick
47 16 60
Edinburgh 12
③
Glasgow
24 15, 59
33 25
Islay Kintyre 48
44
Ayr 2
② 58
34 ⑧
Dumfries
43
56 54
42 ⑨
ENGLAND

Sixty Golf Courses in Nine Regions of Scotland

30

CHAPTER TWO

Where to Go

The map on the facing page represents my sense of the relative popularity of regions where tourists go to play golf in Scotland. All but one of these are coastal regions that feature "links" golf, though all the courses in a coastal region are not necessarily links courses. The *numbers in dark circles* (e.g., ❷) indicate the relative popularity of each region, from #1 (Fife - St. Andrews) to #9 (the South Coast). The smaller numbers from 1 to 60 correspond to courses described and arranged alphabetically in *Part III, The Directory of Courses.*

A large percentage of Scotland's eighteen-hole golf courses are located within these nine regions. *Virtually all the courses most visitors want to play are within these nine regions.* I have not included golf courses in Glasgow and Edinburgh. Does that mean no courses there are worthy of play? Of course not. It's just that most visitors don't want to play golf when they're in those cities. They want to see the cities.

Think of these regions as building blocks for itineraries. In describing itineraries, I use the term, "base," interchangeably with "region." With these bases clearly defined, we can start creating trips featuring various combinations of bases.

Want to get off the beaten path?—then focus on the highest numbers. Maybe you'd like a combination of classic courses and less-traveled byways—then pair a low number with a high number (e.g., 1 and 7, 2 and 8, 2 and 9). Each of these provides foundation for a six to ten-day itinerary combining well-known courses with courses and regions off the beaten path.

Geographic Arrangement of Sixty Courses *(located by number on map)*
+ = British Open Qualifying Course
* = Current or historic venue for British Open

Region #1 - Fife (from Tayport, south along coast and back)
Scotscraig+ (53)
The Duke's Course (52)
St. Andrews Old*/New/Jubilee (49, 50, 51)
Kingsbarns (26)
Crail (7)
Golf House Club - Elie (20)
Lundin Links+ (32)
Leven Links+ (30)
Balbirnie Park (1)
Ladybank+ (28)

Region #2 - Ayrshire (north to south)
Irvine - Bogside (24)
Glasgow Gailes+ (15)
Western Gailes+ (59)
Kilmarnock - Barassie+ (25)
Royal Troon* (48)
Prestwick* (44)
Belleisle - Ayr (2)
Turnberry Ailsa* (58)

Region #3 - East Lothian (west to east)
Royal Musselburgh (47)
Longniddry+ (31)
Gullane #1+ (22)
Honourable Company of Edinburgh Golfers - Muirfield* (23)
North Berwick - West Links+ (39)
The Glen - North Berwick (16)
Whitekirk (60)
Dunbar+ (12)

Region #4 - Angus/East Coast (from Dundee north to Edzell)
Downfield (10)
Monifieth (35)
Panmure (40)

Carnoustie* (6)
Letham Grange (29)
Montrose+ (36)
Edzell (13)

Region #5 - *Inverness/Dornoch (south to north)*
Kingussie (27)
Boat of Garten (4)
Nairn (38)
Fortrose & Rosemarkie (14)
Tain (57)
Royal Dornoch (46)
Golspie (21)
Brora (5)

Region #6 - *Northeast/North Coast (south to north to west)*
Stonehaven (55)
Royal Aberdeen (45)
Cruden Bay (9)
Duff House Royal (11)
Moray Old (37)

Region #7 - *Perthshire/Central (south to north)*
Gleneagles - King's/Queen's/PGA Centenary (17, 18, 19)
Crieff (8)
Blairgowrie Rosemount (3)
Pitlochry (41)

Region #8 - *Kintyre/Islay*
Machrie (34)
Machrihanish (33)

Region #9 - *South Coast (west to east)*
Stranraer (56)
Portpatrick (42)
Southerness (54)
Powfoot (43)

Constructing Itineraries

Where you go depends upon three factors—your personal preferences, the length of your trip, and, most likely, how many times you've been to Scotland. If you're a first-timer, you're probably not going to choose the Kintyre Peninsula over St. Andrews. On the other hand, if you've visited St. Andrews and played the Old Course, you may be quite keen to make the pilgrimage to Machrihanish on remote Kintyre.

For the typical seven or eight-day trip I recommend limiting yourself to one or two bases. Beyond one week, the number of bases can increase as the length of a trip increases. With ten to fourteen days, a third or even fourth base might be added to the mix. If you are among the lucky ones who can spend three or more weeks, then you can cover more ground and your options increase dramatically.

This is such an important topic, I want to restate and amplify the central idea of the preceding paragraph. *If you are making a one-week trip, limit yourself to one or two bases.* On a two-base trip, this means three or four nights in each locale. With three or four nights in one place, you'll feel more like you're "at home." You can get unpacked and stay unpacked for awhile. You can get to know your lodging hosts. You can get to know the streets and shops, the restaurants and the corner bartender. Most important, you can spend your time playing golf instead of packing up, driving for several hours, then finding your next place to bunk down. The last thing you want to do on a golf trip is get into the tourist trap: "If this is Tuesday, it must be Carnoustie."

Some tour operators sell a seven-day package touting the world-famous courses at Troon, Dornoch, Cruden Bay, Carnoustie, and St. Andrews. That kind of routing is absurd—five bases in seven days, covering about 800 miles, requiring you to spend most of your free time in a car or bus and leaving no time to "savor the clubhouse" (not to mention the countryside). This is not the right way to tour Scotland.

Likewise, some golfers will fly into and out of the airport at Machrihanish in one day just to say they've played that great course. They don't understand they've missed the best part of the Machrihanish experience—namely, the process of *getting there* by sea or land and, once there, exploring the wild and remote reaches of the Kintyre Peninsula. The golfer who flies in and out of Kintyre in one day will never know the thrill of driving down a one-lane road to Southend where, on a clear day, you can see all the way to Ireland; or of stopping at the Dunaverty Golf Club for a quick round on a course that will take you back to the nineteenth century as a reminder of the way golf used to be played. At unattended Dunaverty you'll be asked to drop your fee in an "honesty box" before leaving the first tee. You'll probably "play through" several bovine hazards as well. That's the kind of experience a traveler can savor long after the buzz of a championship course is forgotten. But it's not an experience a *hurried* traveler will ever have. This is the single most important piece of advice I can give: *Don't hurry. Slow down and savor the clubhouse* (the golf equivalent of "smelling the roses").

The Case for "Stay and Play"

One-base, one-week golf trips are becoming increasingly common in Scotland. Tourism councils and hotels in Aberdeenshire, Angus, Ayrshire, Fife, and the Highlands are making the pitch to "stay and play," often accompanied by package deals that reduce costs at participating golf courses and accommodations (e.g., see *www.golfhighland.com)*. As one can see on the map and the Geographic Index at the beginning of this chapter, there is no shortage of courses in any area when a decision is made to stay and play. Case in point: on a seven-day trip, with five days dedicated to golf, you could play *two* excellent courses a day in Fife and still leave courses untouched. Start with five courses in St. Andrews (Old, New, Jubilee, Eden, Duke's), then add Kingsbarns, Crail, Elie, Lundin Links, and Leven Links. That still leaves courses like Scotscraig, Balbirnie Park, Ladybank, and the courses at St. Andrews Bay to play on another trip. Another benefit of a one-base trip is that you can almost always negotiate a multi-night discount at your B & B or hotel. Following are the five most popular bases for a one-week stay:

- Region #1 – St. Andrews/Fife
- Region #2 - Ayrshire
- Region #3 - East Lothian/Edinburgh
- Region #4 - Angus/East Coast
- Region #5 - Inverness/Dornoch

One-week, two-base trips: combine from above bases or from additional bases. In combining bases to make one-week, two-base trips, add four more bases to the mix:

- Region #6 - Northeast/North Coast
- Region #7 - Perthshire/Central
- Region #8 - Kintyre/Islay
- Region #9 - South Coast

These four additional bases could be in the stay-and-play category but, as a practical matter, they are far down the list for most golfers. It's conceivable, for example, to base for a week in Perthshire (Region #7) and play the parkland courses at Gleneagles, Blairgowrie, Pitlochry, Crieff, etc., but I've never encountered a first-time traveler to Scotland who has chosen to do that rather than go to St. Andrews, Troon or North Berwick. On the other hand, combining several of the Parkland courses in Perthshire with courses in Ayrshire (#2) or Angus (#4) makes an excellent itinerary offering variety and some salutary movement around the countryside. Likewise, a great trip comes from combining several days playing the historic courses in Ayrshire with an excursion to Machrihanish in Kintyre and Machrie on Islay (#8).

Now let's take a closer look at a few popular two-base combinations, still within the parameters of a one-week trip:

. *Itinerary #1 - Fife (#1) and Ayrshire (#2)* - the most popular duo, combining the courses in and around St. Andrews with Royal Troon, Turnberry, Western Gailes, and Prestwick in Ayrshire.

. *Itinerary #2 - Fife (#1) and East Lothian (#3)* - this combination includes easy access to Edinburgh and features the Fife courses plus the Lothian courses at North Berwick, Dunbar, Gullane, and Musselburgh.

. *Itinerary #3 - Fife (#1) and Angus/East Coast (#4)* - again we start with Fife but add the courses near Carnoustie as far north as Montrose.

36

This is a good time to answer the common question, "Couldn't I do North Berwick, St. Andrews, and Carnoustie in a one-week trip?". The answer is "Yes, you can." Carnoustie is within an hour's drive of St. Andrews—easily reachable from that base. The problem comes when you are trying to ballot for play on the Old Course and a pre-booked round at Carnoustie interferes. If your name were chosen in the ballot and you already had a tee time on Carnoustie, you would be faced with the unenviable predicament of having to give up a *prepaid* round at one championship course to play another championship course. The solution? Leave one or the other for another trip or resign yourself to one less day in the Old Course lottery. A North Berwick-St. Andrews-Carnoustie itinerary, then, might look like this:

- D Day - depart
- Day 1 - arrive, settle, and rest; optional golf
- Day 2 - *North Berwick West Links*; perhaps a half-day or evening in Edinburgh
- Day 3 - *Gullane #1* or *Dunbar;* transfer to St. Andrews
- Day 4 - ballot the Old Course for Day 5; play *Kingsbarns* or *Scotscraig;* Fife sightseeing
- Day 5 - *Old Course* (if chosen); optional pre-booked other course in Fife;
- Day 6 - play *Carnoustie*
- Day 7 - depart

This itinerary is fine and workable. It involves three bases—which is to say, my two-base limitation is only a guideline. The important point is to try to maintain focus in your itinerary. Avoid the "one-night stands." Hang on for a few days and get to know a place. You'll enjoy the pace more and you'll probably play better golf!

Multi-base Trips: Ten Sample Itineraries

Following are ten itineraries best suited to trips of ten to fourteen days (or more). Most of these trips could start in either Glasgow or Edinburgh. Though surprisingly few travelers fly into Inverness or Aberdeen, those cities also can be used as the beginning and/or ending point of an itinerary. Itinerary #8 is an example of a trip that starts and ends in Aberdeen. Itinerary #s 9 and 10 traverse the length of

Scotland, either beginning or ending in Inverness—ideal for someone traveling to or from England.

While browsing through these ten itineraries, bear in mind they are only suggestions designed to stimulate your thinking. If you have fewer than ten days to travel, maybe some *portion* of one of these itineraries will appeal to you. With more than two weeks for travel and golf, some combination of itineraries might appeal. My purpose here is to include all the regions where you'll find the golf courses described in *Part III, The Directory of Courses.*

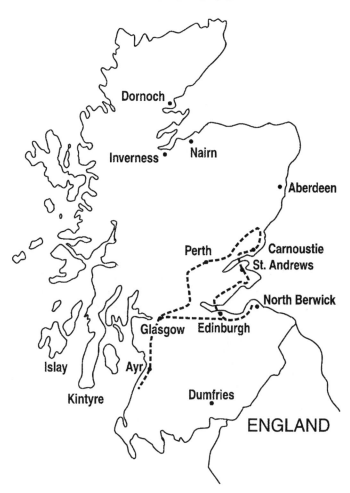

Itinerary # 1 - The Open "Rota" Courses: *Combining Ayrshire (Region #2), Angus/East Coast (Region #4), Fife (Region #1), and East Lothian (Region #3).* This trip might include the following courses: *Ayrshire:* Prestwick, Royal Troon, Turnberry; *Angus:* Montrose, Carnoustie; *Fife:* St. Andrews Old, Crail; *East Lothian:* Muirfield, North Berwick, Old Musselburgh. The focus here is golf on seven past and current venues of the British Open. With St. Andrews' Old Course and Muirfield in the picture, *considerable advance planning (twelve to eighteen months) would be required to actually accomplish this trip.* Variations on the theme can be accomplished with less lead time (i.e., without advance booking at St. Andrews and Muirfield).

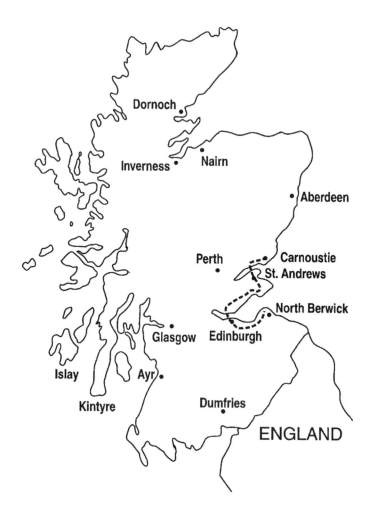

Itinerary #2 - The Historic Homes of Golf - Edinburgh and the East Coast: *Combining East Lothian (#3); Fife (#1); and Angus/East Coast (#4).* Rivaling Itinerary #1 in popularity, this is a highly-focused trip featuring relatively little driving to and from Scotland's oldest courses at Musselburgh, North Berwick, St. Andrews, and Carnoustie. Locations provide easy access to Edinburgh for sightseeing and shopping (a good itinerary for non-golfers).

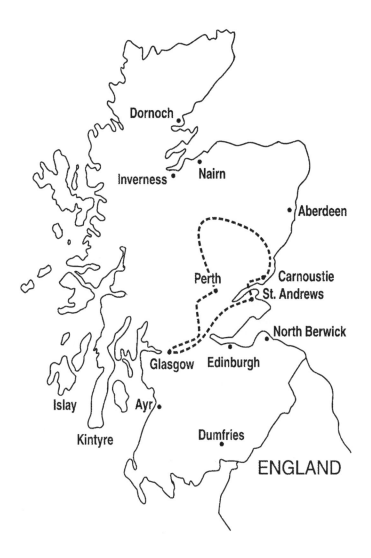

Itinerary #3 - Parkland to Seaside: *Combining Perthshire (#7), Angus/ East Coast (#4), Fife (#1).* This trip might include the courses at Gleneagles, Pitlochry, and Blairgowrie; then on to Montrose, Carnoustie, and Letham Grange, with a finish in and around St. Andrews. This appealing itinerary combines scenic variety with golf course variety and a strong touch of history at Montrose, Carnoustie, and St. Andrews.

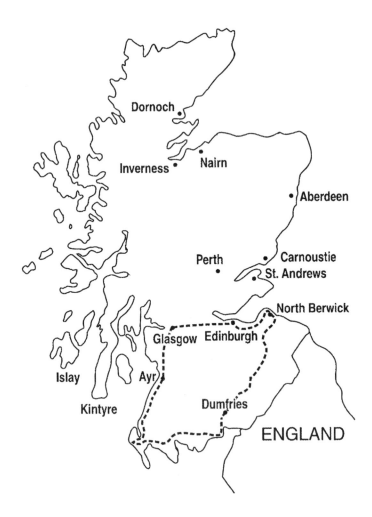

Itinerary #4 - The Southern Loop: *Combining Ayrshire (#2), South Coast (#9), East Lothian (#3).* We start with the historic courses of Ayrshire, then combine them with scenic driving and golf in the less-traveled south of Scotland. The courses of the South Coast are accessible and bargain-priced. The courses of East Lothian are both historic and relatively good bargains. For those of literary bent, this trip traverses the haunts of Robert Burns and Sir Walter Scott. Easy access to Edinburgh also figures into the equation.

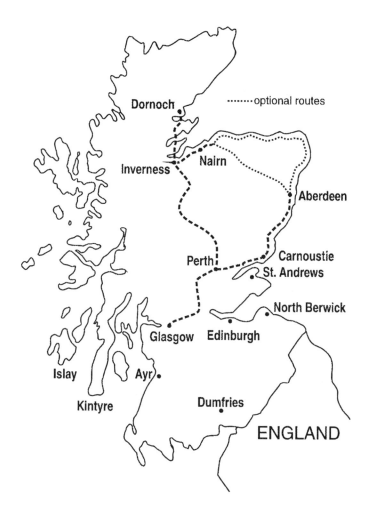

Itinerary #5 - Highlands Loop to the East: *Combining Perthshire (#7), Inverness/Dornoch (#5), Northeast/North Coast (#6), Angus (#4).* This trip moves away from the populated midlands to increase the drama of both the golf experience and the travel experience. Starting again in the lush midlands of Perthshire, we push on to the Highlands at least as far north as Dornoch, fifty miles above Inverness. Then down to Cruden Bay (Scotland's most dramatic dune-filled linksland) either through the Cairngorm Mountains or along the north coast, then southward to visit the courses of Angus, especially Carnoustie, before departing from Glasgow or Edinburgh.

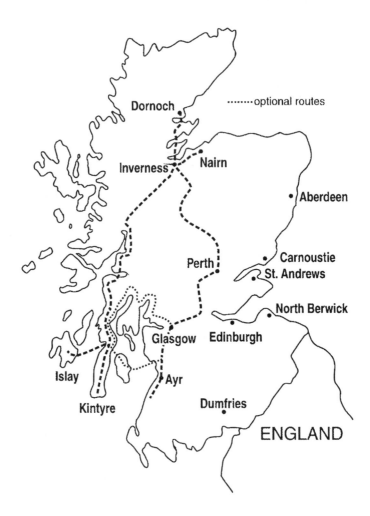

Itinerary #6 - Highlands Loop to the West: *Combining Perthshire (#7), Inverness/Dornoch (#5), Kintyre/Islay (#8), and Ayrshire (#2).* A variant on Itinerary #5, this features the dramatic scenery of the west coast and islands. At least ten days (preferably two weeks or more) are needed to do justice to this itinerary. Optional routes by ferry or land to the Kintyre Peninsula are indicated. Getting to Islay requires ferry travel to and from Kennacraig. Additional western islands to explore: Iona, Mull, and Skye. The perfect itinerary for a long stay.

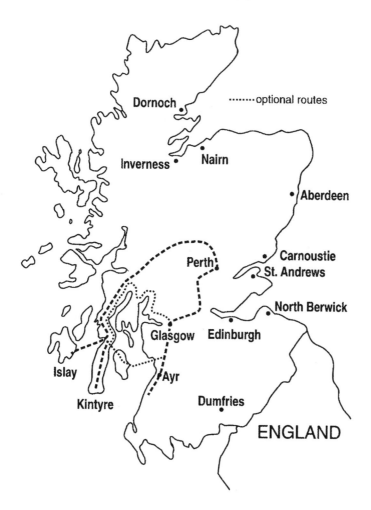

Itinerary #7 - Ayrshire and Scenic Scotland: *Combining Ayrshire (#2), Kintyre/Islay (#8), and Perthshire (#7).* A variant on Itinerary #6—for those on a shorter trip—this trip features the historic courses of Ayrshire, then sets out for the wild and wonderful Kintyre Peninsula (either driving or by ferry). Islay is reached by ferry from Kennacraig. From Islay, return to the mainland for sightseeing and golf in beautiful Perthshire before departing from Glasgow or Edinburgh. This itinerary includes many of the features of Itinerary #6 without the expansive loop into the Highlands.

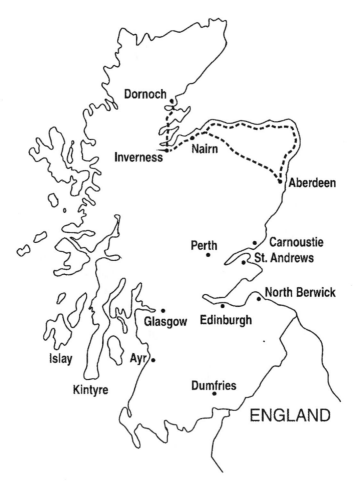

Itinerary #8 - The Highlands and the Northeast: *Combining Northeast/North Coast (#6) and Inverness/Dornoch (#5).* Here's an example of a highly-focused trip encompassing all the best Scotland has to offer: great golf, the "Castle Trail," the "Whisky Trail," plus the dramatic scenery and friendly people of the Highlands. This trip starts and ends at Aberdeen, Scotland's third largest city. After links golf near Aberdeen, it's across the broad Cairngorm Mountains and around the Whisky Trail before exploring the courses and historic sites of the Inverness/Dornoch area. Then back to Aberdeen, but this time along the Northern Coastal Route for a look at small fishing villages and rugged links courses. The best part: a leisurely pace on "roads less traveled."

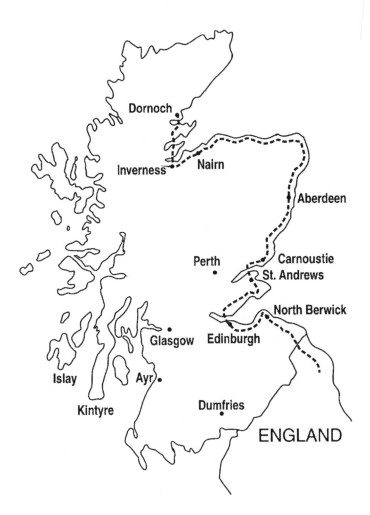

Itinerary #9 - East Side: A One-Way Trip to the Highlands.
*Combining East Lothian (#4), Fife (#1), Angus/East Coast (#3) North-
Northeast (#6) and Inverness/Dornoch (#5).* Coming from England? Here's
a way to follow your star northward playing links golf all the way. Just
imagine: Dunbar, North Berwick, Gullane #1, Lundin Links, Crail, St.
Andrews, Carnoustie, Montrose, Cruden Bay, Moray Old, Nairn, and Royal
Dornoch. You may think you've died and gone to golfer's heaven. Leave
your vehicle in Inverness and fly home or back to London.

47

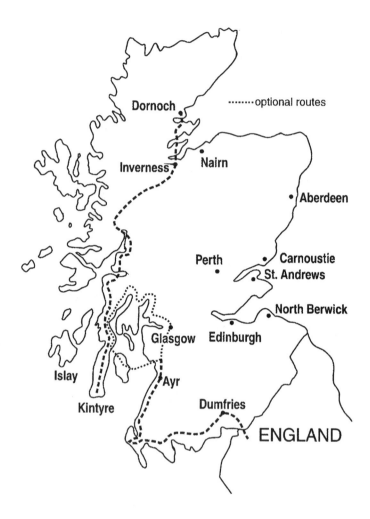

········optional routes

Itinerary #10 - West Side: A One-Way Trip to the Highlands.
Combining the South Coast (#9), Ayrshire (#2), Kintyre/Islay (#8), and Inverness/Dornoch (#5). A variant on #9, but this time up (or down) the craggy and wild west coast. Links golf is featured at Southerness, Portpatrick, Turnberry, Prestwick, and Troon, with Royal Dornoch and other northern courses the icing on the cake. With history and scenery and gardens galore, this is a strong itinerary for the non-golfing fellow traveler.

In Anticipation of Chapter Three

St. Andrews is included in four of the ten itineraries laid out above. As a practical matter, for first-time golf travelers to Scotland, St. Andrews is included in most itineraries. Rarely do I encounter a first-timer who doesn't want to visit the Auld Grey Toon and have a look at the Old Course, take a shot at the daily ballot, and at least play next door to it on the New Course or the Jubilee. And that's fine. As we shall see, "Everyone Wants to Go—and Why Not!".

Fortunately, even in the dead of summer it's not as hard to get a tee time at the Old Course as it is at some of the other well-known Scottish courses. I'll have a lot more to say about that in the ensuing pages. In the context of this chapter, it is more important to answer the common question, "*Among the historic and current 'rota' courses, which are the hardest courses to get on?*". In my experience, in order of degree of difficulty in high season, they are: (1) Muirfield; (2) Royal Troon; (3) St. Andrews' Old Course; (4) Turnberry; (5) Prestwick; and (6) Carnoustie.

Due to its exclusivity, Muirfield will lead the pack any time of year. Royal Troon is more difficult than St. Andrews because it is a private club where visitor play is limited to three days a week. St. Andrews is third due to sheer demand; if all things were equal (i.e., access policy), it would rank sixth. The Ailsa at Turnberry is tied to the resort hotel and, as long as there's room in the hotel and you're willing to pay up, you can be assured of a tee time. Prestwick and Carnoustie are a tossup. Demand at Carnoustie is greater, but Prestwick's more restrictive visitor policies sometimes make it a bit more difficult to manage.

You'll find more course-specific information in *Part III, The Directory of Courses.* But before we get to the details of trip planning, it's time to take a closer look at the place everyone wants go—St. Andrews.

CHAPTER THREE

St. Andrews:
Everyone Wants to Go—and Why Not!

Traveling to St. Andrews carries with it an undeniable sense of drama. I think of it as a modern-day pilgrimage to Shangri-La or Oz. You know there's a shining city upon a hill awaiting, and you're pretty sure there's a pot of gold at the end of this rainbow. And, you know, you're right. St. Andrews does not disappoint. It's everything one hopes for and maybe a little more.

From Edinburgh, you cross the Forth Bridge (nine miles from the Edinburgh airport) on the M90, leaving airports and cities and crowds far behind. Only a few minutes along, the A92 branches eastward off the M90 and then sharply northward into the Kingdom of Fife. Now, shedding another layer of modernity, the dual carriageway disappears near Glenrothes as you press on through rolling farmland past Freuchie and Ladybank to join the A91 just fifteen miles outside St. Andrews. Time elapsed: only about forty minutes to this point but so different as to be in some other time and place.

Getting to this point from Glasgow takes a little longer—about ninety minutes, first northward on the M80, then eastward along the length of the A91, skirting Stirling and the golden bluffs of the Ochil Hills, slowing at tiny farm villages, driving ever more deeply into the peaceful countryside of Fife. The tensions of travel ease and the drive begins to feel like a pilgrimage. You're on your way to the place where the game of golf was conceived, nurtured, and codified. You're ever so close to St. Andrews.

Now the A91 takes you straight through the bustling market center of Cupar, ten miles east of your destination. After clearing Cupar, a few miles along, you cross a flowing stream marked, "Eden." Could this place name be entirely coincidental?

Now, as the A91 slides gracefully to the southeast, you round a bend or two and there St. Andrews appears on high ground above the Fife countryside. You wind your way into town past university playing fields, take a left on Golf Place at the second roundabout, and . . . there you are. In an instant all you've seen in books and on television is before your eyes. In one grand sweep you take it in: the vast, flat field encompassing the first and eighteenth fairways of the Old Course; the golden beach curving off into the distance; the intimidating first tee exposed for all to see; the mammoth eighteenth green ringed around by white fence and idling observers; the imposing Royal and Ancient clubhouse, looking as though it has stood since time immemorial.

Now more details catch your eye: the British Golf Museum across the street behind the R & A; the starter house, the caddie pavilion and putting green bounded by more white fence; the Victorian stone buildings alongside the eighteenth fairway; Tom Morris's golf shop; Rusacks Hotel; the Old Course Hotel off in the distance near the seventeenth hole. There's "Grannie Clark's Wynd" where people are walking and cars are driving right across the middle of the first and eighteenth fairways! And, beyond it, the Golfers' Bridge across Swilken Burn.

Eventually you make your way down the West Sands Road to the car park and the Links Clubhouse where you find all the golfer's amenities for a stay in St. Andrews—information desk, changing rooms, pro shop, and the starter's office for the New Course and Jubilee. Maybe it's time for some refreshment in the handsome lounge, or a jaunt up to the rooftop observatory for a bird's-eye view over the linksland.

Finally, you've arrived at St. Andrews! Now it's time to find your accommodations, get settled, and explore the Auld Grey Toon.

The Lay of the Land

St. Andrews, with a permanent population of about 20,000 including university students, is compactly laid out and entirely walkable. Six golf courses spread out in the shape of a giant fan on the flat, low ground to the west/northwest of town. Town buildings occupy high ground above the linksland and rocky cliffs that separate the West Sands (golf courses) from the East Sands about a mile away around a bend in the coastline.

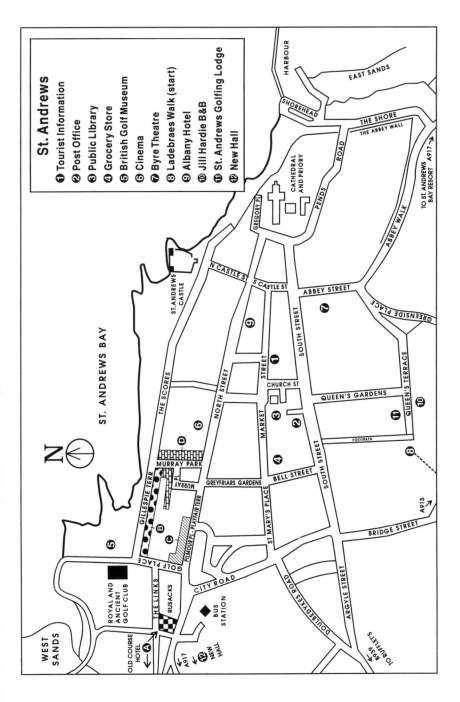

St. Andrews

1 Tourist Information
2 Post Office
3 Public Library
4 Grocery Store
5 British Golf Museum
6 Cinema
7 Byre Theatre
8 Ladebraes Walk (start)
9 Albany Hotel
10 Jill Hardie B&B
11 St. Andrews Golfing Lodge
12 New Hall

Looking at a town plan of St. Andrews, the medieval character of the place is plain to see. Once the ecclesiastical center of Scotland, the heart of the old city was at the east end of town where the dramatic cathedral and cemetery grounds meet the coastline. Here, along Abbey Walk, Castle Street, and the Pends, one can trace the remains of old city walls that lead to the ruins of a 13th-century castle—first the bishop's home—perched on a promontory above the rocky shore.

Just as the town's golf courses fan out from the first tee of the Old Course, four streets fan out from the cathedral grounds to define the commercial and spiritual core of modern St. Andrews. Three of these streets—North Street, Market Street, and South Street—offer up a lot of traffic and most of St. Andrews' shops and restaurants, pubs and other public places. None is longer than about three-eighths of a mile. A fourth street, between North Street and the coast, is called "The Scores." This street leads directly and symbolically from the bishop's castle to the first tee of the Old Course and is remarkable for its peaceful contrast to the trio of commercial streets just mentioned. To the east of Murray Park, The Scores is a leafy, lightly-traveled, one-lane track lined by ivy-covered walls and university buildings. Between Murray Park and the R & A clubhouse, The Scores and its university roots give way to a long block of offices and relatively expensive ocean-front hotels.

Marked on the map on the previous page, on Market Street and South Street, are several places of special interest to golfers and non-golfers alike. At 70 Market St., you'll find the Tourist Information Office ❶. Start here for information about "What's On" in Fife and St. Andrews during your stay. It's a well-stocked TI with excellent staff. Next, on the north side of South St. between Church St. and Bell St. is the main Post Office ❷ where you can go to send postcards to all your golf buddies back home (and, incidentally, pick up a BT phone card). Other nearby practical destinations are the public library ❸ and the Tesco food store ❹ near the corner of Market and Bell.

Looking for entertainment in St. Andrews? There's golf history at the British Golf Museum ❺ near the R & A clubhouse. Try a feature film at the local cinema ❻ or performing arts at the Byre Theatre ❼. But the best entertainment in St. Andrews is all around you—that is, in pounding the paved streets of this enchanting town. It's a place with ancient roots and, as author Michael Tobert advises, "Look up when you walk the streets of St. Andrews. That's where the history is. It's in the details of the buildings." And, finally, my favorites: for peaceful relief from the streets, there are the beaches and the shady walk along Lades Brae ❽ through quiet neighborhoods where the land falls off precipitously to the south behind Queen's Terrace.

Accommodations In and Around St. Andrews

A prospective client once called me in considerable confusion and frustration. He didn't have a lot of money to spend and said a travel agent had told him, "The only hotels in St. Andrews are the Old Course Hotel, Rusacks Hotel, and Rufflets." Of course, nothing could be farther from the truth. As one of Scotland's major tourist destinations, St. Andrews is blessed with a wealth of lodging options in every price category. St. Andrews is not just for the well-heeled.

In this section I want to give you an overview of your choices and direct you to internet sites where you can get more information. To that end, I've organized my comments on St. Andrews lodging generally by proximity to the golf courses and, among the first four groups, generally by price. Proximity and price tend to coincide around the links so, rather than locate all the individual hotels on the map, I've indicated four main *areas* (A, B, C, D) of lodging choices near the links. All price estimates are double occupancy 2003 (exchange rate £1 = $1.55).

The Crème de la Crème (area A)
In town that would be *The Old Course Hotel* (01334-474-371; *www.oldcoursehotel.co.uk*) and *Rusacks Hotel* (0870-400-8128; *www.macdonaldhotels.co.uk*). *Rufflet's Country House Hotel* (01334 -472-594; *www.rufflets.co.uk*) is about a mile and one-half west on Strathkiness Road. A newcomer to this group in 2002, the monumental *St. Andrews Bay Resort Hotel,* rises on high ground two miles south of town (01334-837-000; *www.standrewsbay.com*). The least expensive double room in these places will cost you about £160 ($250) a night. Want to face the Old Course from suites at Rusacks or The Old Course Hotel?—that will be about £220 ($340) per night. Of course, if you want to use the helipad, that's a whole 'nother ball game.

The Scores (Gillespie Terrace) (B)

Eastward from the corner of Golf Place and The Scores, four hotels offer million-dollar views from oceanfront windows at rates a cut or two below the *crème de la crème*. In order, from the corner to Murray Park, these are: The Scores Hotel, the St. Andrews Golf Hotel, the Hazelbank Private Hotel, and the Russell Hotel.

The *Scores Hotel* (01334-472-451; *www.bestwestern.com*) has thirty rooms and a classy pub called the "The Chariot Bar"—so named to honor the feature film, "Chariots of Fire," filmed primarily on the West Sands of St. Andrews. On the cherry-wood walls of the Chariot Bar are hung photographs, sketches, and oil portraits of 127 famous Scots from several centuries and all walks of life. High-season rates at The Scores for a double room: about £150 to £170 ($230-$265).

The *St. Andrews Golf Hotel* (01334-472-611; *www.standrews-golf.co.uk)*, a bit farther along, is a family-run hotel with twenty-two comfortable rooms, a first-class restaurant, and strikingly handsome public rooms. Prices here are virtually identical to those at The Scores Hotel, though their dining requirements are a major turnoff.

Near the corner of The Scores and Murray Park, are the *Hazelbank Private Hotel* (01334-472-466; *www.hazelbank.com)* and the *Russell Hotel* (01334-473-447; *www.russellhotelstandrews.co.uk*). Each is family run and has ten rooms that cost about £100 to £110 ($155-$170) per night. The Russell Hotel has a popular dining room, but you don't have to stay at the hotel to use it.

In every case here, we're talking location, location, location. I've quoted a range of prices because you pay more for an ocean-view room than for an "inside" room. The best idea: save these hotels for the shoulder season or off-season when special offers are available at significantly reduced rates.

Pilmour Place/Playfair Terrace (C)

Eastward from the other corner of Golf Place are three more small hotels. They are the *Dunvegan Hotel* on the corner of Golf Place and Pilmour Place; the *Ardgowan Hotel* a little farther along on Playfair Terrace; and *The Inn on North Street* up by Murray Park. These are small hotels run in the best Scottish tradition—popular gathering places with full bar and restaurant facilities. They frequently show up on mid-price tour packages and, given their popularity and small size, one should book well in advance. Prices are similar to those at the Hazelbank and Russell, though in a wider range. Expect to pay from $140 to $200 double occupancy in high season with the Ardgowan at the lower end of that range and the Dunvegan at the upper. The *Dunvegan Hotel* (01334-473-105; *www.dunveganhotel.com*) is St. Andrews' most famous small hotel, and in 2002 it got bigger fast when it acquired the three "Auchterlonie Suites" in the historic corner building across the street from the main hotel. Layered onto the hotel's popular golfers' lounge and Claret Jug Restaurant, these spacious rooms increase still further the Dunvegan's appeal to small groups of golfers. The owners here are Jack and Sheena Willoughby. Jack is a transplanted Texan (A & M) who first lived in Aberdeen where he was involved with North Sea oil exploration and drilling. When the opportunity came to buy the Dunvegan in 1994, he settled in St. Andrews and has since become a local institution and minor celebrity in international golf with hundreds of clients returning annually to enjoy his and Sheena's welcoming little inn.

Audrey and Roderick Grieve, a mother-son combination, run the *Ardgowan Hotel* (01334-472-970; *www. ardgowanhotel.co.uk)* at #2 Playfair Terrace. With doubles starting around £90 ($140) in high season, this one is popular on many "budget" golf tours. The hotel has its own restaurant and an attractive lounge, "Playfair's Bar."

A serious up-and-comer in the same price category is the *Inn on North Street* (01334-473-387; *www.theinnonnorthstreet.com)*. There's nothing new about the building but, under new management, the old place has found new life as a sophisticated sleeping-eating-meeting place for locals and visitors alike. The evening menu in the "Cidsin" dining room is among the most extensive in town.

Murray Park and Murray Place (D)

The most affordable lodging near the golf courses is on Murray Park and Murray Place. These two Murrays are lined entirely by B & Bs ranging in quality from two-star to four-star. We're not talking fancy here—but clean, well-lighted places near town centre, within easy walking distance to the golf courses, priced from about £55 to £70 ($85-$110) double occupancy in high season. Every bit the bargain for a town as pricey as St. Andrews. Most of these establishments have their own web site, but they also can be found on one of the promotional associations (e.g., *www.smoothhound.co.uk).* There are too many to mention, but among them are the *Annandale Guest House, Arran House, Burness House, Cameron House, Craigmore Guest House,* and *Glendarran Guest House*—all good choices for the savvy traveler (tip for singles: Cameron House has three small rooms priced at £30). When considering these, keep in mind that address numbers ascend from North Street to The Scores— so, while Burness House at #1 is up by busy North Street, the Annandale at #23 is on the corner at the relatively quieter Scores across from the Russell Hotel. Also, note that the square fronting Murray Place is a parking lot—not exactly St. Andrews most scenic view—and a corner space is taken by Ziggy's Bar, a student hangout that can get a wee bit rowdy at times. Ask for an inside room.

Parking in the Golf Quadrangle

With the exception of the luxury hotels, what I've described to this point is lodging in the quadrangle of blocks directly east of the R & A clubhouse and the first tee of the Old Course. A major problem for all these establishments—thus, for *you* and, indeed, for all of St. Andrews—is parking. The medieval streets in the central part of this fair city are simply not designed to accommodate the modern auto-mobile in anything like the numbers vying for space every day. What to do? First, take whatever advice and help your lodging host can provide. Second, take whatever space you can find and be damned glad you got it. Third, before getting into your car, think about the possibility of walking.

Alternatively, consider other accommodations where the parking challenge is not so severe. To that end, following are suggestions in two more lodging groups—the first, in St. Andrews but outside the Golf Quadrangle; the second, literally outside of St. Andrews.

Other options in St. Andrews

In the small-hotel category is the *Albany Hotel* ❾ on the cathedral end of North St. (ph 01334-477-737; *www.standrewsalbany.co.uk).* The Albany is comparable to the hotels in Group C above. It's a restored Georgian with about ten rooms—popular on mid-price golf tours and, though on busy North St., just far enough away from town centre to improve the parking odds. Cost: about $170 for a double.

Excellent B & Bs in private homes are scattered throughout the St. Andrews area. This is where the budget traveler will find some of the most interesting properties and the lowest rates in town (typically £20 to £25 singles, £30 to £40 doubles). Most belong to the St. Andrews Private B & B Association (*www.standrewsbandbs.com*).

Another step up are the luxury B & Bs of St. Andrews. Representative of this class are two properties on Queen's Terrace, one block off South Street. *Jill Hardie's B & B* ❿ at 18 Queen's Terrace (01334-478-849; *ww.aboutscotland.com/fife/queensterrace*) is a Victorian row house where the weary traveler is surrounded by good taste and personal attention. Entirely renovated in 2000 before the British Open, all the rooms feature heirloom antiques, fine art, and top-of-the-line fixtures. And, yet, the atmosphere is relaxed. Guests have the run of the house, including an enclosed conservatory just off Jill's colorful kitchen. At £45 single and £70 double occupancy ($105), this is the kind of special place available in St. Andrews at about one-third the cost of the five-star hotels and, for that matter, considerably less than the three-star hotels.

Across the street from Jill Hardie's B & B, at *The St. Andrews Golfing Lodge* ⓫ (01334-477-676; *www.st-andrews-golf-lodge.com*), Chris Toll and Claire Cook preside over the newest concept in St. Andrews lodging—it's a private home, renovated in sleek Scandinavian modern in 2002, and available to groups for a fixed price by the night (£600 B & B in 2003). Rather like "self catering," but with the option of breakfast service, this is a perfect arrangement for eight to twelve golfers who want their own place with a kitchen, lounge, private parking, and back garden. Split the cost eight or more ways and it's no more expensive than a hotel room in the Golf Quadrangle.

Finally, in its own category, I want to mention housing available in the summer through the University of St. Andrews (01334-462-000; *www.st-andrews.ac.uk).* These include the *New Hall* ⓬ —not far from the Old Course and three-star rated by VisitScotland—and *Hamilton Hall,* right next to the Scores Hotel, overlooking the Old Course. A special word about Hamilton Hall: this building is almost as famous as the Royal & Ancient clubhouse. It's the five-story, turreted sandstone directly behind the eighteenth green of the Old Course. Most people think the building is an expensive hotel. *Au contraire.* Singles start at £27.50 ($43) and, for £65 ($100), though the lodging is dorm style sharing bath facilities, two can have the best view in town in a "premier" twin room overlooking the linksland. In America this grand building in its incomparable location would have been torn down long ago. But not in Scotland. Hamilton Hall lives on.

Outside St. Andrews

In *The Directory of Courses* I have cited popular lodgings at Glenrothes (see *Balbirnie Park*); Lundin Links (see *Lundin Golf Club*), and Crail (see *Crail Golfing Society*). To these I would add:

• *Eden House Hotel* (01334-652-510; *www.eden-group.com*) in Cupar, on the A91 ten miles east of St. Andrews. A good "golfers' hotel" on the train line to and from Edinburgh.

• *Inn at Lathones* (01334-840-494; *www.theinn.co.uk*). Great location just five miles outside St. Andrews on the A915. A 400-year-old coaching inn with a popular restaurant; pricey but special.

So, you see, there's a lot more to lodging in and around St. Andrews than the Old Course Hotel, Rusacks, and Rufflets. And I've just hit the highlights. The main point is, you can pay a lot or a little. Demand is high, but competition is keen, and that works to the benefit of the tourist. Consider your preferences, then start digging. There's something for everyone in St. Andrews.

The Golf Courses at St. Andrews

The St. Andrews Links Trust and Links Management Committee

In 1974 the St. Andrews Links Trust was established by an Act of Parliament to deal with the increasing numbers of visitors descending upon St. Andrews to play golf on the ancient links. The Trust was charged with maintaining the courses as *public* courses with assured access to all and with particular regard for the citizens of St. Andrews.

In carrying out its charge, the Links Management Committee has taken a variety of actions—some popular, some controversial. Surely the most popular was wholesale redesign of The Jubilee Course by Donald Steel in 1988-9, thus giving St. Andrews three championship-level courses side by side. Next, to accommodate beginning and high-handicap golfers, a new 18-hole course (The Strathtyrum) and a nine-holer (The Balcove) were opened in 1993. Additionally, a Golf Practice Centre was carved out of The Eden Course (some say to the everlasting ruin of the little track adjacent to the Old Course). A large clubhouse to accommodate visiting golfers was built in 1995 ("unnecessary," grumbled the old-timers). A smaller clubhouse at The Eden was finished in 2000. In 2000-01 an extensive, expensive, and controversial irrigation system was installed on the Old Course. In 2003 the committee announced plans for a seventh public course—this one of championship quality—on ground situated one mile south off the A917 between the St. Andrews Bay Resort Hotel and town centre.

To pay for all these changes, the Links Management Committee revised fee structures (constantly upward, of course), with special attention to visitors' wallets. Case in point: In the mid-1970s a visitor could play the Old Course for about £5; by the mid-1980s the cost was £15; by the late 1990s, the fee reached £60. In 2001 the rate was pegged at £85. In 2003 it jumped to £105. Has inflation increased twenty times in thirty years?—no. Is the Old Course twenty times better than it was thirty years ago?—of course not. Is demand twenty times greater?—yes, probably so, and then some.

Devising a system responsive to visitor demand, while continuing to guarantee democratic, affordable access to the Old Course *and* some preference for local residents, required the wisdom of Solomon. The Management Committee's multipart answer was the advance reservation system, the now-famous daily ballot for visitors, and the local ballot for residents. Unfortunately, the committee created serious controversy in 1995 when, to maximize revenue and simplify administration, it entered into a ten-year contract with a London-based travel agency to manage and sell about 1,000 tee times annually to the public and to "the trade" (i.e., tour operators and travel agencies) *without* retaining control over the agency's pricing policies (see my discussion of *The Old Course Experience* below). This action introduced elitism and obscurity to the previously democratic, straightforward booking process at St. Andrews.

The net result of links management history since 1974: lots of money for the Trust; a booking system that manages demand reasonably well, though not so democratically or cleanly as one would hope; a basketload of controversy over the years; and, at bottom,

Europe's largest golf complex with ninety-nine holes on six courses. Thanks to the Links Management Committee, comprised over the years of individuals dedicated to golf at St. Andrews, there's something for everyone at The Home of Golf. That much is not debated. Detailed information about the courses at St. Andrews, links news, and management policies can be found at the Links Trust's excellent web site, *www.standrews.org.uk.*

Getting a Tee Time on the Old Course

When I begin to explore itinerary options with a potential client, early in the conversation I ask one key question: *How important is the Old Course to your trip?* The answer to that question influences all aspects of trip planning. Before addressing that question here, I want to provide some context for the discussion—namely, an explanation of how to get a tee time on the Old Course. You have *seven options:*

✓ *Make an advance reservation.* For May to September dates, a request should be made approximately twelve to eighteen months prior to date of play. For example, in mid-September 2002 the Links Management stopped taking advance reservation requests for peak-season 2003. As demand for the Old Course increases, the cutoff date continues creeping toward the middle of the calendar year. *Best advice*: the sooner you can submit a request, the better. Applications are held and acted upon by date of receipt. Then, in the fall of the year preceding date of play, the Links Management allocates times. Applicants are contacted by the end of December. If you've secured a time, you can proceed to plan the rest of your trip. If your bid has failed, you can weigh your other options.

This is a process more easily described than accomplished. Making an advance reservation at St. Andrews requires considerable forethought, as well as the freedom to make a date-specific commitment more than a year away. The Links Management requests information that may be a challenge to present. They want to know: (1) the names of all golfers; (2) their handicaps; (3) their club affiliations; (4) a "lead golfer" to receive all correspondence and make payment; (5) a specific date of requested play (Monday through Friday; all play on Saturdays is by ballot); and (6) your choice of a second course to play (an advance date on the Old Course requires play on another of the St. Andrews courses). This level of detail is required to help prevent speculative booking by tour operators. A minor modification might be made along the way (e.g., substitution of one player for another), but wholesale variations from the original request are not tolerated. Application must be made in writing by mail, fax, or Email. See *The Directory of Courses* for contact information. A single golfer may apply for an advance reservation. Depending upon the month, from May to September something like ten to fifteen slots per month are allocated to singles.

In *Part II, Chapter One,* I stressed the importance of checking the Old Course calendar for conflicts and closure dates, with the admonition that, "You can't play the Old Course if it's not open." I reiterate that admonition here. Check the Links Trust web site and/or call the reservations office if you have any doubt about the availability of a date. If you request a date when the Old Course is not available by advance reservation, you will be notified and asked to re-submit for another date. In 2003 the Links Management announced a policy of no advance reservations during June and September due to frequent conflicts with scheduled tournaments and other special events (e.g., autumn meeting of the Royal and Ancient).

✓ ***Enter the daily visitor ballot.*** On this subject I quote directly from the Links Management web site:

> Around 50% of all starting times over the year are put into the daily ballot (lottery) which is drawn every day for next day's play except Sunday—the Saturday draw is for Monday play. Success in the ballot is not guaranteed and chances vary according to the time of year, how busy the course is, and the weather. A minimum two golfers can enter. Either telephone or apply in person before 2 p.m. on the day before play. The results are shown by 4 p.m. on the web, at the clubhouses, the starters' boxes, the caddie pavilion, local golf clubs, and the tourist information office.

This is the way most visitors to St. Andrews get a tee time on the Old Course. Odds are about even in April and October; odds are more like one in six in the peak months May to September.

✓ *Enter the daily local ballot.* Each day, tee times from 8-9 a.m. and 5-6 p.m. are reserved for residents of St. Andrews. The pool of applicants in the local ballot is much smaller than in the visitor ballot. Thus, if you can get into the local pool, your odds of getting onto the Old Course improve. To enter the local ballot, you need to pair up with a resident of St. Andrews who will play a round of golf with you and who will enter your names in the ballot. How do you that? Maybe you already know someone who lives in St. Andrews or belongs to one of the golf clubs there. If not, when you get into town, start talking to people. Chat up the bartender, the shopkeeper, the waiter, or a university student. Most important, talk to your lodging host. He or she most assuredly will know a local resident who might be looking for a game. This method of getting on the Old Course is not "by the book" (except when you buy this book), but it's entirely legitimate. It's a great way for a single golfer to avoid the walk-on queue.

✓ *Walk on.* Though a few advance reservation slots are allotted to singles, joining the walk-on queue is the most common way single golfers get on the Old Course. Since many advance reservations and ballot applications are made for two or three golfers, each day the starter has a varying number of open slots. And, because many Scots play in twos and threes, this is also your best shot at playing with locals who know the course. With a first tee time of 7 a.m. in the summer, single golfers, often with coffee and continental breakfast in hand, start queuing up at the Old Course Starter House at about 5:30 a.m. (or earlier). Alternative to the morning queue, one might check with the starter mid-to-late afternoon to inquire about the possibility of evening play. Inclement weather can bring the best opportunity for walking on any time of day. While a little rain won't stop visitors who have traveled thousands of miles to play the Old Course, locals, who can play any time, may prefer to sit out a rainy day.

The cost of these first four methods of getting on the Old Course is the current green fee plus, in the case of advance reservation, another green fee on the New Course, Jubilee, or Eden. From here on, the options get considerably more expensive.

✓ *Buy a St. Andrews hotel package that includes an Old Course tee time.* Each year the hotels of St. Andrews are allocated about one hundred tee times (total). These are pooled and administered by a committee of innkeepers chaired currently by Louise Hughes of the St. Andrews Golf Hotel. Most of the times go to the largest, most prestigious hotels—the Old Course Hotel, Rusacks, Rufflets, The Scores Hotel, and the St. Andrews Golf Hotel. Small hotels like the Dunvegan or The Russell get only a handful (four or five) to sell. The allocation is made in the fall when the Links Management allocates other advance reservations. You can request a reservation at a hotel contingent upon receiving one of their allocated tee times. Should they decide to sell to you, for a package price putting a premium on the Old Course round, they will require play on two courses, a minimum three-night stay, and dinners at the hotel. They'll also be looking for a full contingent—that is, four golfers with four non-golfing spouses—to maximize their revenue from these little nuggets of golfing gold. In practice, most of the hotel tee times go to longtime patrons—people who come back year after year to vacation in St. Andrews—or to favored tour operators who bring trade to the hotels. This is the *least* likely way to get on the Old Course.

✓ *Buy a tour package.* The Links Management has created a class of "protected operators" who get a small allocation of tee times. These are Scottish operators or the UK offices of American companies like PerryGolf and InterGolf. Of course they only sell the tee times as part of a larger tour package. Generally speaking, the Scottish operators run more reasonably-priced tours than their American counterparts. To get a list of these protected operators, inquire at the Links Management office.

Other tour operators buy Old Course tee times at "trade" prices from the Keith Prowse Agency (see *The Old Course Experience* below). They then wrap the tee times into package tours and re-sell them to the public. As you saw in *Part I Chapter One*, the problem with these tours is their cost. You can get a tee time on the Old Course this way, but, to get it, you will probably have to stay at the Old Course Hotel, not to mention Gleneagles, the Marine Hotel in Troon, and the Turnberry Hotel. In other words, you can play the Old Course, but only by paying top dollar all the way through your tour of Scotland's luxury resorts.

✓ *Buy "The Old Course Experience."* Tour operators can be removed from the picture by dealing directly with the Keith Prowse Agency. You can read in detail about The Old Course Experience at *www.oldcourse-experience.com*. Before we get to price, here's a summary of what you get when you buy The "Old Course Experience," circa 2003, June to September: (1) tee times on the Old Course and another St. Andrews course; (2) two nights lodging at the St. Andrews Golf Hotel, Rusacks, or the Old Course Hotel plus a night at Carnoustie's Golf Hotel; (3) two dinners; and (4) a photograph of your group. Oh, yes, you also get "full use of the links clubhouse" (open to the public at no charge) and "souvenir video and merchandise." The price? The least you'll pay for this "experience" is £1595 (about $2,472) with accommodations at the St. Andrews Golf Hotel. If you want to stay at the Old Course Hotel, the cost will be £1800 ($2,790). And, by the way, that's *per person,* not per room.

If a person could get a tee time on the Old Course in any other reasonable way—e.g., by advance reservation or through the daily ballot—the actual cost of the OCE package described here would be about $800 to $900. In other words, the Keith Prowse Agency is selling that tee time on the Old Course for about $1,600. Is any golf course worth $1,600? I don't think so.

Surprisingly enough, there are times when I recommend The Old Course Experience as a way of playing the Old Course without buying into a longer and still more expensive trip offered by a tour operator. That subject and others are taken up in the next section.

How important is the Old Course to your trip?

With some context in place, let's take another look at this question. For many people, playing the Old Course is the "bottom line" of a trip to Scotland. The guarantee has to be in place. Without it, they'd rather stay home. If you fall into that category, you have four options: (1) *successfully* make an advance reservation; (2) persuade one of the hotels to sell a package to you; (3) sign up for a tour package; or (4) buy the Old Course Experience. None of the other methods of getting on the Old Course carries a guarantee of success.

If you can plan far enough ahead to apply for an advance reservation and succeed, you're miles ahead of everyone else. In my view, it's the only reasonable way to buy a "guaranteed" tee time.

But most people either don't know they need to apply twelve to eighteen months ahead of anticipated play or they just start planning too late. Every January and February I get calls from people who say they want to go to Scotland in the summer and, of course, they *must* play the Old Course. These are the times when I suggest consideration of The Old Course Experience rather than a package tour. With this approach, one can pay the Keith Prowse piper, while retaining the flexibility to plan the rest of a trip for a reasonable price—in effect, creating a "tour within a tour." But it doesn't make much difference. Either way, it's expensive. When it comes to the Old Course, guarantees cost a lot of money.

Most often, golfers simply cannot or will not buy into the outrageously priced Old Course Experience. Yet the Old Course remains their primary objective. In this case, if the idea of a package tour also has been rejected, the options become: (1) the daily visitor ballot; (2) the daily local ballot; or (3) walking on as a single. In the first two cases, I recommend an itinerary that keeps you within striking distance of St. Andrews so that the Old Course bell can be answered when it rings. This means a "stay and play" itinerary in Fife (see Trip #1 in *Part I, Chapter Two*); or a circumscribed itinerary combining, for example, Fife with East Lothian or Angus (see Trip #3 in *Part I, Chapter Two*). Your objective is to ballot the Old Course for a full week, if necessary. Given that much time, your success in getting on the Old Course is virtually assured. Here's what I recommend to make this approach work most effectively and efficiently:

• Arrive in Scotland on Saturday; ballot the Old Course for Monday play (or have your hotel do it for you). Check the ballot results after 4 p.m. If you have been chosen for

Monday play, call your pre-booked Monday course to cancel or rearrange the tee time.

• On Sunday, since the Old Course is closed, play an expensive priority course like Kingsbarns or Carnoustie.

• If you were not chosen in the ballot on Saturday, ballot again on Monday for Tuesday play and continue that process throughout the week if necessary.

• For Monday through Friday play, book yourself at courses that require a minimal deposit or no deposit. In Fife, these could include Crail, Elie, Lundin Links, Leven Links, Ladybank, and Scotscraig (see *Part III, The Directory of Courses* for more ideas).

• Toward the end of the week, leave some unbooked time for the possibility of play on St. Andrews' New Course or Jubilee. Though pre-booking these courses is an option, I don't usually recommend it because (a) 100 percent pre-payment is required and (b) due to frequent cancellations, it's normally an easy walk-on during the week. I'd rather have the flexibility than the pre-booked time.

This approach to the Old Course, almost assuredly, will get you a tee time and, more important, an affordable trip focused on a small area of Scotland. Believe me, even if you don't get on the Old Course, you'll have a great trip and play a lot of good golf.

Closing words on the Old Course

This is my basic advice regarding the Old Course and Scottish golf: *To the extent that you can disenthrall yourself of the Old Course, you will have a greater range of itinerary options.* In other words, fixation on the Old Course limits your ability to discover the rest of Scotland.

To be more specific: *without an advance reservation* on the Old Course, it is not logically consistent to say that, in seven days, your main priority is to play the Old Course, but you also want to play Royal Troon, Prestwick, Turnberry, Carnoustie, and Royal Dornoch. If your main priority is to play the Old Course, then you need to plan accordingly—and that doesn't mean buzzing around the country from east to west, south to north. But, with the Old Course in proper perspective, you can schedule all those great courses mentioned above.

So, what is "proper perspective"? Ideally, the Old Course should be treated as icing on the cake. If you get on, fine. If you don't, fine—maybe next time. I can understand those situations that truly are once-in-a-lifetime trips—a father and son's last opportunity to play golf together; an 80-year-old's birthday trip to the Old Country; a dying golfer's last wish. Those are special occasions that deserve extraordinary measures to get on the Old Course.

Otherwise, why take a once-in-a-lifetime approach to Scottish golf? If you like Scottish golf—and most likely you will—then you can go back time and time again. And, if you can afford to go once, surely you can afford to go twice—particularly if you've read this book and have avoided the tours. At bottom, the entire case I've made to this point is that you can make two trips for the price most people pay for one trip. In that context, the Old Course takes on "proper perspective"—ONE of many great Scottish courses to be played on more than one trip.

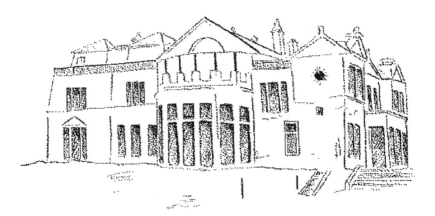

CHAPTER FOUR

The Four Elements of a Golf Trip:
Air Travel, Vehicle Rental, Tee Times, and Lodging

Air Travel

These days everyone has their own approach to purchasing airline tickets. Some people use their trusty travel agent. Others prefer to call an airline straight away. An increasing number of people are booking via the internet. Some people use frequent-flyer miles. Others use miles accumulated through credit-card purchases.

Given all these options—and the ever-changing dynamics of the airline industry—it would be foolish to print specific information on prices and routes in a book like this. What I *can* do is give you some advice, partly specific to current conditions, but generally based on the bigger picture that comes from personal experience.

Frankly, it bothers me a bit when clients plan a trip to Scotland only to delay buying their airline tickets until they can get "the best deal." To put this phenomenon in perspective: some people will blithely spend something like $500 for one night at the Turnberry Hotel but put off buying an airline ticket with the hope of saving $100! I guess it's the fun of playing Russian Roulette with the airlines. But I digress.

Following are two pieces of advice to guide your air arrangements. Both these items are based on an important principle: *it's no fun for a golfer to be in Scotland without golf clubs.* Barring a traffic accident, the worst thing that can happen on your trip is for you to arrive at your destination while your clubs are in London, Paris, Brussels or Amsterdam—not just for a few hours but for a few days.

If you are on a five or six-day trip and you don't get your clubs until the third or fourth day, you are going to be a decidedly "unhappy camper." Unfortunately, it happens. Why? The main reason is spelled H-e-a-t-h-r-o-w. This is another subject on which I've become an expert through personal experience.

The largest percentage of visitors to Scotland arrive via London's Heathrow Airport—mainly because most major cities in the U.S. are served by routes to London and the cheapest flights are to that great city. At London Heathrow one can connect via British Midland to airports at Glasgow, Edinburgh, Aberdeen, and Inverness in Scotland. Now, here's my first piece of advice:

> ✔ *If you fly through London's Heathrow International Airport, leave at least **three hours** between arrival time and your connecting flight to Scotland.*

London is the world's second largest city. The airport at Heathrow is huge. Literally thousands of people are "processed" through Heathrow every hour. Given the size of the airport and the crush of humanity there, it seems to be logistically impossible to get oversize luggage (i.e., golf clubs) from Point A (International Arrivals) to Point C (Domestic Departures) in less than two hours.

Actually, it's nearly impossible to get *yourself* from Point A to Point C in less than two hours. I say, "Point C," advisedly because in between Point A and Point C you have to clear Customs (Point B). Along the way you'll endure two bus rides through a labyrinth of Heathrow's back streets and byways. What a welcome to the UK!

In short, if your travel agent says, "I have your ticket to Glasgow and you only have to wait *one hour and thirty minutes* to connect in London," your reply should be, "Go back to the drawing board and give me three hours to make that connecting flight." To be safe, I would offer the same advice regarding all the major connecting points. The most frequently used are Amsterdam (KLM), Paris (Air France), and Frankfurt (Lufthansa).

Having allowed enough time for you and your luggage to make a connection, if your bags still do not arrive in Scotland when you do, you will need to go the "Baggage Claims" office where, bleary-eyed from lack of sleep, you will fill out claim forms and your patience will

72

be taxed to the limit. Most often your luggage will arrive on the next flight and will be forwarded at the airline's expense to your first lodging address. Ironically, *if you choose an international flight with a connection, there is clear advantage to connecting through London rather than through a city outside the UK.* The reason: through most of the business day, British Midland (your most likely connecting airline) runs flights every two hours from London to Glasgow and Edinburgh. Thus, your luggage most often will be delayed for only two hours. From cities outside the UK, with fewer flights each day, the wait most assuredly will be several hours at best.

All this rather depressing discussion of connecting points and delayed or lost luggage leads to my second (and best) piece of advice:

✓ *Fly nonstop to Glasgow if you can* (Glasgow because currently no nonstop flights are offered from the U.S. or Canada direct to Edinburgh).

When you fly directly into Glasgow you'll arrive at a relatively peaceful, pleasant place, without the "cattle car" environment of major airports. More important, you'll have an umbilical link with your golf clubs and clothes that were put on the plane at your point of departure. At this writing (February 2003), nonstop flights to Glasgow originate from the U.S. at Chicago (American Airlines) and Newark (Continental Airlines). Air Canada flies direct from Toronto.

Two other painless ways to get to Glasgow without going through London are on Aer Lingus with stops at Shannon and/or Dublin, and on Icelandair via Reykjavik. Aer Lingus offers flights to Dublin from Baltimore-Washington (BWI), Boston, Chicago, Los Angeles, and New York (JFK). From Dublin, three Aer Lingus flights depart daily to Glasgow and Edinburgh. There are no direct flights to Scottish cities from Shannon Airport (Limerick) except on Ryanair.

NOTE: Low-fare airlines (Ryanair, easyJet) might serve the golfer who wants to hop across the Irish Sea in one direction or the other for a few rounds but, due to baggage restrictions and the point-to-point nature of these airlines, neither is a good option for transatlantic connections.

Icelandair operates flights to Glasgow through Reykjavik from Boston, Baltimore-Washington (BMI), Minneapolis-St. Paul, and New York (JFK). The layover in Reykjavik is only one hour, thirty minutes, so it's nearly as good as a direct flight. Following is telephone and web site information for the airlines mentioned above.

Aer Lingus	800-474-7424	*aerlingus.com*
Air Canada	888-247-2262	*aircanada.com*
American Airlines	800-443-7300	*aa.com*
British Midland	800-788-0555	*flybmi.com*
Continental Airlines	800-525-0280	*flycontinental.com*
easyJet	0870-600-0000	*easyjet.com*
Icelandair	800-223-5500	*icelandair.com*
Ryanair	0871-246-0000	*ryanair.com*

For toll-free numbers to other airlines, see *www.inter800.com*.

Vehicle Rental

Self-drive versus chauffeur-driven trips
This is an important question probably influenced most by group size. The larger the group (8-12+ golfers/nongolfers), the more likely you are to use a coach and chauffeur. The accent is upon togetherness, socializing, and getting a big group safely through a trip. Cost is not much of a factor because per-person cost diminishes as the number of travelers increases. Per-person cost in a group of twelve will not be much different than per-person cost for four on a self-drive trip.

For groups of four to eight, the issue is a tougher call. For eight, the cost differential increases to about 2:1. Assuming you rent your vehicle from the right place (see below), a group of eight on a self-drive trip will spend about $25-30 per person per day on two minibuses. The same individuals on a chauffeur-driven trip will spend about $45-50+. The ratio for a group of four will be more like 3:1. Clearly, self-driving is the most economical way to travel.

The rest of the decision is qualitative. Your choice will affect the kind of trip you have. Personally, I like to drive and I want to see Scotland "where the rubber meets the road." I like the flexibility and freedom to come and go when and where I want. A group of eight, requiring two vehicles, also gains the flexibility to go more than one direction for either golf or nongolf activities. In sum, this approach amounts to more individual freedom and less "group think."

On the other hand, group think is fun too and chauffeuring takes the adventure out of driving on the left side of the road, negotiating roundabouts, and interpreting foreign traffic signs. And, if you get a personable and compatible driver, you can make a friend for life and receive the undoubted benefit of the driver's local knowledge.

If you choose the chauffeuring option, avoid the big tour companies that shepherd herds of tourists around the UK every summer. You can tell who they are by the content of their web sites. With these companies you are more likely to get a comatose driver and, contrary to theories of "economy of scale," these companies are invariably more expensive than the small ones.

Make sure that your coach company is bonded, insured, and has a PCV license (passenger carry vehicle). Look for company-owned Mercedes and Volkswagen coaches as signs of customized quality. Unless your trip is circumscribed and driving distances are minimal, you do *not* want to hire a freelance driver who is going to get a contract and then go out and rent a minibus from a car rental agency. But, with these caveats in mind, there is every reason to choose a small, family-run business where you will receive personal attention and the best price. Scotland is loaded with them and, over the past couple of years, I've made a point of uncovering some in various parts of the country. Here are a few:

• *Executive Travel Company*, Greenock (nr Glasgow), contact Alistair Thomas, ph 01475-790-546, *www.scotexectravel.co.uk*

• *Joe Russell Minibus Hire*, Strathhaven (nr Glasgow), contact Joe Russell, ph 01357-521-553

• *RowanTravel*, Dundee, contact Steve Mackie, ph 01382-320-376, *www.rowantravel.co.uk*

• *Tim Dearman Coaches*, Ardross (nr Inverness), contact Tim Dearman, ph 01349-883-585, *www.timdearmancoaches.co.uk*

Self-Drive Rental

If the choice is a self-drive trip, reserve your vehicle as early as possible. There's no reason to wait. If cancellation is necessary, any deposits made are normally fully refundable with sufficient notice. Penalties are not assessed for changes in pickup/dropoff plans.

This is a major expense item that can cause way too much brain damage and cost way too much money. Call any of the name brands in the business. After you tell them you want to rent a vehicle in, say, Glasgow, the first question they ask is, "For what dates?". Then the fun begins: "Automatic or manual?" "Do you want full insurance?" "Will that be one way or return?" "You want to add another driver?—that will be another £5.50 per day." "Oh, by the way, our price doesn't include a local airport surcharge of £17 and a road tax of £1 per day."

Go through this song and dance with three different companies and you could easily be pulling your hair out. It makes dealing with the airlines seem simple. By the time you get to the bottom line—with all the "add-ons" and surcharges not included in the base price—you can end up with an expensive rental and a giant headache.

My mission in this book is to make travel planning easy. Therefore I want to pass along two words designed to bypass all the rigamarole of shopping for a rental car in Scotland. Those words are: ARNOLD CLARK. Arnold Clark is the largest automobile dealership in Scotland. They are also in the rental car business. They have the biggest and best fleet of vehicles for golfers. Here is their main reservations number:

Arnold Clark Central Reservations   0845-602-1895

Arnold Clark will initiate online booking during 2003 at *www.acfinance.com/rental*. Another site offering Arnold Clark inventory description, prices and booking is *www.rental-cars-scotland.com*. *My advice on this subject: **Forget about the "brand name" companies and go straight to Arnold Clark for your rental.***

I hasten to add, this is *not* an advertisement. The plain truth is that Arnold Clark is so much better than all the rest of the car rental agencies in the market, there really is no other choice and will not be until other companies start to follow their example. Why?

✓ First, Arnold Clark prices typically beat the brand names by twenty to forty percent (see example below).

✓ Second, *all charges* are included in an Arnold Clark quote. As their brochure says, "The price you see is the price you pay." Prices include the value-added tax (17.5%), road tax, full insurance coverage, and unlimited mileage. No surprises here. Everything's on the table.

✓ Third, Arnold Clark has plenty of vehicles with automatic transmission in every class above the compacts, particularly among the minivans and minibuses that golf parties need. Among the larger vehicles, there is no "upcharge" for automatic transmission. In other words, an automatic minivan and a manual minivan carry the same price. Try that one on for size at the brand-name companies!

✓ Fourth, you won't pay an airport surcharge (£17) when you rent from Arnold Clark because they are an off-site agency with branches conveniently located near Scotland's major airports.

✓ Fifth, Arnold Clark has the lowest additional-driver charge in the industry. It's a flat fee of £5 (compared to the £5 or more per-driver-per-day-rate typical of the brand names).

✓ Sixth, Arnold Clark has a low "excess" liability deductible. That's the amount you're liable for in case of damage to your rental vehicle. Arnold Clark's £100 maximum for compact and mid-size vehicles compares to £250 or more in the rest of the industry. Their £250 maximum for minivans and minibuses compares to £500 or more at other companies.

✓ Seventh, with some thirty locations around the country, an Arnold Clark branch is never far away.

✓ Eighth, while other travelers are standing in line, waiting to be served by one clerk at the brand-name agencies, you'll be out the airport door, into a shuttle bus, and off to an agency where you and you alone are the focus of service.

If this sounds too good to be true, all I can say is that when you find a company like Arnold Clark—straight-shooting, no bait-and-switch, no phony advertising—you had best count your lucky stars and take your business straight to their door. You won't be sorry.

Here's an example of how Arnold Clark pricing compared to AutoEurope (a broker for Avis, Hertz, National, and EuropCar) on a given day in February 2003:

The Request: an automatic minivan for 7 days in early July 2003 with one additional driver.

Arnold Clark's no-nonsense, all-inclusive price: £350

    1. one additional driver £5

    TOTAL £355 ($550)

AutoEurope's Response (quoted in U.S. dollars):

    1. Only EuropCar has an automatic minivan.
       Not available through Avis, Hertz, or National.

    2. "Base rate" plus VAT and insurance: $1080
       ($74 collision/theft insurance)

    3. 5% discount on base rate ($857) for purchase before
       March 31 (must be 100% prepaid): - $42.85

    4. 5% AAA discount on adjusted base rate: - $40.71

    5. Airport tax $29 (£17 flat fee)

    6. Road tax $13 (£1.20 per day)

    7. Additional driver $56 ($8 per day per additional driver)

    TOTAL $1,094

Look at the difference for this simple rental—$544. "Apples to apples," Arnold Clark's rate is about half the competition's best "winter sale" price. And, even without buying EuropCar's insurance, the price differential is still $470. With that you could just about pay for a double room at the Turnberry Hotel!

One weakness of Arnold Clark is that the company has only five branches outside Scotland and none at London airports. Another "homegrown" company with branches at most UK airports is Woods Car Rental (01293-658-888; *www.woods.co.uk)*. Woods is more expensive than Arnold Clark but generally below market competition.

The Brand Names

If you want to test my advice on this subject, if you are a loyal Hertz or Avis customer, or you really *want* to shop the brand names, following are two suggestions on how to proceed:

✓ *Always make more than one call.* Why? Your first call establishes a price benchmark. From there you can do some bargaining. If you ask them, rental car companies will usually match the price of a competitor. Most of them have a "beat-rate" supervisor—someone with authority to make a deal. Your goal is to ratchet the price downward as far as it will go—or at least to get add-ons subtracted or reduced. Remember, it never hurts to ask. Ask for a lower price. Ask for a free upgrade. Ask for a specific car. Ask them to eliminate the fee for an additional driver. If you don't ask, you won't get.

✓ *Invoke your affiliations.* Be sure to ask about any discounts you might secure by virtue of associations, memberships, employment, etc. These might include AARP, AAA, frequent flyer memberships, government or corporate affiliation. But don't ask for the discounted rate until *after* you've received a quote for a basic rate. Most often the reply will be, "That is our lowest rate," but the response might be, "I can reduce that rate by five percent." If you ask for the discounted rate first, you'll never know whether you were just quoted a basic rate that got called a "discounted rate."

Who to call? At Scottish airports you'll find the usual cast of characters—Alamo, Budget, National, Avis, Hertz, plus a European agency, EuropCar, brokered through AutoEurope. Here are toll-free telephone numbers for the major car rental companies:

Alamo	877-530-5613
AutoEurope	888-223-5555
Avis	800-331-1212
Budget	800-472-3325
Dollar	800-800-4000
Hertz	800-654-3131
National	800-227-7368
Thrifty	800-847-4389

On the following page is a worksheet to help you track car agency data with the objective of comparing "apples to apples."

RENTAL VEHICLE WORKSHEET

Company _____

Phone Number _____

Airport: On-site _____ Off-site _____

Confirmation # _____

Date of Inquiry _____ Clerk ID _____

Vehicle Size: subcompact, compact, mid-size sedan, large sedan, station wagon, minivan, minibus

_____

Pickup Date: _____ Approx Time _____

Return Date: _____ Approx Time _____

Days _____

Automatic Transmission _____ Manual Transmission _____

_____ Basic Rate (should include 17.5% VAT, unlimited mileage, theft insurance; it may or may not include items below)

_____ Airport surcharge

_____ Road tax _____ per day _____ flat rate

_____ Additional driver(s) _____ per driver _____ per day
OR _____ flat rate

_____ One-way dropoff charge

_____ Collision Damage Waiver (CDW) - this is normally covered by personal insurance or your credit card

_____ **TOTAL** x $1.55 if quoted in pounds sterling = $_____

NOTES:

Common Questions

Do I need an international driver's license to rent a car in Scotland? No. You need a valid driver's license and your passport.

What is the age limit for drivers? Depending upon car size and individual company policy, minimum ages vary from 21 to 25. At the upper end, the age limits vary from 71 to 75.

Is a minivan big enough for four golfers? Generally, no. I recommend a VW Caravelle minibus for four golfers. A minivan usually will suffice for two golfers and two nongolfers.

What should I do if I have an accident? Your rental car company will provide full instructions and contact numbers.

Tee Times

Contacting the Clubs

Before cheap long-distance phone service, fax machines, and email, the common way to make a reservation at a Scottish course was by written request accompanied by a formal "letter of introduction" from your club professional. That is emphatically *not* the case today. The Scots are polite and somewhat more formal than Americans, but they are modern people, quite good at extracting money from tourists as efficiently as possible rather than by "snail mail."

Thus, the quickest, the most effective way to reserve a tee time at most courses is to simply get on the phone and call. If you do that from the west coast of the United States, it means getting up pretty early. The time differential is 8 hours, so you'll need to make calls before 8 a.m. and not later than 9 a.m. Most offices at the well-traveled courses are open until at least 4 p.m. or 5 p.m. At the lesser-known clubs you may find the secretary's hours sporadic or confined to the morning hours. If that's the case, then you'll probably be communicating by fax or email. Here are the time differentials in the United States:

- Pacific Time - 8 hrs. - call before 8 a.m.
- Mountain Time - 7 hrs. - call before 9 a.m.

- Central Time - 6 hrs. - call before 10 a.m.
- Eastern Time - 5 hrs. - call before 11 a.m.

I recommend a phone call because you can get answers most quickly that way and a phone call gives you maximum flexibility to confirm details regarding alternative available times, visitor restrictions, deposits, club rental, caddie hire, directions, etc. You'll also get a feel for the ambience of a club just by talking with people on the phone. If you have trouble reaching someone with authority to book a time for you, then send email or a fax and wait for a reply.

Most often you will *not* talk with the secretary of a club. You'll probably talk with an office assistant or maybe even a bartender. Usually at least two communications will be necessary—the first to formally request a time, then a second to confirm group composition and payment details by fax or email. If it can all be done with one phone call, so much the better.

The Efficiency of Fax Machines and Email
Admittedly, fax machines and email cost less than phone calls, and there's a certain satisfaction gained from firing off a half-dozen communiqués to Scotland at 10 p.m., then waking up the next morning to find that most of your trip was booked overnight while you were sleeping! It's an efficient way to start the process even if some follow-up work is necessary. If you like this approach, on the next page is a sample letter for you to adapt in making a booking inquiry. All detail necessary to customize this letter for individual courses is in *Part III, The Directory of Courses*.

Online Booking Services
Fee-based online booking services have begun to develop. None is satisfactory. The best is *www.teetimescotland.com*. The problem is, "Garbage in, garbage out." Most clubs have only recently entered the cybernet age. At this point in history, at a high-profile golf club, there is no way an online system can substitute for a telephone call and a personal conversation with the booking assistant. Maybe at the Boat of Garten, but not at Royal Troon or Turnberry. Nevertheless, it's something to consider and monitor.

SAMPLE - ADVANCE RESERVATION REQUEST LETTER

Date
ATT: Mr. A Sneddon, Secretary, Golf House Club
RE: Visitor inquiry - advance reservation

Dear Mr. Sneddon:

I would like to know if Golf House Club can accommodate four visiting golfers, preferably with a morning tee time, on 20 June (Wednesday) 2004. If so, following is information to facilitate an advance reservation.

LEAD GOLFER: A Ferguson, hdp 10, Mira Vista GC, Denver CO
CREDIT CARD: MC 0000-0000-0000-0000 Exp 09/05
OTHER GOLFERS: Donald Rex, hdp 13, City Park GC, Denver CO; Robert Thompson, hdp 12, Overland Park GC, Denver CO; Luther Runyon, hdp 17, City Park GC, Denver CO.

THANK YOU in advance for your assistance with this inquiry.

Allan Ferguson
1743 S. Marion St.
Denver CO 80210
ph/fax: 303-722-3441
aferguson@fergusongolf.com

Important Information for Single Golfers

Often a client will say to me, "I've heard that a single golfer can't make a tee time in Scotland." This is a myth. On the contrary, the single golfer has distinct advantages in making tee times.

The only important exceptions to this generalization are at St. Andrews and Carnoustie. Otherwise, virtually all courses will make advance booking for a single; these include Royal Troon, Prestwick, Royal Dornoch, Western Gailes, North Berwick, Gullane #1, Kingsbarns—all the courses most visitors want to play. Understanding this subject is both interesting and instructive because it relates to the Scottish attitude toward golf and course management.

The Scots will *not* routinely "fill a foursome" the way course managers do in the United States. There are two reasons for this: first, they are more interested in the pace of play than they are in filling a course to capacity. They favor two-ball and three-ball groups to four-ball matches (foursomes) and many courses reserve early and late hours for two-ball matches often preferred by club members. The Scots would rather get a dozen two-ball matches around in three hours than six or seven foursomes in four-plus hours. A five-hour round is out of the question.

Second, if two or three golfers have made a tee time during visitor hours, the Scots won't automatically put other golfers with that group until they ask permission of the booked golfers. In other words, you don't have to play golf with someone you don't know unless you agree to do so. What a novel idea!—enough to make an American club pro cringe. This is a broad generalization. The most heavily-played courses *will* pair singles and twosomes with other golfers before date of play.

In the pairing procedure, a single golfer looking for a game normally will be asked for his or her handicap. Why? Because, for the enjoyment of all, the Scots won't put a total duffer out with a single-digit handicapper. Another novel idea American course managers could well emulate.

So, what does all this mean for the single golfer? Well, it's good news. First, it means that at most courses you'll find lots of "holes" in the schedule of tee times—lots of places for a single golfer to slide into a game with two or three other players. Second, it means most often you'll be playing with golfers of comparable ability. The process can lead to hooking up with other singletons during your stay in Scotland.

Since my wife is a nongolfer, I have considerable experience as a single golfer in Scotland. Here's my approach:

✓ If a course is on my "must-play" list, I'll pre-book it.

✓ I'll leave most days unbooked—thus avoiding prepayments and deposits and, at the same time, creating maximum flexibility for golf or nongolf activities depending upon weather, mood, etc. Then I'll have a list of "optional" courses for play and start phoning through the list in priority order until I find a tee time that works best for our schedule.

✓ Normally, I'll call a course the day before I want to play and ask to speak to the secretary, the booking assistant, or the professional. I'll explain that I'm there as a single golfer and would be interested in a game with a club member if that can be arranged. Sometimes I'm successful with that approach to play with an "insider"; sometimes I'm not—but rarely do I encounter a course that is fully booked.

Step-by-Step Booking Advice

Using *Part II, Chapter Two* (*Where to Go*), and *Part III, The Directory of Courses,* pick the courses you want to play and determine their visitor policies. Then take the following three-step approach.

✓ *Arrange your courses in priority order. Start provisional booking from the top down—from "must-play" to "optional."* Certain courses on your ideal itinerary are likely to be "linchpin" courses— ones that either allow the rest of the schedule to work logistically or are at or near the top of a must-play list. For example, if Royal Troon is on your must-play list, it's usually a good idea to schedule the Ayrshire coast early in the week because Troon accepts visitors only on Mondays, Tuesdays, and Thursdays. Your odds of booking are best if you have the flexibility to play either Monday or Tuesday rather than only on Thursday.

✓ *Schedule "daily fee," public, and resort courses on the weekends.* At most private clubs (i.e., most golf courses in Scotland), visitor access on weekends is restricted. Maximum flexibility to play when you want to play on Saturdays and Sundays can be achieved by booking the daily fee, public, and resort courses on those days. Examples of these are: Kingsbarns, The Duke's Course, and Letham Grange in Fife and Angus (Region #s 1 and 4); the courses at Gleneagles (Region #7); Turnberry and Belleisle in Ayrshire (Region #2); and Whitekirk in East Lothian (Region #3). In St. Andrews, the Old Course is closed on Sunday; the other courses are open.

✓ *Secure all your tee times before you make arrangements for lodging.* As Robert Burns wrote, "The best-laid plans of mice and men gang aft agley" (often go awry). All the pieces of the tee-time puzzle must fit before you start booking accommodations. You could have a well-laid plan only to find out that two of the courses on your must-play list are closed to visitor play on the days you want to be there.

What to do? Well, at that point, you either change your priorities or start rearranging the itinerary to accommodate your must-play courses.

Common Questions

Do I have to prepay green fees? That depends upon the course. Some require full prepayment; most require a deposit ranging from a token (e.g., five or ten percent) to a substantial amount (fifty percent); some require no advance payment at all. See the deposit entries in *The Directory of Courses* for details.

Can I use my credit card to book a tee time? With few exceptions, yes. Just make sure it's MasterCard or VISA; American Express won't get you far in Scotland. This is not a commercial; it's the truth.

Can I use a different credit card from each member of my group for deposits? No. They want a "lead golfer" at least per foursome. Charges will be made against one card. It will then be up to the lead golfer to get reimbursed by the other golfers. Once there, you can use individual cards for paying the balances due.

What information do I need to provide? Lead golfer's name, number of golfers, contact information, credit card details. The St. Andrews Links Management will ask for all golfers names, club affiliations, and handicaps. In general, female golfers are more likely to be asked about handicaps than male golfers. Singles and twosomes of either gender are likely to be asked for handicap information in the interest of pairing you with players of comparable ability.

Lodging

Scotland probably has a greater range and quantity of accommodations per capita than any place in the world. The country is dotted with literally thousands of modest bed-and-breakfast operations while boasting some of the world's most palatial international resorts and manor houses. In between are some of the finest small hotels and country houses you will ever hope to find, as well as larger, "purpose-built" hotels and an increasing number of standardized, American-style hotel chains. Tourism is big business in Scotland.

Most of these accommodations are graded and cataloged annually by VisitScotland (formerly the Scottish Tourist Board) in two publications available in any good bookstore or Tourist Information Office in Scotland. These are: *Where to Stay: Bed and Breakfast (year)* and *Where to Stay: Hotels and Guest Houses (year)*. See *Appendix E* for complete citations. VisitScotland also publishes volumes on camping and "self-catering" (rental) accommodations. To obtain these volumes in the United States or Canada, contact the British Travel Book and Map Shop, 128 Evans Rd., Bloomfield NJ 07003 (toll free 1-866-338-6867; *www.btb-books.com.)* Other travel planning materials and free consultation are available in the United States and Canada from the British Tourist Authority: 551 Fifth Avenue, Suite 701, New York NY 10176 (ph: 212-986-2200) or 111 Avenue Road, Suite 450, Toronto, Ontario MRS 3J8 (ph: 416-925-6326/fax 416-961-2175).

Of course, the VisitScotland publications are not guidebooks. They are inclusive listings of all member establishments. Guidebooks, by definition, are selective, though I find the most popular of the general guidebooks (Fodor's, Frommer's, Lonely Planet) unsatisfactory when it comes to accommodations. Specialized publications are better. But here's another idea: when you call your courses to make tee times, ask the secretary or booking assistant about accommodations in your price range. Usually they'll give you good recommendations and you'll be getting those recommendations from a local source.

Internet Searching

Many hotels, guest houses, and B & Bs have their own web sites. Certainly that is the trend. But the vast majority—particularly among guest houses and B & Bs—do not have their own sites. Rather, they gain access to the web via one or another promotional group. Primary among these is the tourist board's *www.visitscotland.net*. Less comprehensive but well organized is *www.smoothhound.co.uk*. Others are *www.aboutscotland.com* and the Automobile Association's site, *www.theaa.com*. These can provide a good overview of lodging options and prices. See *Appendix B* for more listings.

B & Bs, Guest Houses, and Hotels

The distinction between B & Bs and guest houses in Scotland is blurry but, essentially, the difference is that a B & B is a bit smaller than a guest house. By tourist board definition, a B & B may accommodate no more than six people. A guest house normally will have at least four letting rooms. In times past, there was a further distinction: many guest houses offered an evening meal. Today, some still do—but not many. With few exceptions, an evening meal is not an option at a B & B. Virtually all hotels—even small hotels (up to twenty rooms)—will have (a) a liquor license and (b) a dining room for evening meals and probably lunch as well. Most hotels have a public sitting room or lounge, something that may or may not be a feature of a guest house or B & B. All, of course, serve a traditional "Scottish Breakfast." These days you'll also have healthier fruit and cereal options.

The Star System and Pricing

VisitScotland grades all establishments on a five-star scale. Among hotels, five stars are reserved for "world-class" establishments—the Turnberrys and Gleneagles of the world. Four stars mean "excellent;" three stars are "very good;" two stars indicate "good;" and one star—well, you don't want to go there.

Four stars are often found at large country-house manors and mansions adapted to the hotel trade—in fact, you can look for those magic words, "Country House Hotel," and be pretty sure you're going to have an extraordinary lodging experience.

Three-star hotels are consistently good, frequently full of character, and most price-attractive to the majority of tourists. I've cited a dozen or so of this class in *Part III, The Directory of Courses* and in *Appendix B* as favorites of golfers, including The Udny Arms in Newburgh, Red House Hotel in Cruden Bay, and South Beach Hotel in Troon. *Typically, a three-star hotel will be priced in a range of £35 to £45 ($55-70) per person per night.* From this benchmark, price extrapolations can be made downward and upward (i.e., two-star £20-30; four-star £50-£60+ per person per night).

Prices in each category vary—not surprisingly, rather dependent upon location. For example, Edinburgh is significantly more expensive than Inverness and the three-star hotels in St. Andrews are £10-20 more than the three-star norm. The best bargains will often be found at the two-star hotels, but you need to be careful in that group. These tend to be the smallest of hostelries and they can be either very good or a bit tawdry.

Interestingly enough, while four and five-star hotels are pricey and few in number, you'll find lots of guest houses and B & Bs with these rankings. Typically, they are priced in the same range as the three-star hotels and, for my money, they offer the best value and best personal experiences for golfers and nongolfers alike. This is a class where you'll find the distinctive, small mansions like *Glebe House* in North Berwick or historic row houses like *Jill Hardie's B & B* in St. Andrews. Compared to hotels, these B & Bs offer more spacious lodging and the personal touch of hosts who "know the territory."

Making Reservations

After consulting guidebooks, browsing the internet, and talking to folks at the clubs, you should be ready to contact your chosen hostelry. Again, I prefer the flexibility and personal contact afforded by a telephone call. Here's what to ask about or consider before you call:

✓ *Per person or per room?* The aggravating European tradition of pricing per person, per night (pppn), hangs on in Scotland and is worth special comment. A single traveler will find lodging in Scotland a good bargain—remember, those £35 (more or less) are buying you a breakfast so big that you can easily skip lunch. On the other hand, even ordinary lodging quickly gets expensive for two people in a room (naturally, the most common configuration). This pricing tradition is slowly changing due to pressure from chains like Holiday Inn, Travel Inn, and TraveLodge—all of whom offer space on a per-room basis. Be sure to ask whether quoted prices are *per person* or *per room.*

✓ *Multinight stay discount.* Many lodgings will give a modest discount on stays of three nights or more. Some will offer that verbally or in writing but more often you have to ask.

✓ *Bed sizes; twin-bedded or double-bedded room.* Many double rooms have two single beds or a single and a double—ideal for same-sex golf parties. Others have one double bed. Some can be converted from one configuration to another ("zip and link" twins convert to a king-size double). Apart from the zip and links, you won't find many queen or king-size beds typical of American motels. Among couples, if one person is a picky sleeper, the twin-bedded room may be preferable. In a similar vein, if you're used to space afforded by a king-size bed, a standard double probably won't do. Whatever the case, this is something to ask about.

✓ *Bath/shower facility.* Most Americans are partial to showers. If this is important to you, be sure to ask about inclusion of a shower in the quoted room. Most hotel rooms have showers, though they may be jerryrigged rather than built-in. Some B & Bs only have bathtubs.

An alternative to booking accommodations yourself is to use the services of VisitScotland's *Tourist Information Offices* (TIs). For a small fee, these offices will make bookings for you at member hotels, guest houses, and B & Bs. This is a particularly useful service for those traveling without advance reservations, but it's a service available to anyone at any time.

One final note: I firmly believe *the more money you spend on accommodations the more you separate yourself from the ordinary people, the customs, the heart and soul of Scotland* (or, for that matter, any other place). Taken to extreme, this philosophy might point you towards flea-bag hotels and youth hostels. Of course, that's not what I mean. I mean simply that you can find many accommodations in the mid-price range of $45 to $65 per person per night (or less). That's why I don't recommend places like the Old Course Hotel or

Rusacks in St. Andrews; the Carnoustie Golf Course Hotel; the Marine Hotel in Troon; or the Newton Hotel in Nairn. These places are popular with tour operators. But they are places where you're just another number—one of thousands of tourists (usually Americans) to pass through their relatively impersonal doors every year.

Scotland is one of the special places in the Anglo-American world where a traveler can still experience a tradition of small hotels of distinction, unique character, and highly personal service—a tradition all but extinct in the United States. That's the kind of tradition a savvy traveler will seek out rather than choose a hotel one might as easily find at Myrtle Beach, Palm Springs, or Dallas, Texas.

Common Questions

Do I need to make reservations? Just as with golf courses, if you want to stay at a specific hotel on a specific day, you should make a reservation. If you are trying to maintain maximum flexibility in your itinerary and are open to taking a room where you find it, then don't make a reservation. The decision you make also depends upon the time and place. If you want to stay on the Isle of Skye in August, for example, you would be foolish not to make a lodging reservation. This holds true from June through September in all those locations where accommodations are scarce and tourism is intense (i.e., most of the Highlands and Western Islands). On the other hand, in a large town or city like Inverness, Aberdeen, Glasgow, or Edinburgh, a stop at the local Tourist Information Office will get you a room at *almost* any time of year. Edinburgh in August is another time to make a reservation. That's when the International Festival draws crowds from all over the world, taxing the resources of that fair city.

On balance, the best advice for golfers is to reserve lodging and leave the flexible part of the schedule to golf courses and nongolf activities. If you follow my advice from *Chapter Two* in this section, you'll be basing in one location for at least several days, so why not have that base pinned down in advance? There's no particularly good reason to avoid booking accommodations unless you are truly flying on a wing and a prayer.

Do I have to stay at the Turnberry Hotel to play the Ailsa course? Technically, no. But it's a very busy hotel and residents have priority at the course. In high season, a single or twosome can usually slip onto the Ailsa. It's tougher for a foursome. For more information, see *The Directory of Courses - Turnberry Hotel.*

Do I have to stay at the Carnoustie Golf Course Hotel to play the championship course at Carnoustie? No. For more information, see *The Directory of Courses - Carnoustie Golf Links.*

What does "en suite" mean? It's a silly, highfalutin' term picked up from the French and it means a bath/shower and toilet are in the room. Even though virtually all hotel rooms in Scotland include toilet and bath/shower these days, the term hangs on from an earlier age when the "WC" was down the hall or around the corner.

Should I take a hairdryer? You'll find them in most rooms, though they may be hidden in a dresser drawer. If there is none, ask at the desk. Nine out of ten times they'll have one for you. Bottom line: don't bother to pack one.

Will I have a shower in my room? And what about water pressure? I've heard it's awful. If having a shower is important to you, ask before you book. Most hotels now have showers, but many B & Bs do not. Most of the time you're probably going to be disappointed in the Scottish idea of water pressure. As the kids say these days, "live with it"—that's just the way it is. Look at it this way: you'll probably have a heated towel rack in your room and, unlike in America, each room will be unique.

More Questions/Advice

If you would like to see a topic or question added to this chapter in a future edition of *Golf in Scotland,* send your suggestions my way at aferguson@fergusongolf.com or to Ferguson Golf, 1743 S. Marion St., Denver CO 80210.

CHAPTER FIVE

A Miscellany of Travel Tips

General

✓ *Passport.* Don't forget it. You'll need it to get in and out of the UK. Also good to have with you when shopping.

✓ *Luggage.* Read your carrier's guidelines. Current international rules for most airlines: (1) checked luggage - 70 lb. limit; (2) golf bag - 33 lbs; use it to pack shoes, sweaters, and other bulky items; (3) a carry-on no larger than 9" x 14" x 22" (45"). Extra weight is allowed, but you will be charged for it.

✓ *Carry-on Luggage.* Unfortunately, luggage and golf clubs don't always arrive when you do. Just in case, pack a change of clothes in your carry-on luggage. You can rent or borrow clubs, but it's no fun to go shopping for clothes on your first day in Scotland.

✓ *"Left Luggage."* This is a British term for short-term storage of luggage. No longer available at American airports, luggage storage is common in Europe. This is something to consider if you carry golf clubs in a hard-shell case. I'm not going to get into the hard-shell vrs. soft-side carrier debate, but what do you do with all those hard-shell cases when you get to your destination? One solution is to leave them behind at Left Luggage for about £3.50 per piece per day. You'll find Left Luggage at all the major airports as well as the train stations in Edinburgh and Glasgow.

✓ *Protect your golf clubs.* If using a soft-side carry bag, tie the heads of the irons together and turn the woods upside down in your golf bag. Prevent theft: don't leave clubs in an exposed place in your vehicle.

✓ *Flight Survival Kit.* Earplugs, blind fold, water, thermos, breath mints, eyedrops, aspirin or equivalent, towelettes. Pack your toiletries kit in your carry-on; that toothbrushing can sure feel good midway over the Atlantic.

✓ *Jet Lag.* Lots of advice out there about how to deal with jet lag. You'll probably arrive at your Scottish destination sometime late morning. Once you get to your hotel, here's what I recommend: get unpacked; lay down; take a nap, but set an alarm and *don't allow yourself to sleep for more than about 1-2 hours*; get up; exercise; have dinner; go to bed at a normal time. You should sleep well and be ready to play golf the next day.

✓ *Money management for threesomes, foursomes or more.* Designate a "treasurer" to manage a fund for cash payment of incidentals like lunch, a round of drinks at the 19th hole, etc. This eliminates check-splitting and hassling over minor expenses. When the "kitty" is empty, ante up a set amount per person and start over.

✓ *Water.* Carry it wherever you go. The Brits just don't believe in public water fountains. You won't find any on most of the golf courses either. Ask for water in restaurants. Keep hydrated.

✓ *Directions.* Take a compass with you. It can come in handy when hiking in the countryside, walking in a town or city with winding streets, or regaining your bearings while driving.

✓ *How much will you spend above and beyond air fare and "land package" (lodging, golf, rental car)?* Here's a rule of thumb: add 1/3 to your air + land package cost. Example: $900 air + $1600 land package = $2500; add $835 more or less for food, petrol, additional golf expenses (trolleys, strokesavers), and miscellaneous spending. How much "more or less"?—that depends on how much you drive, how expensively you eat, and how many souvenirs and gifts you buy.

✓ *Traveler's Insurance* - Some people buy it; some don't. Some prepaid golf and hotel deposits will be refunded if adequate cancellation notice is provided. The big factor is air fare. Check with your travel agent.

✓ *Prepaid telephone calling cards* for domestic and international use are available at phone stores, pharmacies, grocery stores, and post offices. Cell phones can be purchased at grocery superstores and phone stores starting at about £60.

Driving in Scotland

✓ Somewhere on the dash or visor, your rental car may have a reminder, "drive left" or "stay left." I advise you to use a sticky note or its equivalent and put another sign on the dash: "**look right**." North Americans are so used to looking left before turning at intersections, it's a difficult habit to reverse. One lapse could be your last lapse. Obviously, it's best to look both ways, but *always* look right.

✓ To really enjoy driving in Scotland, get onto the "B" roads and the "single tracks." On the single tracks, the going is slow but, after you've adjusted to the pullover protocol for oncoming traffic, you'll enjoy the pace and see parts of the countryside that most tourists never see. The protocol? If you're closest to a pullover, then pull over; flash your lights to signal the oncoming driver to proceed.

✓ *Drive times* are more important than drive distances. Here are the basics on popular point-to-point routes:

Edinburgh - North Berwick: 45"
Edinburgh - St. Andrews: 1 hr

Glasgow - Edinburgh: 1 hr
Glasgow - Troon: 45"
Glasgow - Turnberry: 1 hr, 15"
Glasgow - St. Andrews: 2 hrs
Glasgow - Inverness: 3 hrs, 30"
Glasgow - Aberdeen: 3 hrs

Inverness - Dornoch: 55"
Inverness - Aberdeen: 3+ hrs
Inverness - Machrihanish: 6+ hrs

St. Andrews - Carnoustie: 55"
St. Andrews - North Berwick: 2 hrs
St. Andrews - Gleneagles: 1 hr, 15"
St. Andrews - Troon: 2 hrs, 45"

Carnoustie - Aberdeen: 1 hr, 30"
Aberdeen - Cruden Bay: 35"
Cruden Bay - Inverness: 3 hrs"
Aberdeen - St. Andrews: 2 hrs, 15"

Dornoch - Tain: 10"
Dornoch - Golspie: 15"
Dornoch - Brora: 25"

✔ *Roundabouts* are designed to keep traffic moving. Those who live in the New England states know they work pretty well most of the time. You'll see few intersections controlled by traffic lights in Scotland. Protocol: yield to traffic in the roundabout. Remember, "Might is right." In two lanes leading to a roundabout, stay left if turning left. Use the right lane if turning right. Either lane may exit straight ahead. How ingenious!

Food

✔ For *best values,* look for "Bar Meal" signs. Protocol: go to the bar to read the menu and place your order; pay at the bar; your food will be brought to you or your name will be called for pickup at the bar. Tipping? Ten percent is plenty.

✔ *Portions* are large and the Scots don't mind your sharing. No extra plate charge. Money-saving advice: order two soups and one entree; share the entree and you'll have lunch or dinner for two for about $25.

✔ Virtually every golf course has an informal lounge with a respectable menu of soup, sandwiches and other fare. The Scots have a way with soup. The soup's always on and almost always good and hot (*very* hot - watch out).

Clothing and Dress—for Golf and Otherwise

✔ *Dress in layers.* The least useful article of apparel: a short-sleeve golf shirt, but take a couple anyway for a bottom layer. Most often you'll be most comfortable in a long-sleeve, lightweight jersey of some kind. Then layer with variously-weighted sweaters, windbreakers, etc.

✔ *Men - pack a tie and a sport jacket and take them with you to the course.* The key here is to be prepared for that moment when you meet a local club member and get invited into what is usually called the "members' dining room" or "members' lounge" where jacket and tie are mandatory. All courses have a less formal lounge/dining area for visitors and members. At most hotels you'll find the atmosphere quite relaxed. Just as at home, "dressy casual" is the watchword.

✓ *Shorts*. Leave them at home. They're not often seen on the street, on the course, or in the clubhouse.

✓ *Shoes*. My greatest space saver—black leather tennis shoes suitable for any occasion, including golf. I don't even pack golf shoes—just a pair of ribbed galoshes for waterproof covering. Incidentally, steel spikes are still ok at most clubs.

✓ *Hats off!* Remember to take your hat off upon entering the clubhouse. Failure to do so is a "pet peeve" of the Scots.

✓ *Laundry*. It always pays to travel light. The best way to do that is to leave all the extra clothes at home. Take enough for one week. Then, on longer trips, have your laundry done for you weekly at a *laundry service*. Drop your clothes off and pick them up a few hours later—cleaned, pressed, and folded. I've never paid more than £10 pounds for a load of wash. CAUTION: Do *not* have your laundry done by a hotel. You will pay an arm, a leg, and several other appendages. Following are laundry services in some of Scotland's golf centers:

Carnoustie - Kleenomat, #2 Dundee St., 01241-853-676
Inverness - New City Laundrette, 17 Young St., 01463-242-507
North Berwick - Dry Cleaning Center, Quality St. at High St.
Pitlochry - Laundrette & Dry Cleaners, 3 Moulin Rd., 01796-474-044
St. Andrews - SA Laundry Service, 14B Woodburn Terrace,
    01334-475-150
Tain (nr Dornoch) - Tain Dry Cleaners, 13 King St., 01862-894-443

Nongolf Activities/Shopping and Money
✓ *Make a Tourist Information Office (TI) and/or bookstore one of your first stops.* Good information is the key to a good trip. Maps, history books, golf guides, tourist site brochures, specialized publications—all can enhance your travel experience. Far better than relying upon Frommer or Fodor.

✓ Good *hikes* can be found close by, no matter where you are. Look for "Forest Enterprise" signs; ask your lodging hosts or the nearest Tourist Information Office.

✓ Tour *distilleries* during the week, if possible. They may be open to visitors on the weekend, but they won't be operational. Most distilleries are "quiet" during July (though still open for tours). For information on the whisky industry, see ***www.scotch-whisky.org.uk***.

✓ *Shop Hours/VAT.* Most shops open at 9 a.m. and close by 6 p.m. You can reclaim the Value Added Tax (VAT) of 17.5% on goods carried out of the country (not on hotel or green fees). When you make relatively expensive purchases (e.g., £20 or more), ask for a Tax-Free Shopping Form. Shopkeepers administer this program. VAT reimbursement forms issued by shopkeepers at their discretion *must* be processed at your point of international departure. For more detail, ask for Customs and Excise Notice 704, *Traveller's Guide to the Retail Export Scheme.* Is it worth the hassle? If you spend a lot of money, it is. Otherwise, I'm not sure.

✓ *Credit cards* are accepted at most stores and restaurants. American Express is the *least* widely accepted. Purchasing on credit is the best way to track major expenses. With widespread availability of ATMs, travelers' checks are practically a thing of the past.

PART III

THE DIRECTORY

OF

COURSES

Preparing for Play in Scotland

Linksland Golf

Many of golf's great writers, including Herbert Warren Wind and Bernard Darwin, have tried to define links golf—its unique qualities and history. Is it seaside golf?—yes. But is all seaside golf links golf?—clearly not. Is it always "out and back," like links in a string of sausages?—maybe in its purest form, but not always. If there are trees or an artificial lake on a course, is it a true links course? Questions like these propel discussion. Ultimately, the most interesting question is, "Is seaside links golf in Scotland unique? Is it different than seaside golf in Florida, California, Spain, or Portugal?" Certainly, one can make the case that the environment is different—the air, the temperature, the precipitation—and these combine to make Scottish links golf qualitatively different than golf in other places. But then what about links golf in Ireland and England? Well, as you see, this topic can generate an essay or book—and it has.

To be brief, links golf in Scotland has both locational and qualitative aspects. Locational: yes, near the sea—in purest form a relatively narrow strip of sandy, non-arable lowland between settled and/or arable land and the sea. The narrow characteristic of linksland led to the familiar "out and back" design of many Scottish courses (e.g., Royal Dornoch, Nairn, Western Gailes, Cruden Bay)—basically two fairways wide.

But always narrow? No, exceptions abound. The key word in the previous paragraph is *low*land—lowland near the sea that, over centuries and eons, was subject to periodic inundation and continual sedimentary processes. Thus the land became sandy and non-arable— "waste land" fit mostly for grazing and for golf. So, being seaside is not enough. Linksland might well extend some distance inland due to the character and geologic history of the land. And high ground near seaside, never subject to the ebbs and tides of sand and sea, may not be

101

linksland at all. The soil might be rich, giving rise to a great variety of plants, grasses and trees.

So, we come to the qualitative aspects: sandy soil that drains water and does not allow lakes to form; salt-water air and residues in the soil that prevent or retard the growth of trees; hardy grasses and plants capable of growing in sandy soil and salt air; dunes, hillocks, and depressions associated with the blowing and drifting of sand. The cumulative effect of these—along with those environmental aspects of mild temperatures, the likelihood of strong winds, and frequent rains—all add up to golf on a Scottish links course.

Does it add up to golf unique in all the world? Now we approach the literary territory explored with such effect by Wind and Darwin, Longhurst and Campbell, Finegan and Bamberger. Fortunately, you can go to Scotland and form your own opinion on this subject.

Parkland and Heathland Courses

Often these descriptors are used interchangeably, though, in fact, they describe different conditions. It's another sticky wicket, but I'll try: Generally, parkland and heathland (or moorland) courses are inland, away from the sea—though not necessarily far inland (e.g., Belleisle, Royal Musselburgh). The defining differences between parkland and heathland have to do with (a) soil and (b) vegetation supported by the soil. Parkland soil is relatively rich and retentive of moisture, giving rise to a variety of deciduous trees, wild grasses, and even lakes—in short, the kind of land associated with pastures and woods. Heathland has more in common with linksland—sandy, peaty soil, quick to drain, and relatively poorer in nutrients, thus supporting scrubby heather and evergreens but not much more. According to David Allan, secretary at Ladybank Golf Club, the real tip-off is in the rough: grass on the parkland courses; heather on the heathland courses. Most inland courses fall clearly into one camp or the other. For example, Ladybank and Glasgow Gailes are heathland courses through and through, just as there's no doubt about the parkland status of Letham Grange and the courses at Gleneagles. Others, like Panmure near Carnoustie, have qualities of linksland, heathland, and parkland. In these cases, in *The Directory of Courses*, I've indicated that a course is a "hybrid." The most common hybrid combines linksland features with parkland features (e.g., Lundin Links, The Glen, Longniddry).

Handicap Certificates

Virtually every course will indicate in its statement of visitor restrictions, "handicap certificate required." Some courses are more specific: "Handicap certificate required - men 24, ladies 36." The St. Andrews Links Trust Management is even more specific: "All golfers wishing to play over the Old Course must be in possession of a current, official handicap which should be presented to the Starter on the day of play and the maximum handicap is 24 for men, 36 for ladies . . . . **Proof of handicap must be in the form of a handicap card or handicap certificate, a letter of introduction from a golf club is no longer acceptable as proof of handicap"** (their bold emphasis).

In all the years I've been going to Scotland, *except at St. Andrews,* I have *never* been asked to show a handicap certificate or GHIN card. Nevertheless, one should be prepared. It's not hard to do. If you haven't done so already, register for a GHIN card at your nearest USGA-affiliated course. Seniors and women are most likely to be "carded."

Buggies (Golf Carts)

The Scots call them "buggies." Americans call them "carts." Whatever they're called, you'll see few of them in Scotland where, thankfully, golf is still considered a *walking* game. And, if the day ever comes when that can no longer be said, that day will bring an end to the game of golf as it has been played for centuries. In the United States, under the influence of golf professionals and golf management companies who think their economic lives depend upon "cart revenue," that game is already seriously ailing, if not dead.

The Scots will tell you their courses are "not suitable" to accommodate buggies. In fact, cart paths *could* be installed at most courses. But, God bless 'em, the Scots won't do it. They won't build concrete runways on their beloved linkslands. So we are given the gift of peace and quiet on the golf courses of Scotland, without the visual and auditory pollution visited upon us by the infernal machines that have ruined American golf for the traditionalist.

This is not to say buggies are entirely unavailable. Almost every course has a few, though policies regarding their use vary. In *The Directory of Courses* I have indicated specific buggy policy and even numbers of buggies available where that information could be ascertained. The following is offered in summation:

✓ *Some* courses do not allow buggies at all (e.g., St. Andrews Old Course, Kingsbarns, Royal Troon, Prestwick, Carnoustie).

✓ *Some* courses have a few buggies available for people with a *verifiable* medical infirmity or physical disability (e.g., Crail, Dunbar, Gullane). In a few cases, age alone may be a qualifier (e.g., St. Andrews New). You must be able to document your age or condition.

✓ *Many* courses have a few buggies available for general hire. This number rarely exceeds four, so it is advisable to reserve one well in advance of play.

✓ A *few* courses have a stable of buggies available for general hire. For whatever reason, if you must use a buggy to enjoy a round of golf, you might want to include one or more of the following courses on your itinerary: *Letham Grange, Gleneagles' PGA Centenary Course, St. Andrews - Duke's Course,* and *Whitekirk.* At these courses, advance reservation of a buggy probably won't be necessary.

Practicing for play on a Scottish links course

In North America, to my knowledge, a golfer cannot prepare for an encounter with the prickly gorse (whins) bushes of Scotland or, for that matter, even the low-lying, tough, woody heather. There are plenty of "links style" courses now that feature long, wispy, natural grasses. But, to put them all together—with an admixture of wind and rain, blind shots, deep pot bunkers, and rolling fairways—I'm not sure there's any way to fully prepare for golf in Scotland. In bad weather, the courses can be positively brutal but, even in benign conditions, most visiting golfers are going to play five or six shots above their index. A mid-handicapper should be happy with scores in the 80s. Someone who normally shoots in the high 80s probably will card scores in the 90s and low 100s. The low handicapper may have his or her ego rearranged. Having said that much, you can still go to your nearest practice range and get a jump start on good golf in Scotland. Here's what to do:

✓ Hit mid-iron (5,6,7) "knock down" shots to targets from 100 to 160 yards. This will help you prepare to play in the wind.

✓ Find an area of thin lies and practice with all clubs. The links fairways will tend to catch the leading edge of your clubs; you have to work on "nipping" the ball.

✓ Especially for the St. Andrews courses, practice the longest putts you can find; some of the double greens there are nearly as big as a football field. More important, you'll find plenty of opportunity to use the "Texas Wedge" from well off the greens.

✓ When you get a blast of lousy weather, think of it as a chance to practice for golf in Scotland. Grab your clubs and head for the course.

Equipment

To help my clients anticipate the necessary equipment for play in Scotland, I give them a "Golf Readiness Checklist" duplicated here in *Appendix A*. From that list, I want to emphasize three items:

✓ Unless you carry your golf bag, you'll probably be using a pull-cart or "trolley." If so, take a two to three-foot *bungee cord* to secure your golf bag to the trolley. If you don't you'll be cursing all day as your bag repeatedly falls off the trolley amongst the hillocks and uneven rough.

✓ If you wear glasses, the worst element to deal with in golf is rain. In Scotland, where rain is likely sometime during your trip, you'll be thankful you took a *washcloth* to tuck into a pants pocket. A washcloth is easier to handle and stow than a towel.

✓ Follow the advice of every seasoned traveler to Scotland and *dress in layers*. During the typical three to four-hour round of golf, dramatic variations in cloud cover, temperature, wind speed, and precipitation are common. Here's a good way to layer: start with a short-sleeve golf shirt and/or long-sleeve, lightweight jersey; carry a sweater, a windbreaker, and a waterproof rain jacket. In the spring (April - May) and fall (September - October), I don't even bother packing short-sleeve golf shirts. I start with a long-sleeve pullover and carry a windbreaker, sweater, and rain suit for extra cover.

At the Course

✓ Call your scheduled course a day or two before play. This is the time to confirm your presence, change a tee time, request a caddie, or reserve a buggie. The Scots will appreciate your thoughtfulness. At some clubhouses the front door or locker room door will be locked. Don't take it personally. It just means this is a private club where you need to be a member or guest to use the clubhouse facility. *Protocol:* Go to the pro shop to register and pay your green fee. You'll be given a code to punch into a box near the front door or locker room door. That's your passkey to club facilities for the day.

✓ *Caddies.* Top courses may make a distinction between caddies and bag carriers—and charge accordingly. Caddies typically cost between £25 and £35. Bag carriers typically cost £15 to £20. It's fine for two or three golfers to split the cost of a caddie. Four golfers may be pushing the issue a bit, but that's a negotiable point. You just need to make it clear the caddie is there to advise more than one golfer and ante up for the additional service. Tipping? A £10 note is typical. Check with the caddymaster or pro.

✓ *Stroke Savers.* Every course has some kind of "stroke saver"— a yardage book with schematic drawings of each hole. They vary in quality but are uniformly indispensable because you won't find yardage markers on most courses. Cost: about £1-3. It's the best scoring investment you will make and an inexpensive souvenir of your trip.

✓ *Trolleys* ("pullcarts") are universally available and typically cost £2.50 to £3.50.

✓ If you don't hit consistently well with a driver, consider leaving it at home. Direction is more important than distance.

✓ From the heather and long grass, your first objective should be to get the ball back in play. Don't be a hero and don't hurt yourself. Take a firm grasp and swing smoothly through the ball; don't thrash at it. If your ball goes into the gorse, take a penalty drop and play on.

✓ Use the toilet before teeing off. You won't find any facilities on most courses.

✓ Take water with you. You won't find that on most courses either. And if you're used to a hot dog "at the turn," forget about it. In most cases, there ain't no "turn" anywhere near the clubhouse.

✓ Take your hat off upon entering the clubhouse. It's the Scots' second biggest complaint about Americans and they'll not be shy about reminding you of your manners.

✓ The biggest complaint?—loud conversation on the putting greens. Remember, in Scotland the tees are close to the greens. Sshhh!

Sixty Great Courses:
A Directory with Profiles

All information needed for booking at sixty of Scotland's finest golf courses can be found in this directory: *address - phone - fax - email - web site - key contacts - visitor restrictions - green fees - deposits.* Of course, any selective list of courses is fraught with danger. The aficionado of Scottish golf will say, "But you've left out Ballater, Braid Hills, and Bruntsfield Links." And I would simply say, ninety-nine percent of golfers visiting Scotland go to play a handful of courses; they don't go to play Ballater, Braid Hills, and Bruntsfield Links. Maybe they should, but my aim here is to provide useful information rather than to change the profile of Scottish golf tourism.

My emphasis is on seaside courses because that is what most visitors to Scotland want to play. In priority order, most golfers want to visit (1) St. Andrews; (2) The Ayrshire coast: Troon, Prestwick, Turnberry; (3) Carnoustie; (4) North Berwick - Gullane; and (5) Inverness - Dornoch. In those locations, they are interested mainly in about ten to twelve courses: St. Andrews' Old/New/Jubilee, Kingsbarns, Royal Troon, Prestwick, Turnberry, Carnoustie, North Berwick, Gullane #1, Royal Dornoch, and Nairn.

If I can get a visitor to Scotland interested in a second tier of lesser-known courses, either on that first trip or on a follow-up trip, I consider it a victory. These courses might include Lundin Links, Crail, or Elie in Fife; Western Gailes, Glasgow Gailes, and Belleisle in Ayrshire; Montrose, Royal Aberdeen, and Cruden Bay along the northeast coast; Golspie, Brora, Tain, and the Boat of Garten in the north; Crieff, Blairgowrie, and Pitlochry in the middle of the country. In short, there's plenty of golf here for both the first-timer and the guy or gal who's "been there, done that" and now is ready to dip more deeply into the reservoir of great Scottish courses.

Notes on the Entries

✓ *Club name and date.* Each entry starts with the proper name of a club or managing entity. The date in parentheses (1897) is the year the club was formed or was thought to have been formed. The date may or may not be the year when a course was created.

✓ *Course Yardage: member tees and visitor tees.* In the course data area of each entry, note that a range of yardage is usually given (e.g., 5850-6177 yds). The first number is yardage from the "visitor" tees. The second number is yardage from the "member" or "medal" tees. At most courses, tee markers for visitors are yellow; tee markers for members are white. Usually there's also a set of forward tees (red) presumed to be for female golfers. *Unless informed otherwise, a male visitor will be expected to play from the yellow tees.* If you would like to play from the "medal" tees, ask the starter for permission. The answer will probably be, "I'm sorry, we reserve the medal tees for member play," but you can try. The Scots are finicky about this.

✓ *SSS: Standard Scratch Score.* Scotland's "SSS" is comparable to the USGA's course rating. Just as it sounds, the SSS rating on a course is what the scratch golfer should achieve relative to par. If the SSS is 73 against par 69 (e.g., Southerness), you can look forward to one tough round of golf. If, on the other hand, the SSS is 68 against par 70 (e.g., Portpatrick), you're probably looking at something like a stroll in a lovely park.

✓ *Booking Contact(s) and Secretary:* Though this information is subject to frequent change, I have included it because I think it's nice to be able to make a call and know to whom you might be talking. Generally, you will *not* speak with the club secretary but rather with a booking secretary or assistant or even the club professional. It depends upon the club.

✓ *Phone - Starter/Pro Shop.* This number is included because most courses turn over their "diary" to the starter or pro shop within a week of play. Thus, to check in before your appointed tee time, this is the number to call.

✓ *Profile.* Following the club data, comment on each course follows. Most often, this comment has as much to do with the location, the ambience and feel of the place, as with course description. Detailed course descriptions of major courses are available in other books dedicated to that purpose. My aim here is to convey the flavor of the place, put it in perspective, and answer the question, "Why should I want to play this course?". In some cases, area accommodations and nongolf activities are discussed. Web sites noted throughout this section are cumulated in *Appendix B*.

✓ *Arrangement and Indices.* Course entries are numbered from one to sixty. They are arranged alphabetically because most people are more familiar with course names than with their exact locations or the names of Scotland's political subdivisions. To help navigate the alphabetical entry, several indices preceding the directory give guidance:

• First, there's a *geographic* index in directional order so that you can identify locations in the direction you most likely might be traveling (away from Edinburgh and Glasgow).

• A second index lists the courses by *type* and, here, I've distinguished among (1) parkland/heathland courses; (2) links courses with a sea view; and (3) links courses where the ocean is neither in play nor particularly visible. This links distinction is worth making because, for example, many people don't realize they won't see much of the ocean when they play Carnoustie or the Old Course at St. Andrews. On the other hand, the golfer has magnificent sea views at courses like North Berwick, The Glen, and Kingsbarns. This may or may not be critical in choosing courses to play, but it is useful information.

• *Course architects* are recognized in a third index. The giants of Scottish golf architecture are Tom Morris and James Braid and it is remarkable how many of the courses listed here are either complete works of their expertise, their imaginative extensions of nine-hole courses, or their redesigns of existing layouts. Students of Scottish golf may find this index particularly rewarding because it suggests a way of organizing an itinerary—perhaps an all-Braid excursion or an all-Morris pilgrimage. Better yet, consciously combining the two may allow comparison and contrast in design philosophies.

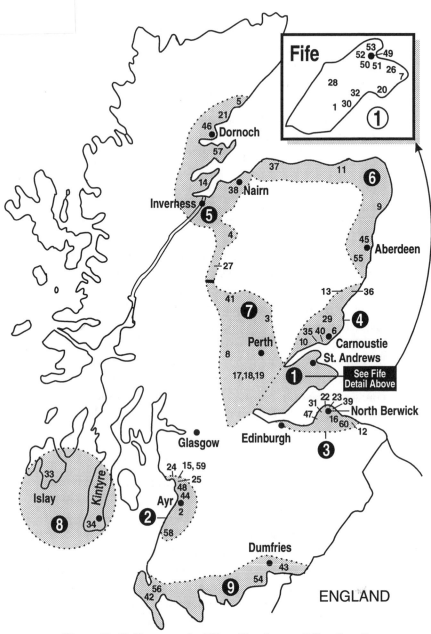

Sixty Golf Courses in Nine Regions of Scotland

Index 1 - Geographic Arrangement of Sixty Courses
(located by number on map)

+ = British Open Qualifying Course
* = Current or historic venue for British Open

Region #1 - Fife (from Tayport, south along coast and back)
Scotscraig+ (53)
The Duke's Course (52)
St. Andrews Old*/New/Jubilee (49, 50, 51)
Kingsbarns (26)
Crail (7)
Golf House Club - Elie (20)
Lundin Links+ (32)
Leven Links+ (30)
Balbirnie Park (1)
Ladybank+ (28)

Region #2 - Ayrshire (north to south)
Irvine - Bogside (24)
Glasgow Gailes+ (15)
Western Gailes+ (59)
Kilmarnock - Barassie+ (25)
Royal Troon* (48)
Prestwick* (44)
Belleisle (2)
Turnberry - Ailsa* (58)

Region #3 - East Lothian (west to east)
Royal Musselburgh (47)
Longniddry+ (31)
Gullane #1+ (22)
Honourable Company of Edinburgh Golfers - Muirfield* (23)
North Berwick - West Links+ (39)
The Glen - North Berwick (16)
Whitekirk (60)
Dunbar+ (12)

Region #4 - Angus/East Coast (Dundee to Edzell)
Downfield (10)
Monifieth (35)

Panmure (40)
Carnoustie* (6)
Letham Grange (29)
Montrose+ (36)
Edzell (13)

Region #5 - *Inverness - Dornoch (south to north)*
Kingussie (27)
Boat of Garten (4)
Nairn (38)
Fortrose & Rosemarkie (14)
Tain (57)
Royal Dornoch (46)
Golspie (21)
Brora (5)

Region #6 - *Northeast/North Coast (south to north to west)*
Stonehaven (55)
Royal Aberdeen (45)
Cruden Bay (9)
Duff House Royal (11)
Moray Old (37)

Region #7 - *Perthshire/Central (south to north)*
Gleneagles - King's/Queen's/PGA Centenary (17, 18, 19)
Crieff (8)
Blairgowrie Rosemount (3)
Pitlochry (41)

Region #8 - *Kintyre/Islay*
Machrihanish (34)
Machrie (33)

Region #9 - *South Coast (east to west)*
Powfoot (43)
Southerness (54)
Stranraer (56)
Portpatrick (42)

Index 2: Links Courses with Ocean in Play
or in Sight *(alphabetical within each region)*
Region #1 - Fife
Balcomie Links - Crail
Golf House Club - Elie
Kingsbarns
Leven Links
Lundin Links
St. Andrews Jubilee

Region #2 - Ayshire
Prestwick
Royal Troon
Turnberry
Western Gailes

Region #3 - East Lothian
Dunbar
The Glen (North Berwick East Links)
Gulllane #1
Longniddry
North Berwick West Links

Region #4 - Angus/East Coast
Montrose

Region #5 - Inverness/Dornoch
Brora
Fortrose and Rosemarkie
Golspie
Nairn
Royal Dornoch

Region #6 - Northeast/North Coast
Cruden Bay
Moray Old
Royal Aberdeen
Stonehaven

Region #8 - Kintyre/Islay
Machrie
Machrihanish

Region #9 - South Coast
Portpatrick
Powfoot
Southerness

Index 3: Links Courses – Minimal/No Ocean View
Carnoustie
Glasgow Gailes
Irvine - Bogside
Kilmarnock (Barassie)
Monifieth
Panmure
St. Andrews Old Course
St. Andrews New
Tain

Index 4: Parkland/Heathland Courses
Region #1 - Fife
Balbirnie Park
Ladybank
St. Andrews - Duke's

Region #2 - Ayrshire
Belleisle

Region #3 - E. Lothian
Royal Musselburgh
Whitekirk

Region #4 - Angus/East Coast
Downfield
Edzell
Letham Grange

Region #5 - Inverness/Dornoch
Boat of Garten
Kingussie

Region #6 - Northeast/North Coast
Duff House Royal

Region #7 - Perthshire/Central
Blairgowrie Rosemount
Crieff
Gleneagles - Queen's/King's/PGA Centenary
Pitlochry

Region #9 – South Coast
Stranraer

Index 5: Courses by Tom Morris, Sr. (1821-1908)
Crail (9 holes - 1895; 9 holes - 1899)
Dunbar (15 holes - 1856)
Luffness New (1894)
Moray Old (1889)
Muirfield (1891)
St. Andrews New (1894)
Scotscraig (1892)
Tain (1890)

Partially Designed or Expanded
Elie (1895)
Ladybank (1879)
Prestwick (12 holes - 1851)
Royal Dornoch (9 holes - 1887)

Index 6: Courses by James Braid (1870 - 1950)
Belleisle (1927)
Boat of Garten (1936)
Downfield (1932)
Gleneagles - King's/Queen's (1919) with C.K. Hutchison
Irvine - Bogside
Powfoot (1903)
Royal Musselburgh (1926)
Stranraer (1950)

Remodeled or Expanded

Blairgowrie Rosemount (1934)
Brora (1920)
Carnoustie Championship (1926 - 1936)
Elie (1921)
Fortrose and Rosemarkie (1935)
Nairn (1938)
Prestwick (1918)
Royal Troon (1923)
Scotscraig (1904)

1. Balbirnie Park Golf Club (1983)

Region #: 1   **Category:** parkland
Architect(s): Fraser Middleton
Length: 5994-6210   **SSS:** 69-70   **Par:** 71

Address: Balbirnie Park, Markinch by Glenrothes KY7 6NR
Directions: off A92 N of Glenrothes

Reservations phone: 01592-752-006 **Fax:** 01592-752-006
Email: bpgc@aol.com   **Website:** no
Booking Contact(s): professional shop
Administrator: Steve Oliver   **Professional:** Craig Donnelly
Phone - Starter/Pro shop: 01592-752-006
Fee(s) (2003): wkday £27, £35; wkend £33, £45; jrs £15 all wk
Deposit (2003): £5
Visitor Policies: all week   **Buggies:** 4 - general hire

The most important asset of Balbirnie Park is its location near Glenrothes just off the A92 at Markinch Junction midway between Edinburgh and St. Andrews (and on the rail line). This is a perfect location for the traveler who wants to combine proximity to the golf courses of Fife with easy access to Edinburgh. Twelve minutes will get you to the coastal courses at Leven and Lundin; it's ten minutes to Ladybank; thirty to St. Andrews; and from Markinch Junction you can be in central Edinburgh on the train in less than forty-five minutes (the *best way*—i.e., without having to worry about driving and parking).

Just as it sounds, Balbirnie Park is a parkland alternative to the rigors of seaside golf. Situated in a huge woodland park, this is a recent addition to Scottish golf (1983). Consequently, you'll feel quite at home here—that is, it looks and plays like a lot of American courses. This is one place where you may play (and a mid-to-low handicapper *should* play) from the "Back Gents Tees." At 6200 yards, with minimal trouble to negotiate and with three par 5s under 500 yards, Balbirnie is what it is—a mildly-challenging municipal course in a very pretty setting. It's literally and figuratively a stroll in the park and a good golfer can "go low" here. In short, this is a good course, not a great course. Among Fife's inland courses, Ladybank will be the golfer's obvious first choice. But, if you're staying near Glenrothes and looking for another break from links golf, there's every reason to make a date with this beauty created by Scottish designer Fraser Middleton.

Accommodations: The countryside surrounding Balbirnie is lovely and offers two outstanding "country house hotels" that cater to golfers and deserve special mention. One is the mid-priced *Balgeddie House Hotel* (*www.balgeddiehouse.co.uk*), located two miles north-east of Glenrothes just off the A912. The other is the more expensive *Balbirnie House Hotel* (*www.balbirnie.co.uk*) located, as you might guess, at Balbirnie Park. Each draws visitors from miles around to their award-winning dining rooms. Together, they represent a class of establishments found throughout Scotland, typically transformed from a country manor house to a modern hotel with character and class. It's a kind of hostelry simply unavailable in the United States. Thus, these hotels can help make a trip to Scotland special, each in its own unique and memorable way.

Barassie: *See Kilmarnock Golf Club*

2. Belleisle Golf Club (1927)
Region #: 2   **Category:** parkland
Architect(s): James Braid
Length: 6040-6431   **SSS:** 70   **Par:** 71

Address: c/o S Ayrshire Council, Burns House, Burns SQ, Ayr KA7 1UT
Directions: 1 mi S of Ayr off A719

Reservations phone: 01292-441-258   **Fax:** 01292-442-632
Email: no   **Website:** no
Sr. Staffer: T Culter   **Professional:** D Gemmell
Phone - Starter/Pro shop: 01292-441-258
Fee(s) (2003): wkday £19.50, day tkt w/ Seafield £29;
wkend £26, day tkt £38
Deposit (2003): £5
Visitor Policies: all week - public course   **Buggies:** no
Other: Seafield Course adjacent

Partisans of Fife may disagree but, arguably, Ayrshire on Scotland's southwest coast has the greatest concentration of important links courses in the country. Visitors from around the world flock to play Turnberry, Prestwick, and Royal Troon—three past and present sites of British Open history within a coastal span of less than thirty miles. Then there are the increasingly popular courses at Gailes, not to mention a half dozen other first-rate courses between Ayr and Irvine.

Against this constellation of stars, it's no wonder Belleisle is the Ayrshire golf course most overlooked and underplayed by visitors. In that sense, it qualifies· as a true "hidden gem" among Scottish courses—one many consider the finest of Scotland's parkland courses.

And in that word "parkland" lies the truth of Belleisle's anonymity. Though less than a mile from seaside, this is not a links course. Through some quirk of nature, rich forest ground won a victory over sandy links turf in this spot just south of Ayr town center. The fairways are lush. Trees are full and present. Forest OB threatens. This is Belleisle—as full-bodied and robust a parkland course as you're likely to find. If it weren't for the occasional view of the Isle of Arran off in the distance (a *belle isle),* you might think you were miles inland, far away from the sea.

Apart from the fact that it's one of the best bargains in Scottish golf, the main reason to visit Belleisle is to play a course that is pure James Braid, Scotland's most prolific golf architect. Much of Braid's work involved redesigning or extending existing golf grounds. At Belleisle, Braid was given a clean slate. The result was a "signature" parkland course with a look and feel of modernity. You'll find all the Braid trademarks at Belleisle—challenging par 3s to all points of the compass; long two-shotters that make or break the round; judicious bunkering to indicate the line of play. No tricks. No blind shots. Everything in full view. And the golf is superb. Is this James Braid's finest inland course? I'm not sure. I like to think of it as one of the "Four Bs"—the Braid quartet of Belleisle, Blairgowrie, Boat of Garten, and Bogside (at Irvine). The setting of each course is different. Each is a gem.

Nongolf and accommodations. For those of literary bent, Ayr is the center of the Robert Burns industry in Scotland. That fact cannot escape when you are there. It's "Burns this and Burns that." Beneath the hype is the reality of Burns's primary place in Scottish cultural history. Burns enshrined dialectic Scots Gaelic. He celebrated common people. He preserved and lyricised Scottish folk music. For all these reasons, "Robbie Burns" became and remains a national folk hero. His

119

birthplace is now an informative museum on the main street in Alloway and is well worth a visit. On a broader scale, you can follow the "Burns Trail" through the villages and countryside of Ayrshire.

Just north of Turnberry, south of Ayr, you'll find Culzean (pronounced Cull-LEAN) Castle, the most heavily-visited of Scotland's "National Trust" properties. This perfectly-preserved Georgian mansion, built by Robert Adam, Scotland's leading architect of the eighteenth century, is surrounded by forest walks, expansive grounds, and formal gardens worth the price of admission. It was an elegant office site for General Dwight Eisenhower during World War II and, despite the heavy traffic, should be seen when you're in the area. On and around the A719 south of Ayr, between Belleisle and town center, you'll find a host of excellent small hotel, guest house, and B & B accommodations. This is a good base for exploring Burns country and Ayrshire golf. Out in the countryside, at the village of Dunure, consider *Dunduff Farm* (Mrs. Agnes Gemmell, ph 01292-500-225), a comfortable farmhouse set on a 650-acre estate.

3. Blairgowrie Golf Club (1889) - Rosemount
Region #: 7   **Category:** parkland
Architect(s): Tom Morris, Alister MacKenzie, James Braid
Length: 6229   **SSS:** 72   **Par:** 70

Address: Golf Course Rd, Rosemount, Blairgowrie PH10 6LG
Directions: A923 from Perth, turn rt at Rosemount sign; from A9, to Dunkeld and 1 mi S of Blairgowrie

Reservations phone: 01250-872-622   **Fax:** 01250-875-451
Email: admin@blairgowrie-golf.co.uk   **Website:** blairgowrie-golf.co.uk
Booking Contact(s): Melanie Collins
Secretary: John Simpson   **Professional:** Charles Dernie
Phone - Starter/Pro shop: 01250-872-594/873-116
Fee(s) (2003): April - £35, day tkt w/ Landsdowne 55; May-Oct £55, day tkt w/ Landsdowne £75
Deposit (2003): £10 nonrefundable
Visitor Policies: all wk; Wed, Fri, Sat club competitions; hdcp - men 26, women 36
Other: Landsdowne companion course   **Buggies:** 6 - general hire

Carved out of a mature forest, each hole at Blairgowrie is lined with silver birch and pine and trimmed by borders of gorse, heather, and broom. It's always beautiful, but especially so in late May and early June. What I remember most about playing golf at Blairgowrie is the springy turf and the peaceful quiet of the forest. There's a peace here both auditory and visual—no housing developments, no golf carts—just you, your companions, and the forest. Even when the course is entirely filled, it can seem you are alone with the golf and the forest. The opening hole, "Black Tree," sets the tone: it's a long par 4 requiring two powerful shots to a large, accepting green. Lots of bunkers, expertly placed by Alister MacKenzie and James Braid (at different times), add challenge and define the greens. A straight shooter can score well here. If you spray the ball, you're in for a long day and a lot of lost balls. The one-shotters are among the finest you will see anywhere. Simply beautiful.

A note on the Landsdowne course: This companion course to the Rosemount is not so highly regarded as the main attraction. But, at 6500+ yards, with narrow fairways and challenging greens, it was far more than a "relief course" designed by Peter Alliss and Dave Thomas during the 1970s. A day ticket will get you on both courses for a very reasonable fee. If you're up to thirty-six, I recommend this approach when the days are long and you can enjoy a respite between rounds.

4. Boat of Garten Golf and Tennis Club (1898)

Region #: 5 **Category:** heathland/parkland hybrid
Architect(s): James Braid (1931-2)
Length: 5650-5866 **SSS:** 69 **Par:** 69

Address: Boat of Garten, Nethybridge Rd, Inverness-Shire PH24 3BQ
Directions: 5 mi N of Aviemore, 2 mi E of A9; through town, turn left at Boat Hotel, then next rt

Reservations phone: 01479-831-282 **Fax:** 01479-831-523
Email: boatgolf@enterprise.net **Website:** boatgolf.com
Booking Contact(s): Heather Bantick
Secretary: Paddy Smyth **Professional:** James R Ingram
Phone - Starter/Pro shop: 01479-831-282
Fee(s) (2003): wkday £28, day tkt £33; wkend £33, day tkt £38
Deposit (2003): none **Buggies:** 2 - general hire

Visitor Policies: all week; wkend between 10-4; no 4-ball on wkend
Other: 36-hole open championship 1st Sat in August; jrs £15

For me, the Boat of Garten brings to mind the old Sara Lee slogan: "Nobody doesn't like Sara Lee." A double negative equals a positive. There's nothing you won't like about "the Boat." Incidentally, the unusual name comes from Garten's historic past: the golf course sits above the place where in times past a boat ferried people, carts, and livestock across the River Spey. This is one of my favorite courses in all of Scotland.

Garten exemplifies two aspects of Scottish golf. First, this is a fine example of James Braid's approach to golf course design. Here you can see clearly how Braid used bunkers to indicate a preferred line of play. You can see how he so cleverly and sensitively routed holes through natural landscape to achieve changes of direction, visual appeal, and challenging golf. There's also a rhythm to this course in the sequence of the holes that, in no small measure, is due to Braid's genius. Second, the Boat of Garten is a case study in how a course can be short yet still challenging. Many Americans look at the yardage on a course like this and say something like, "It's only 5866 yards from the back tees. How can that be considered a real golf course?". But then you look at the details and realize there's only one par 5, the par 4s are difficult, and par is 69. Case in point: the amateur record on this course is 67. Does that give you an idea of how difficult it is?

Some specifics: The course increases in difficulty as the round progresses. An opening one-shotter, unlike the rest of the course, is flat, short, and dull, but at least it gets you off to a quick start. From there, shots across banks of heather and shots from elevated tees to mogul-filled fairways and elevated greens give the feel of a hilly links course set in a Highland forest of silver birch. After a relatively easy go of it on the outward nine ("Avenues," #6, is a major exception), you encounter the inward nine featuring several doglegged par 4s where hitting a green in regulation can be accomplished only with two long, perfect shots (e.g., "Tulloch," #13, 422 yards, uphill, dogleg right). The locally-famous "Gully" (#15) requires a mid-iron tee shot to a plateau overlooking a gully, leaving 150 yards to a small green on the other side. At the nineteenth hole you'll probably be asked, even by nongolfers, how you played Gully. To finish the challenge, "Road"

hole (#18) is a punishing 426-yarder to an elevated green. Go
It's great fun.

Now for the rest of the Boat story: this is my idea of great golf in the Highlands. It's in a small town with a good hotel, a steam railway for atmosphere, and an incomparable natural setting in the beautiful Spey Valley. It's reasonably priced, visitors are welcome all week, and the clubhouse and staff are unpretentious and welcoming. I can go to the Boat for a round of golf in the morning, have a hot lunch in the attractive bar of the Boat Hotel, then in the afternoon go for a hike with my wife in the nearby Abernethy Forest. That's my idea of heaven on earth.

Accommodations: Recreation tourism is Boat of Garten's *raison d'être*. Just twenty-five minutes from Inverness, this is a good base for Highland fun. First-rate lodgings throughout the area can be viewed at the excellent web site *www.boatofgarten.com*.

5. Brora Golf Club (1891)

Region #: 5   **Category:** seaside links
Architect(s): John Sutherland (1891); James Braid (1924)
Length: 5854-6110   **SSS:** 69   **Par:** 69

Address: Golf Rd, Brora, Sutherland KW9 6QS
Directions: 5 mi N of Golspie on A9; 1st rt after bridge in village center

Reservations phone: 01408-621-417   **Fax:** 01408-622-157
Email: secretary@broragolf.co.uk   **Website:** broragolf.co.uk
Booking Contact(s): secretary
Secretary: James Fraser   **Professional:** none
Fee(s) (2003): wkday £27, day tkt £35; wkend £32, day tkt £40
Deposit (2003): no
Visitor Policies: any time   **Buggies:** 2 - general hire

Brora and Golspie—Golspie and Brora. Only five miles apart, just north of Dornoch, these two courses frequently are mentioned in the same breath as if they were one. They may as well be, for they are the northernmost courses golfers normally play when staying for several days in the Inverness-Dornoch area. If one must choose between Brora and Golspie, then the choice should probably be Brora—as pure a seaside links as you'll find in Scotland. Choosing between Tain and Brora is another matter. It's a toss up and a decision I would avoid by refusing to do anything but play both.

The attractions of Brora are many. First, we have a perfect seaside links setup—nine holes out and nine holes back—over rolling topography similar to that at St. Andrews and North Berwick rather than the dune-dominant terrain of Cruden Bay or Western Gailes. Add to that the genius of James Braid who came here in 1924 to re-work and extend a course already touched by Tom Morris of St. Andrews and John Sutherland of Dornoch. Finally, there is a pastoral touch unequaled among Scotland's most famous courses: due to ancient grazing rights maintained to this day, this is the course you will always remember for its electric fences that protect the greens from wandering cattle and sheep, as well as the local rules that treat cow pies as "casual water." This really is rural Scottish golf at its best.

As for individual holes, it's the usual Braidian stew—short, but challenging, and great fun. There are imaginative par 3s to each point of the compass; only one par 5; and the usual "monster" two-shotters (five at 400+ yards). If you're a fan of courses by James Braid (count me in), you'll love this one. Another of those fans, golf writer Jim Finegan, counts Brora "among my dozen favorite seaside courses in Scotland . . . as fine an example of Braid's work at the sea as we are likely to find today." Appropriately enough, Brora is home to the James Braid Society, dedicated to preserving the memory and spirit of James Braid, especially, as they note in their charter, "by playing the lesser-known 'village' courses" (see *www.thebraidsociety.com*).

See also: Golspie, Royal Dornoch, Tain.

6. Carnoustie Golf Links (1842) - Championship *

Region #: 4   **Category:** seaside links - no view
Architect(s): Allan Robertson, Tom Morris, Willie Park, James Braid
Length: 6692-6941-7400   **SSS:** 74   **Par:** 70

Address: Links Parade, Carnoustie, Angus DD7 7JE
Directions: well signposted 3 blks from High St in ctr of town

Reservations phone: 01241-853-789   **Fax:** 01241-852-720
Email: carnoustiegolf@aol.com   **Website:** carnoustiegolfclub.com
Booking Contact(s): Carol McKewan, Nan Hay, Kathleen Blair
Secretary: EJC Smith   **Professional:** Lee Vannet

Phone - Starter/Pro shop: reservations
Fee(s) (2003): £82 all wk; day tkt with Burnside £95; 17.5% VAT applied if booked by 3rd party (i.e., tour operators); jrs (14-18) - 50%
Deposit (2003): 100% prepayment, non-refundable
Visitor Policies: wkdays; not Sat am or before 11:30 Sun; Carnoustie Golf Course Resort Hotel & Spa preference hrs: M-F 9-10; 1:30-2:30; Sat 2-3:00; Sun 11:30-12:30
Buggies: no
Other: fairway mats in use mid October-April; no trolleys Nov-Apr; course closed to visitors 1st wk Sept for annual "Tassie" tournament; hdcps - men 28, women 36

Visitors to Scotland usually mention Carnoustie somewhere in the same breath as St. Andrews' Old Course, Royal Troon, Turnberry, and Muirfield—the famous courses on the "rota" of the British Open. Particularly since the return of the Open to Carnoustie's hallowed ground in 1999, the Championship Course has risen in stature. Golfers want to play this course. They've heard about the legendary difficulty of Carnoustie. And, in 1999, they were able to watch on television as professionals flailed away in knee-high rough and as Jean Van de Velde imploded on the "Home" hole with the claret jug all but inscribed with his name. For years into the future, Carnoustie will see golfers taking photographs down in the Barry Burn and measuring their success on the infamous eighteenth against Van de Velde's brilliant flameout. After a period of relative decline since the Open was held here in 1975, Carnoustie has re-emerged as a place where golf history is made.

Among the Open rota courses, there is probably more misinformation about Carnoustie than all the others combined. What about Carnoustie's legendary level of difficulty? First, this course is made difficult primarily by the vagaries of wind and weather. This part of the Angus coast does not get the "micro-climate" benefits of St. Andrews and North Berwick. Nasty weather just seems to cling to Carnoustie like a wet blanket. Second, you'll be playing off the visitor tees at around 6600 yards. That's not exactly a stroll in the park, but neither is it the "Tiger" championship tees that stretch to 7400 yards. To be sure, over 110 bunkers, punishing rough, and plenty of gorse, not to mention Jockie's Burn and Barry Burn, await the mis-hit ball.

This course is no pushover under any conditions. But in fine weather, it's not the monster it's made out to be.

Many times I've heard Carnoustie called "boring," "a wasteland," "uninteresting." I would characterize those comments as hasty if not dead wrong. It's true that most of Carnoustie's middle fourteen holes are relatively flat. But a course cannot be labeled boring if it boasts at least a half dozen superb golf holes, flat or otherwise. And, in that category, I would put Carnoustie's #1 "Cup" hole at the top of my list of the Best Holes in Scottish Golf. It's a complete golf experience and, what's more, it's followed by another par 4, "Gulley," that would rank close to the top of that list too. To have such a strong start is unusual in Scottish golf. And I don't think I need to say anything at all about the now-famous closing holes at Carnoustie!

Now to the important part: How hard is it to get a tee time at Carnoustie? In recent years, an accommodations myth has grown up around Carnoustie—namely, that to get a tee time you have to stay at the Carnoustie Golf Course Hotel. *Not true!* Let me try to make the proverbial long story short: In 1998-9 the Angus Council put a lot of money into the big (and expensive) Carnoustie Golf Course Hotel & Spa Resort that sits behind the eighteenth green and first tee. The structure was "purpose built" to accommodate the Open in 1999 and put Carnoustie back on the map of international golf. After the Open, three to four hours of prime tee times were reserved daily for the hotel. If the times went unsold, they had to be returned to the Links Management for re-sale *nine weeks prior to date of play.*

Naturally, local hoteliers went ballistic. Meetings ensued. Hair was torn. Breasts were pounded. Lawsuits were threatened. But not to worry. After the Open, business returned more or less to its normal level in Carnoustie and the big hotel was left with lots of empty rooms and lots of tee times that had to be returned unsold to the Links Management. Consequently, other hotels in town, late applicants, and freelancing golfers were able to secure tee times fairly easily.

The situation improved still further in 2003. Only two hours per day Monday through Friday were reserved for the hotel. Now Carnoustie is as easy to book as it was pre-1999—and that means just about the easiest "rota" ticket to get.

The Town: Frankly, Carnoustie is not a particularly attractive town. Its narrow, straight High Street is a monotonous slog of dingy

126

buildings with little to excite. As far as nongolf time goes, two days here will be plenty, though it makes a fine base for seeing the tourist sites of Angus (e.g., Glamis Castle). One definite "birdie": the town boasts value accommodations in B & Bs and several good, mid-price hotels, including the *Carlogie House Hotel* (01241-853-185; *www.carlogie-house-hotel.com*), *Carnoustie Links Hotel* (01241-853-273; formerly *Hogan House*), and *The Lochlorian Hotel* (01241-852-182).

Interestingly enough, dining in Carnoustie can be a gourmet treat. Folks come from miles around to be served by the Harris family at the *Lochlorian Hotel* in the heart of town at 13 Phillip St. A few blocks away, at *11 Park Avenue*, you'll find an award-winning restaurant of the same name (01241-853-336). Finally, at Burnside and High Street is *Ristorante Belmonte* (01241-853-261) and, I kid you not, this is one of the great Italian restaurants in the world. Owner "Luciano" and his wife moved to Scotland about nineteen years ago and have been cooking up an Italian storm in Carnoustie ever since. There's nothing pretentious or fancy here—just the freshest of ingredients cooked and presented with love and passion.

See also: Monifieth, Panmure.

7. Crail Golfing Society (1786) - Balcomie Links

Region #: 1   **Category:** seaside links
Architect(s): Tom Morris (1895 - 9 holes; 1899 - 9 holes)
Length: 5453 - 5922   **SSS:** 69   **Par:** 67-69

Address: Balcomie Clubhouse, Fifeness, Crail KY10 3XN
Directions: Well signposted 2 mi NE of Crail off A917

Reservations phone: 01333-450-686   **Fax:** 01333-450-416
Email: crailgs@hotmail.com   **Website:** crailgolfingsociety.co.uk
Booking Contact(s): Margaret Hunter, Doreen Mayes, Frances Robertson
Secretary: Alasdair Busby   **Professional:** Graeme Lennie
Phone - Starter/Pro shop: 01333-450-278; 01333-450-960
Fee(s) (2003): £32 wkdays, £53 day tkt; £40 wkend, £63 day tkt; jrs - 50%
Deposit (2003): 50%
Visitor Policies: wkdays; restrictions wkends   **Buggies:** 3 - med/phys
Other: Craighead Course - 6250 yds (1999)

I like to book clients at the Balcomie Links (pronounced Bal-COMB-ee) in Crail for three reasons: First, hard against the sea, this is Fife's most scenic course. Second, at just under 6,000 yards, it's a throwback to nineteenth-century holiday golf—a shotmaker's course—that contrasts nicely with the brawnier par-72 tracks at St. Andrews and Kingsbarns. Third, a trip down the road to Crail from St. Andrews gets the traveler onto Fife's Coastal Route and into the pretty fishing villages of the "East Neuk" between Crail and Leven.

The village at Crail is ten miles south of St. Andrews, just three miles on from Kingsbarns. The Balcomie Links are situated another two miles out past Crail on the easternmost promontory of Fife where the shore makes its westerly turn along the firth. Thus, Balcomie is not only the most scenic course in Fife, it's also the one most exposed to wind and rain from the North Sea. And, to put it mildly, this simple fact tends to have a lengthening effect on a rather short course.

Tom Morris came down here from St. Andrews to lay out nine holes for the Crail Golfing Society (Scotland's sixth oldest club) in 1895. Then, in 1899, he came back to add another nine. This was some of Morris's last work, closing out a productive decade when, well into his seventies, he completed Muirfield, Elie, Luffness New, Scotscraig, and Tain.

Balcomie's layout is odd, with the last four holes laid off on a terraced area west of the clubhouse a bit removed from the rest of the course. It's almost as if Old Tom laid out a perfect fourteen and then had to figure out how to cram another four into the picture.

You can survey the entire layout from the high ground at the Crail Golfing Society's comfy clubhouse. The first hole, "Boat-house," plays down a slope leading to the sea for holes two through five. These latter are among the most stirring in Scottish golf and they will certainly remind one of Pebble Beach, particularly the #5 "Hell Hole," a brutal beauty that plays to 459 yards over the rocky shoreline. Holes six through fourteen—all with sea views—play along an OB stone wall that lends more atmosphere to the round. After fourteen, you make a hike of about two hundred yards to the fifteenth tee to begin the "terrace four" that take you home.

Throughout this layout you'll find the presence of Tom Morris in a raft of bunkers, testing par 3s (three on the back nine extend to more than 200 yards), challenging greens, one double green, and, in effect, one triple green where hole #s 1, 10, and 12 converge. In short, the Balcomie at Crail is a unique course designed by a unique individual in a unique setting—emblematic of all the reasons we go to Scotland to play golf.

Accommodations: For some, lodging in Crail or any of the villages in Fife's East Neuk will make an attractive alternative to busy and pricey St. Andrews. A basic golfers' hotel near the links is the *Balcomie Links Hotel* (01333-450-237; *www.balcomie.co.uk*) and the best B & B in town is *The Hazelton* run by Karen and Jerry Dawe (01333-450-250; *www.thehazelton.co.uk*). For more about the East Neuk, see the web site *www.eastneukwide.co.uk*.

See also: Elie, Lundin Links, Leven Links.

8. Crieff Golf Club Ltd. (1891) - Ferntower Course

Region #: 7   **Category:** parkland
Architect(s): various, incl James Braid, Robert Simpson, John Stark
Length: 6052-6402   **SSS:** 71   **Par:** 71

Address: Perth Rd, Crieff PH7 3LR
Directions: 1 mi NE of Crieff town centre on A85

Reservations phone: 01764-652-909   **Fax:** 1764-655-096
Email: davidmurchie@crieffgc.ssnet.co.uk
Website: crieffgolf.co.uk
Booking Contact(s): professional
Secretary: Scott Miller   **Professional:** David W Murchie
Phone - Starter/Pro shop: reservations
Fee(s) (2003): wkday £22-27 depending upon month, day tkt £34-44; wkend £27-37, no day tkt
Deposit (2003): none
Visitor Policies: all wk   **Buggies:** 4 - general hire
Other: 9-hole relief course, "Dornock," SSS 63, 4642 yds

Completed in 1980, only a few years before the PGA Centenary at Gleneagles, neighboring Ferntower at Crieff (about twenty minutes away) offers golf over terrain similar to that at Gleneagles at about one-fourth the price. In other words, this is a good choice for the golfer on a budget or the golfer already familiar with Scotland's pricier tourist magnets. Replete with B & Bs, guest houses, and hotels, Crieff the best base for those planning to play at Gleneagles without ⸗ at the hotel.

Directly north of Stirling, no more than an hour from the airports at Edinburgh and Glasgow, Crieff has long been a strategic crossroads on routes to and from the Highlands. The ancient feel of this attractive hill town (population 6,500) is pervasive in its twisting streets and old stone buildings. When not on the golf course, visitors to Crieff can find historic sites (a Roman road has been uncovered south of town); natural history afforded by superb hiking around Loch Earn to the west; or the commercial history of Scotland's whisky trade at the Famous Grouse Experience (formerly the Glenturret Distillery). Only one and one-half hours from St. Andrews, Crieff makes an excellent day-trip destination from that fair city.

The Ferntower Course plays east to west along the south-facing slope of a hill called the "Knock," a local landmark. From those heights, the golfer can enjoy superb views over the Strathearn Valley while hoping (usually in vain) for a level lie. A rather short course from the visitor tees (6052 yards), I would politely request play from the "member" (white) tees at this course. Ferntower's three par 5s and four par 3s offer pleasing variety. Course maintenance is first-rate. Incidentally, the former pro at Crieff is John Stark, who gained a certain measure of immortality as the key figure in Michael Bamberger's delightful book, *To the Linksland.*

So, why not make a stop at Crieff? Or a day trip from St. Andrews? You'll be glad you did. This is one of Scotland's best-kept golf secrets.

9. **Cruden Bay Golf Club (1899)**

Region #: 6   **Category:** seaside links
Architect(s): Tom Simpson
Length: 6022-6395   **SSS:** 72   **Par:** 70

Address: Aulton Rd, Cruden Bay, Peterhead AB42 0NN
Directions: 2 mi off A90 on high ground S of village

Reservations phone: 01779-812-285   **Fax:** 01779-812-945
Email: cbaygc@aol.com   **Website:** crudenbaygolfclub.co.uk
Booking Contact(s): administrator
Administrator: Rosemary Pittendrigh

Professional: Robbie Stewart
Phone - Starter/Pro shop: 01779-812-414
Fee(s) (2003): wkday £55, day tkt £75; wkend £65, no day tkt
Deposit (2003): none   **Buggies:** none
Visitor Policies: not before 10 M, T; wkend pm only and not before 4:30 on club competition days
Other: Closed wk of Brit Open for club event; visitors ok from white tees

Here's a measure of how good Cruden Bay is: After one of my clients has finished a golf trip, I send a "post-trip evaluation" asking, among other things, for a list of courses played and a ranking of the courses. In these post-trip evaluations, among golfers who have played it, Cruden Bay has never been less than #2. Usually it is #1—and that's compared to Carnoustie, Dornoch, Turnberry, Troon, and all the courses at St. Andrews. Pete Dye has cited Cruden Bay among his five favorite courses in the world! Readers of *Golf World,* as reported in *Best Courses in Scotland,* rank Cruden Bay sixth among Best Courses and fourth among Best Value Courses. For myself, I put Cruden Bay in my Top Five in Scotland with Machrie, Machrihanish, North Berwick, and Western Gailes (not to play favorites, in alpha order).

Many golf writers have described Cruden Bay in loving detail. Suffice to say here, the overwhelming impression made at Cruden Bay is that of a lunar landscape laid down on the gentle curve of an ocean bay. This is nothing less than pure links golf played on the wasteland between fertile soil and raging sea. The course, routed into the natural terrain by architect Tom Simpson (of the Carnoustie Simpsons), traces an elongated "figure eight" from the elevated clubhouse to the equally elevated #10 tee at the far end of the course and back again. In between, it's, "Nelly, bar the door!" Everything you want to find on a Scottish links course is here: long rough, gorse, burns, gullies, dells, dunes, blind shots, elevated tees, raised greens. Golf writer Jim Finegan summarizes: "One of the most awe-inspiring stretches of linksland in Scotland, indeed, in all of the British Isles." I would say Cruden Bay is simply *the* most dramatic duneland in all of Scottish golf. And, what's more, it's the most *fun* to play. It's so much fun, you hardly care about your score when you reach the comfortable nineteenth hole—incidentally, one of the finest in Scottish golf.

So, why isn't Cruden Bay played by more visitors? The obvious reason is that it's in the northeast corner of Scotland—not exactly the crossroads of most itineraries. At the same time, Cruden Bay has grown in stature as the golf experience there has spread by word-of-mouth from one visitor to the next. Consequently, more and more golfers are making the pilgrimage to this special place.

Accommodations: Cruden Bay lies about thirty miles north of Aberdeen, Scotland's third largest city, and ten miles south of Peterhead. If an urban base is the goal, one should stay in one of those cities where accommodations are plentiful. For more information, see *www.granite-city.com.*

Outside Aberdeen, two excellent choices catering to golfers deserve special mention: First, midway between Aberdeen and Cruden Bay, at the village of Newburgh, is the *Udny Arms* (01358-789-444; *www.udny.co.uk)*, run by Guy Craig, his family, and staff. The Udny has a wide and well-deserved reputation as a first-rate "golfer's hotel." It's warm and attractive, with attention to detail, but without being either pretentious or particularly expensive. Most important, the Udny offers five-star dining in a three-star setting. The Craig family's long history of culinary excellence shines in the dining room. Second, in a priceless location right at Cruden Bay on the high ground overlooking the golf course, you'll find the *Red House Hotel* (01779-812-215; *www.redhousehotel.com)*. The Red House is a bit of a splurge (just under £50 per person per night in 2003), but when you check into one of the rooms overlooking the golf course (ask for Room #s 1, 2, or 5) you'll quickly forget about the price. Furthermore, the Red House is home to one of the most voluble, expansive, lovable characters in Scottish golf—and that would be Ian Devenish, man of many businesses, many accents, and many tall tales. If you're lucky enough to catch Ian on duty and available for conversation, you'll probably remember the Red House as the best bargain on your trip. The important point: both of these establishments are one-of-a-kind, family-run hotels of the sort long removed from the American scene—another reason to savor the travel experience Scotland offers in this cookie-cutter age of chain formulas.

10. Downfield Golf Club (1932)

Region #: 4   **Category:** parkland
Architect(s): C K Cotton (expanded to 18 holes - 1969)
Length: 6247-6803   **SSS:** 70-73   **Par:** 70-73

Address: Turnberry Ave, Dundee DD2 3QP
Directions: NW of Dundee; Exit A923 off ring Rd; left on Harrison Rd to
T-junction; left to Turnberry Ave

Reservations phone: 01382-825-595   **Fax:** 01382-813-111
Email: downfieldgc@ukonline.co.uk   **Website:** downfieldgolf.com
Booking Contact(s): secretary
Secretary: Margaret Stewart   **Professional:** Kenny Hutton
Phone - Starter/Pro shop: 01382-889-246
Fee(s) (2003): Apr & Oct wkday £29, day tkt £31; May-Sept wkday £34,
day tkt £36; wkend Apr & Oct £35, May-Sept £45; jrs - 50%
Deposit (2003): £15   **Buggies:** 2 - general hire
Visitor Policies: not on Sat; Sun after 2:30

Downfield is a course that visitors to Carnoustie or St. Andrews
might consider as a parkland respite from linksland golf. Situated in
northeast Dundee, midway between those two golf Meccas, the course
is easily accessible in about twenty minutes from either location.

Relatively new to Scottish golf, Downfield was designed in 1969
by C.K. Cotton for the City of Dundee. At the time, it created a bit of
a stir. Soon after its opening, the club hosted the Scottish Open in
1972, the British PGA Match Play Championship in 1974, and the
Scottish Amateur in 1978. But, since those halcyon years, Downfield's
star has faded—not for the locals, but for the UK golf establishment
and the international visitor. Today, this condition makes it all the
easier for the cagey traveler to make a short-notice reservation or even
walk on at one of Scotland's finest inland courses.

The outstanding feature of Downfield is its forest setting with
evergreen and deciduous trees unmatched in their multifarious variety
except perhaps at Gleneagles and the Boat of Garten. The setting is
usually described as "mature woodlands," but that antiseptic
description does not do justice to the beauty of Downfield. This is rich,
midland Scotland at its very best, and it's a good example of why a
parkland course should be mixed into an itinerary focused on linksland
courses. After playing golf at the links courses—never described as
"pretty" or "lush" or "graceful"—it can be a relief to visit a course
where all those adjectives apply.

The irony and oddity of Downfield is that, if it's challenge you are seeking, this is a course where you should relish playing off the visitor tees at 6250 yards rather than the medal tees at 6800 yards. The reason: three relatively easy par 5s on the medal course become very long, difficult par 4s on the shorter track. The medal par 73 (unusual in golf anywhere) is reduced to par 70 from the visitor tees. Fairways at #s 4, 5, 7, 15, and 16 are alleys cut through forest; landing areas are generous; and the course is always in "top nick." As golf writer Jim Finegan puts it, Downfield offers "good, honest golf . . . in an exquisite parkland setting, but it is no occasion for hat tossing and dancing in the streets." Well, yes, that's about right: Downfield will not be the highlight of your trip to Scotland. But it can be a welcome break from the links, and it's a lot less expensive than Gleneagles.

Nongolf: Dundee is Scotland's fourth largest city. Approaching from Fife, its setting is dramatic—on a high hill tumbling down to the Firth of Tay. In days past, jute, journalism, and shipbuilding made Dundee's reputation. Today, that reputation is associated with high unemployment and related maladies of the modern economy. Dundee has become the place where most visitors take a right turn at the north end of the Tay Bridge to get from St. Andrews to Carnoustie. Near that bridge is anchored Dundee's highest-profile tourist attraction. For a memorable experience, take a left (instead of a right) along the waterfront and you'll find Captain Robert Scott's vessel of Antarctic exploration, *The Discovery.* This ship is now a remarkable museum. It will leave you in awe of the indomitable spirit of the Scots. An audio-visual introduction precedes a tour of the ship. *The Discovery* is a useful reminder that the Scots were a seafaring people who built great ships and were willing to go places others feared to tread (or sail). This is one of the best nongolf expeditions I can recommend and its 5-star rating from VisitScotland corroborates my experience.

11. Duff House Royal Golf Club (1909)
Region #: 6   **Category:** parkland
Architect(s): Alister MacKenzie (1923)
Length: 5991-6161   **SSS:** 69-70   **Par:** 68

Address: The Barnyards, Duff House, Banff AB45 35X
Directions: 1 mi S of Banff on A98

Reservations phone: 01261-812-062   **Fax:** 01261-812-224
Email: duff_house_royal@bt.internet.com
Website: theduffhouseroyalclub.co.uk
Booking Contact(s): Mrs. Janice Corbett
Secretary: Hamish Liebnitz   **Professional:** R S Strachan
Phone - Starter/Pro shop: reservations
Fee(s) (2003): wkday £20, day tkt 26; wkend £27, day tkt £32; jrs (under 18) - 50%
Deposit (2003): no   **Buggies:** 2 - med/phys
Visitor Policies: wkdays after 9:30; wkend after 11 am

Golf at Banff has a long history but, to make the proverbial long story short, Duff House has been part of that history only since 1910 when Alexander Duff, Duke of Fife, donated his parkland estate to the twin towns of Banff and Macduff. Prior to this magnanimous gift to Scottish golf, the game had been played on nine holes on linksland near the Moray Firth. Coincidentally, the duke was married to the daughter of the Prince of Wales, Princess Louise, who eventually became patroness at Duff House and secured the "Royal" appellation for the club—the seventh and last in the line of Scottish clubs so designated.

To put an even finer point on the pedigree of Duff House Royal, the course we play today actually dates from 1923-5 when Alister MacKenzie was engaged by the club to give them a course worthy of the royal designation. As a last gesture before his relocation to America, where he created Augusta National, that's exactly what the master of wartime camouflage and great golf courses did. And, because Scotland boasts so few MacKenzie courses, Duff House Royal must be included in a selective directory of this sort.

Though not far from the sea, MacKenzie worked with a flat expanse of parkland turf fronting the River Deveron. Here he created a challenging venue featuring huge, double-tiered greens protected by dozens of bunkers. Deceptively short at 6161 yards, the course has only one par 5, leaving us at par 68 against an SSS of 70. This kind of profile promises a collection of long, difficult par 4s—a promise kept on the road home as one encounters #14 (434 yards), #15 (468 yards), and #17 (462 yards). Yes, I skipped #16: that's a 242-yard one-shotter reachable only by the power hitter. The eighteenth home hole will feel like sweet relief after playing this stretch of closing holes that must be among the most punishing in Scottish golf.

Nongolf: For those traversing northeast Scotland's "Coastal Trail," Duff House Royal is situated about twenty-six miles west of Fraserburgh. It's just off the A98 where that highway returns to the coast at Banff-Macduff after an inland bend. Given some time and inclination, this is an area to savor and explore. For example, one can combine a day of golf with art at Duff House itself. The Georgian mansion designed by William Adam is now managed by Historic Scotland and is part of the National Gallery's network of "Country House Galleries" (*see www.nationalgalleries.org*).

The inland attraction of the northeast corner of Scotland is the "Castle Trail." The seaside attraction is the collection of small fishing villages that dot the coastline. One of these is Pennan, twelve miles east of Banff-Macduff on the B9031. I mention this tiny village because a feature film, "Local Hero," starring Burt Lancaster was shot here about twenty years ago. This is a movie I recommend to all travelers to Scotland. Written and directed by a Scot, Bill Forsyth, it captures a part of the spirit of Scotland without any of the usual clichés. It's a movie about North Sea oil and the transformation of a small village or, more precisely, how a small village manages to retain its character in the face of "modernization." In the opening scenes of the movie, two American oil executives—buttoned-down, intense, and efficient—arrive in the small town to "make a deal" and get out as quickly as possible. By the end of the movie these fellows have shed their shirts and ties and are lazing about on the sand with an old beachcomber. I hope this is something like what happens to you on your trip to Scotland. The message: when in Scotland, SLOW DOWN and enjoy the gift of life.

See also: Moray Old.

Duke's Course: *See St. Andrews - Old Course Hotel - Duke's Course*

12. Dunbar Golf Club (1856) +

Region #: 3   **Category:** seaside links
Architect(s): Tom Morris (1856)
Length: 6200-6426   **SSS:** 71   **Par:** 71

Address: East Links, Dunbar EH42 1LT
Directions: SE of town ctr off A1087

Reservations phone: 01368-862-317   **Fax:** 01368-865-202
Email: secretary@dunbar-golfclub.co.uk
Website: dunbar-golfclub.co.uk
Booking Contact(s): Shirley Fairbairn
Secretary: Liz Thom   **Professional:** J Montgomery
Phone - Starter/Pro shop: 01368-862-086
Fee(s) (2003): wkday £37, day tkt £40; wkend £45, day tkt £55; jrs - 50%
Deposit (2003): £10
Visitor Policies: after 9:30 except Th   **Buggies:** 2 - med or phys

About twenty minutes southeast of North Berwick, just off the A1, at the attractive port/resort of Dunbar, golfers will find a classic links where the game has been played since at least the early seventeenth century. It's another course where the long hand of Tom Morris remains; the course has hardly changed since the Great One laid out fifteen holes here in 1856. In 1880 three additional holes (the opening holes) were added to bring the course to the number made standard by that time.

You'll have little trouble recognizing the non-Morris three, for they have little to do with the rest of the course. Unusual in Scottish golf—or golf anywhere for that matter—the first two holes are par 5s. The first hole shoots straight away from the clubhouse and the second, like a boomerang, returns to place. Then #3, a par 3, makes a ninety-degree turn, heading straight to the ocean. After this quirky start, dictated by available land, the Morris holes proceed along a narrow strip of linksland, out and back, in classic fashion. Along the way you'll be treated to exhilarating ocean views and a series of excellent golf holes highlighted by a stone wall on the right side of the outgoing holes. This is no course for a slicer, for, once free of the outgoing stone, you'll have the ocean to deal with coming home. Back at the clubhouse you'll find no warmer welcome in Scottish golf. This is a down-to-earth golf experience—easily in my Top Ten list. And it will be abundantly clear why Dunbar is used as a qualifying course when the British Open is held at Muirfield.

Anyone interested in an additional eighteen holes will find the short but intriguing Winterfield golf course on the opposite (northeast) end of town. This course features a bundle of wild and woolly one-shotters (the first hole across a vast, grass gully is worth the price of admission), played first on the bluffs above the ocean, then out on a promontory fully exposed to the forces of nature. Great stuff.

The Town: Dunbar has always occupied a strategic position relative to England, so you'll see here a collection of castle ruins and historic buildings. Of greatest interest to many Americans is the birthplace of John Muir, the most influential conservationist of our nineteenth century and fountainhead of America's system of national parks. The John Muir Country Park is located outside Dun-BAR and his birthplace, now an excellent museum, is in the middle of town on the main street.

A digressive note: regarding the emphatic spelling in the previous paragraph, locals will warm to you when you pronounce their place as *they* do—with the accent on the last syllable. Same with Inver-NESS, Aber-DEEN, and Dum-FRIES.

13. Edzell Golf Club (1895)

Region #: 4   **Category:** parkland
Architect(s): Bob Simpson
Length: 6042-6299   **SSS:** 71   **Par:** 69-71

Address: High St, Edzell, Angus DD9 7TF
Directions: 4 mi W of A90 on B966; left just past Edzell archway

Reservations phone: 01356-647-283   **Fax:** 01356-648-094
Email: secretary@edzellgolfclub.demon.co.uk
Website: edzellgolfclub.net
Key Contact(s): secretary
Secretary: Ian Farquhar   **Professional:** Alistair J Webster
Phone - Starter/Pro shop: 01356-648-462
Fee(s) (2001): wkday £25, day tkt £35; wkend £31, day tkt £44; jrs £6
Deposit (2001): £5
Visitor Policies: all wk   **Buggies:** 5 - general hire

For golfers in transit from Fife to Aberdeenshire, Edzell Golf Club is an elegant way to break up the drive. For 36-holers staying in Angus, this is a highly-regarded parkland course to pair with one of the historic seaside courses.

Still another way to play Edzell is to combine golf with a drive up Glen Esk on a narrow road that crosses the B966 about a mile north of

Edzell. A twelve-mile jaunt on this road, through the broad, verdant glen, leads to the Glenesk Folk Museum, castle ruins, and abbey ruins on the rim of Loch Lee. A great place for a picnic! Back in Edzell are more castle ruins and gardens. Lots of fishing, hiking, and hunting in this area too. In short, Edzell is a good example of how a savvy traveler can combine golf with excursions into the Scottish countryside in a way that will never show up on the typical operator's itinerary.

As for the golf, it's a challenge on a course laid out by Bob Simpson of Carnoustie. Relatively flat and compact, Edzell is easy to walk despite its location at the foot of hills that rise to 1,000 feet. Pleasant views abound. The River West Walter plays a role here and out-of-bounds is a constant factor—in the case of #15, on both sides of a tight fairway. At 6300 yards Edzell is about average in length for a Scottish course. But, just in case you think that sounds like a pushover, please note the professional course record is 67. Visitors here most often remark about the friendly, welcoming staff; the outstanding food and drink in the clubhouse; and the excellent pro shop kept by Alistair Webster. There's also a new driving range. This one's a *real* hidden gem.

Elie: See *Golf House Club at Elie*

14. Fortrose and Rosemarkie (1892)
Region #: 5   **Category:** seaside links
Architect(s): James Braid
Length: 5555-5875 yds   **SSS:** 69   **Par:** 71

Address: Ness Rd East, Fortrose, Ross-Shire IV10 8SE
Directions: 12 mi N of Inverness; A832 at Tore roundabout; rt at Fortrose police station, follow signs

Reservations phone: 01381-620-529   **Fax:** 01381-621-328
Email: secretary@fortrosegolfclub.co.uk   **Website**: fortrosegolfclub.co.uk
Booking Contact(s): secretary
Secretary: Bill Baird   **Professional:** none
Phone - Starter/Pro shop: 01381-620-733
Fee(s) (2003): wkday £25, day tkt £35; wkend £30, day tkt £40
Deposit (2003): no
Visitor Policies: all wk   **Buggies:** 4 - general hire

Golfers basing in or near Inverness have their sites set clearly on Royal Dornoch, Nairn, and Tain—in about that order. Once those are played, this is a good course to squeeze into the itinerary, maybe on a quick morning or afternoon round but, better yet, on a day outing to the "Black Isle" (actually a peninsula) just a few miles northeast of Inverness. Incidentally, if you like the idea of staying in a small town away from Inverness, Fortrose is a good choice.

Fortrose and Rosemarkie is another James Braid design extended in 1935 from nine holes existing since the golf club was organized in 1888. At only 5555 yards from the visitor tees, with an SSS of 69, the course inevitably will remind one of the short but difficult track designed by Braid at Boat of Garten. But the setting here is dramatically different: the golf course is crammed into a promontory (Chanory Point) jutting into the Moray Firth. Just across the water, on another point of land, you'll see Fort George, a northern outpost of the English army (1769). These two pincerlike points of land aimed at one another form a natural harbor wall between Inverness and the frequently-raging sea.

Golf tour operators like to promote the "Hidden Gems" of Scotland. The trouble is, most of them are not hidden at all. Fortrose and Rosemarkie is an exception and an exceptional hidden gem. At £25 weekday in 2003, it's also one of the bargains in Scottish golf.

15. Glasgow Golf Club (1892) - Glasgow Gailes +
Region #: 2   **Category:** seaside links - no view
Architect(s): Willie Park, Jr. (1892)
Length: 6323-6539   **SSS:** 70-72   **Par:** 71

Address: Glasgow Golf Club, Killermont, Bearsden G61 2TW (Glasgow)
Directions: 2 mi S of Irvine off A737; 6 mi N of Troon town center on the coastal route

Reservations phone: 0141-942-2011   **Fax:** 0141-942-0770
Email: secretary@glasgow-golf.com   **Website:** glasgowgailes-golf.com
Booking Contact(s): Margaret Stygal
Secretary: David Deas   **Professional:** J Steven
Phone - Starter/Pro shop: 01294-311-561; 01294-311-258 (clubhouse)
Fee(s) (2003): wkday £45, day tkt £60; wkend £58, no day tkt

Deposit (2003): £15
Visitor Policies: am and pm restrictions vary allowing about 5 hrs daily;
Sat/Sun 2:30 - 4:06 pm only
Buggies: 2 - general hire
Other: reservations at Glasgow office; white tees for hdcp 6 and below

Glasgow Gailes is among the "dazzling dozen" that line the crescent coast of Ayrshire from Irvine to Turnberry. A feature of them all is the coastal railway that made the courses easily accessible to residents of Glasgow in the late nineteenth century. The Glasgow Golf Club opened its course at Gailes in 1892 to relieve member pressure on its home course at Alexandra Park in Glasgow. Willie Park, Jr., was brought in from Musselburgh to design the course and he did a magnificent job of it.

Western Gailes is situated on the west side of the rail line between the railway and the sea. Glasgow Gailes lies away from the water, on the east side of the line and a little to the north across a service road. In 2003 Glasgow Gailes was joined on the east side of the rail line by Southern Gailes, designed by Kevin Phillips (of Kingsbarns fame). Thus, the two easterly courses are on relatively flatter ground, without the proliferation of seaside dunes and without the sea views. In anticipation of the rush to Troon for the British Open in 2004, this is a powerful collection of courses to rival any in the land.

Realistically, the courses at Gailes will not likely supplant the royal triumvirate of Turnberry, Troon, and Prestwick on the golf traveler's list of priorities in Ayrshire. But, for those who have extra time to give to the Ayrshire coast, this is the place to go. Western Gailes certainly has gained in international notoriety, having appeared on many "Best of Scotland" lists. Southern Gailes is sure to follow. Now, in that Gailesian triumvirate, will Glasgow Gailes play third fiddle?—probably. But this is a fine course that deserves more recognition than it gets.

My recommendation: If you are up to a 36-hole day, make a day of it at Gailes. I particularly like the combination of Western and either Glasgow or Southern Gailes, not only for the proximity of the courses, but for the variety they offer in such proximity. Playing Glasgow Gailes, for example, is a little like relaxing with Debussy after struggling through the brawny Wagnerian experience offered across the road at Western Gailes. Another special attraction of a day at

Gailes: the clubhouses are handsome and warmly welcoming, with particularly fine views from the elevated lounge at Western. The Glasgow clubhouse is a classic. Now, with Southern Gailes in the picture, there's still more reason to make a day of it at Gailes.
See also: Western Gailes

16. The Glen (1906) - (North Berwick East Links)

Region #: 3 **Category:** seaside links
Architect(s): James Braid (1906), Philip Mackenzie Ross (after WWII)
Length: 5791-6043 **SSS:** 68 **Par:** 69

Address: East Links, Tantallon Terrace, N Berwick EH39 4LE
Directions: E of town center off Beach Rd

Reservations phone: 01620-892-726 **Fax:** 01620-895-447
Email: secretary@glengolfclub.co.uk **Website:** glengolfclub.co.uk
Booking Contact(s): Rita Wilson
Administrator: Kevin Fish **Professional:** none
Phone - Starter/Pro shop: 01620-894-596
Fee(s) (2003): wkday £25, day tkt £36; wkend £35, day tkt 45
Deposit (2003): £10
Visitor Policies: all wk 9:30 - 11; Sat after 2 pm; Sun 9-12 and after 2:30
Buggies: no

Among the most scenic courses in Scotland, this track on the opposite end of town from the historic "West Links," is worth a visit either in its own right or paired with the West Links on a day of 36-hole golf.

On a crisp fall day alternating between sunshine and a Lothian burst of showers, I played a round of golf at The Glen with Club Captain John Wellwood and a tour organizer, Willie Wallace of Celtic Legend. Briefly stated, I have never played a more enjoyable eighteen holes in Scotland. The reasons? Apart from the presence of good company, first, The Glen is a course that can really be enjoyed by the average golfer. The mid-to-high-handicapper can play this course without feeling like a lightweight boxer thrown into the ring with a heavyweight. Though you'll find plenty of challenge here, no great banks of gorse or heather lie in wait to swallow up errant balls. Second, even if you're not playing well you'll still enjoy panoramic ocean views encompassing the coastal south, monumental Bass Rock, and The Kingdom of Fife to the north.

When not admiring the scenery, you'll find a collection of memorable golf holes—all consistently good, some outstanding. In the latter category, I would include all the one-shotters, particularly the signature #13, a 144-yarder where a blind shot leads to a green set in a hollow (with beach to the right) in a gully some one hundred feet below the level of the teeing ground. Number fourteen, at 370 yards, requires a solid drive across the aforementioned gully to achieve position for a clear second shot to a small green. Back to the beginning (and the end), the par 4 #1 hole ("The Haugh") plays straight out about 220 yards, then up a steep hill to a blind green. Number eighteen ("Jacob's ladder") traverses the same ground in the opposite direction, plunging from the hilltop to a broad fairway and a narrow, deep green at the home hole. Back at the whitewashed clubhouse you'll receive a warm welcome in unpretentious surroundings. Incidentally, plans are afoot to build a new clubhouse on the high ground beyond the first hole. If and when that happens during the next few years, some re-routing may occur but, in any case, the holes will be re-sequenced so that the current #1 will become #18. This may lead to an increase either in heart attacks or beer sales as tired golfers straggle into the clubhouse after ascending "The Haugh."

See also: North Berwick - West Links.

The Courses at Gleneagles
17. King's Course   18. Queen's Course
19. PGA Centenary Course (formerly Monarch's)

Region #: 6   **Category:** parkland
Architect(s): James Braid (King's, Queen's); Jack Nicklaus (Centenary)
Length: King's 6125-6790; Queen's 5660-5965; Centenary 5605-7081
SSS: King's 73; Queen's 70; Centenary 71-73
Par: King's 68-70; Queen's 68; Centenary 72

Address: Auchterarder PH3 1NF
Directions: well signposted 3 mi S of Auchterarder off A9

Reservations phone: 01764-694-469   **Fax:** 01764-694-387
Email: visitor.golf@gleneagles.com   **Website:** gleneagles.com

Director of Golf: Graeme Marchbank   **Professional:** Sandy Smith
Phone - Starter/Pro shop: 01764-694-362
Fee(s) (2003): Apr & Oct hotel guest £75, visitor £95; May-Sept hotel guest
£90, visitor £110; twilight rate £70 (after 4 pm May-Sept)
Deposit (2003): none for hotel residents; visitors 100% prepay
Visitor Policies: 14-day cancellation ok
Buggies: Centenary - plenty; med/phys on King's, Queen's
with driver-caddie
Other: Scottish PGA early July; will host Ryder Cup 2014

Gleneagles can be described in the plainest of words: This is an international resort with three golf courses. But to put it that way is a little like describing the Empire State Building as a large edifice.

So, let's start over. Only one hour from Glasgow or Edinburgh, Gleneagles is *the* finest international resort hotel in Scotland and, very likely, among the half-dozen classiest golf hotels in the world. With its amenities and grounds, Gleneagles puts Turnberry in the shade. And the beauty of the place is not just in the stately granite walls of the main building or its incomparable natural setting on the edge of the Scottish Highlands. The contemporary beauty of Gleneagles lies in its relatively democratic spirit. This is a place accessible and welcoming to all—rich or not-so-rich, resident or visitor.

As for the golf courses, it might suffice to say that the two courses by James Braid and C.K. Hutchinson (King's and Queen's) and the one course by Jack Nicklaus (PGA Centenary, formerly known as Monarch's) are at or near the top of the list of Scotland's best inland courses. But that would be putting it too plainly also—especially when golf writers have worn their thesauri thin from looking for words to describe these courses in this lovely land. In *Blasted Heaths and Blessed Greens,* Jim Finegan waxes positively rhapsodic in describing the Gleneagles courses as "no less than wonderful, a collection of arresting golf holes painted with bold brush strokes on a canvass of hills and valleys, of heather and bracken and gorse, of majestic hardwoods and equally majestic evergreens." I'll leave the Gleneagles poetry to those who have done it so well over the years. For the visiting golfer, there are more basic facts to convey.

First, if you are looking for a traditional Scottish course design, you'll want to choose, first, the King's Course and, then, the Queen's (vintage1919). The King's Course features half-a-dozen par 4s in the

400+ range and par ranging from 68 to 70 depending upon the tees used. Braid offers *no* par 5s on the 6115-yard track. At 5965 yards, the Queen's Course is the shorter of the two. But don't be fooled. The course has only one par 5. Remember, this is James Braid—lover and master of the long, demanding par 4. The Nicklaus Centenary course is about what you would expect. No matter how you cut it—despite the setting and the fact that he did a magnificent job—it looks and feels like a modern, American course. Distances between green and tee are considerable. Five par 5s make up for their absence on the King's and Queen's. Carved fairways, bunkering, and undulating greens are all "Jack." So, if that's your cup of tea—and a lot of people want to see what Nicklaus has done in Scotland—then the Centenary Course should be your choice. Incidentally, the name change from Monarch's to PGA Centenary occurred in 2001 when the Scottish Professional Golf Association set up permanent shop at Gleneagles.

Second, no handicap or gender restrictions apply here. With five sets of tees on both the King's and Centenary courses, and with four on the Queen's, there's a track for golfers of every level of ability and strength. And, if one must ride over these beautiful though admittedly taxing hills, the Nicklaus course allows carts on concrete paths (the first such in Scotland and still a bit offensive to traditionalists).

Third, though hotel guests have tee-time priority, Gleneagles is open to all. In fact, because the hotel is relatively small for its class (maximum capacity about 450 people) and golf holes abound, it's normally fairly easy to book a time at Gleneagles on *one* of the courses—even on short notice. And you won't be disappointed in any of the choices.

Fourth, relative bargains can be had at Gleneagles if you go at the right time or play at the right time. In April and October rates are reduced in the hotel as well as at the courses. From May through September, the "twilight" golf fee, after 4 p.m., is £70 (from mid-May to late July that gives you plenty of time to complete a full round.). To learn more, see the hotel's exhaustive web site *www.gleneagles.com*.

20. Golf House Club (1875) at Elie

Region #: 1   **Category:** links-heathland hybrid
Architect(s): evolution w/ help from Tom Morris (4 holes - 1895/6)
Length: 6000-6273 yds   **SSS:** 70   **Par:** 70

Address: Elie, Fife KY9 1A5
Directions: well signposted near town center off A917

Reservations phone: 01333-330-301   **Fax:** 01333-330-895
Email: sandy@golfhouseclub.freeserve.co.uk
Website: golfhouseclub.freeserve.co.uk
Booking Contact(s): Moira Lawrie or secretary
Secretary: Alexander Sneddon   **Professional:** Robin Wilson
Phone - Starter/Pro shop: 01333-330-955
Fee(s) (2003): wkdays £40, day tkt £55; wkend £50, day tkt £65; no jr rates
Deposit (2003): none
Visitor Policies: wkdays after 10 am; no Sundays May-Sept
Buggies: none

Whenever I think of Elie, the phrase, "Sherman's March to the Sea," springs to mind. None of the typical links "out and back" along a coast line here. At Elie you start perhaps three-quarters of a mile from seaside at the clubhouse and then you *march*—albeit, to and fro—for six holes before approaching the water. Even then, it's back and forth until, finally, three exquisitely challenging holes present themselves for play along the rocky shore (#s 11, 12, and 13). And, yet, the sea is never out of sight. It's out there—tantalizing and omnipresent. You know you're at a seaside links, but it comes and goes like a lover pursued, then found, then lost. This is a peculiar layout, singular in Scottish links golf. I can only conjure up Montrose in point of comparison. But at Montrose, the interior holes appear at the end of the round, thus losing Elie's feeling of *marching* (or is it *meandering?*) to and from the sea. With all the holes twisting and turning to all points of the compass, I love this layout at Elie enough to put it in my personal Top Twenty among links courses in Scotland. The rhythm of the course—from pastureland to sea and back to pastureland—is thrilling and fulfilling.

Now, if you've ever wondered where James Braid acquired his preference for the long, testing two-shotter, you need look no farther than Elie. This is where Braid was born and raised and, by no mere coincidence, the golf course here has *no* par 5s and only two par 3s! If it weren't for the imagination and variety applied to the par 4s, this could get plain boring. Elie provides the key to understanding Braid: length—incidental; tough but fair; above all, imaginative and fun.

The course at Elie is loaded with memorable features. First, there's the opening blind drive up the #1 fairway ("Stacks") over a sharp rise—but even more memorable, a periscope mounted at the starter house to view play over the rise. You'll only tee off after getting the call, "Play away!" from the starter. This periscope, vintage 1938 and called "Excalibur," came to the club in 1966 and has become a beloved landmark in Scottish golf. Next, you'll be struck by the proximity of town buildings along the fourth, fifth, and sixth fairways—among them, the Golf Tavern, once the meeting site of golf clubs, near the fourth tee. Further along, memorable is the only way to describe Elie's three seaside holes that begin at the precipitously perched teeing grounds at #s 11 and 12 and follow the coast to "MacDuff's Cave"—a mountain cliff rising above the 190-foot-wide green at the #13 "Croupie." In a flight of hyperbole, James Braid called this severely testing seaside two-shotter "the finest hole in all the country." And who are we to quarrel? Not done yet, you'll remember the narrow neck of land, two fairways wide, joining the four holes near the clubhouse to the twelve holes nearer the sea. No surprise, this odd feature has its history too: this was a part of the linksland contested by a landowner on one side and the town golfers on the other. It became the subject of an important legal decision adjudicated in favor of the golfers in 1822 after many years of squabbling—important because it helped establish case law supporting public access to linkslands. Finally, the handsome whitewashed clubhouse with its banks of plate glass windows looking out over the course will leave its impression too. In a word, *memorable*—an important word when it comes to judging golf courses.

See also: Crail, Leven Links, Lundin Links.

21. Golspie Golf Club (1889)

Region #: 5   **Category:** links-parkland-heathland hybrid
Architect(s): James Braid (1905); revisions made in 1967
Length: 5677-5863   **SSS:** 68   **Par:** 68

Address: Ferry Rd, Golspie, Sutherland KW10 6ST
Directions: 10 mi N of Dornoch on the A9; S end of town, hard rt at playing fields

Reservations phone: 01408-633-266   **Fax**: 0148-633-393
Email: secretary@golspie-golf.co.uk   **Website**: golspie-golf.co.uk
Booking Contact(s): Catherine McKay
Secretary: none   **Professional:** none
Phone - Starter/Pro shop: reservations #
Fee(s) (2003): wkday £25, day tkt £35; jrs (under 18) - 50%
Deposit (2003): £10
Visitor Policies: all wk   **Buggies:** 2 - general hire

Just eleven miles north of Dornoch on the A9, you'll encounter the village of Golspie. Brora is another five miles farther along. Golf at Golspie and neighboring Brora is for venturesome travelers who have decided to spend a few days based in the Dornoch-Tain area while exploring the northern reaches of Scotland. Golspie is the least among this quartet of northern courses, yet it is a delightful track well worth playing. At only 5677 yards from the visitor tees, with only one par 5, the course is among the shortest included in this book. Yet, due to its pedigree (another James Braid design), its location, and its unique composition, Golspie deserves its place here. This is the only Scottish course I am aware of that so clearly breaks into an even six holes each of links turf, heathland, and parkland pasture. After the opening holes along the shore, you turn inland and only re-emerge at the close of the round. If your trip has already included Braid's creation at Boat of Garten, Golspie's #9 ("Paradise") will remind you of the testing doglegs there. Paradise is followed by a lovely par 3, "Lochy," playing across a deep hollow to a two-tiered green. Still more enjoyable golf follows in the unusual and strong closing three. Braid gave Golspie two challenging par 3s followed by the "Drum Brae" par 4 at 445 yards—a typical Braid home hole that says to the golfer, "You think this course is so easy? Try making par here".

Nongolf Activities: Another reason for making the trip to Golspie is to visit Dunrobin Castle, home of the Dukes of Sutherland since at least the fourteenth century. One of Scotland's oldest, continuously-inhabited castles, Dunrobin's stately rooms and formal gardens make a great half-day diversion from golf. You'll come away with a greater sense of Scottish history, for this was the land of the Sutherlands—a fact that becomes apparent after a few days here. You cannot help but notice how many Sutherlands and Rosses cross your path in this territory. For more information about Dunrobin Castle and other area attractions, see *www.highlandescape. com.*

See also: Brora, Royal Dornoch, Tain.

22. Gullane Golf Club - Gullane # 1 (1882) +

Region #: 3   **Category:** seaside links
Architect(s): various
Length: 6077-6466   **SSS:** 72   **Par:** 71

Address: East Lothian EH31 2BB
Directions: W side of village on A198; highway bisects the golf courses

Reservations phone: 01620-842-255   **Fax:** 01620-842-327
Email: gullane@compuserve.com   **Website:** gullanegolfclub.com
Booking Contact(s): Linda Ingle
Secretary: SC Owram   **Professional:** Alasdar Good
Phone - Starter/Pro shop: 01620-842-255
Fee(s) (2003): wkday £70, day tkt £95; wkend £85, no day tkt; jrs - 50%
Deposit (2003): £15
Visitor Policies: wkday 10:32 - noon and 2:30 - 4 pm; wkend - 7 available times each day
Buggies: 4 - med or phys only
Other: combo tkts with Gullane #2 & #3 offer good value; hdcp - men 24, women 30

There's no doubt that, at the seventh tee of Gullane #1, you can experience one of the most awesome panoramic views available on a Scottish golf course. To the north sits the Kingdom of Fife; off to the east lies Muirfield; and to the west, on a clear day, you can see all the way to the Forth Bridge on the west side of Edinburgh. There's also no doubt that my somewhat negative view of Gullane #1 was influenced by the persistent sixty-mile-an-hour gale blowing off the North Sea when I played it in 1998. Nevertheless, to my mind, this is the least enjoyable and most overrated of Scotland's marquee courses.

I should be more charitable, but Gullane #1 is really not among my favorite Scottish courses, and I'll tell you why: first, the setting of the courses at Gullane, for all its promise near a pretty village, just past Aberlady (another pretty village), is remarkably pedestrian for its plain openness without the bracing virtue of views to the open sea. The main impediment to a sea view is Gullane hill where the championship-level golf is played. (By the way, it's advisedly pronounced "GILL-ann" according to Mrs. Sheila Montgomery, former assistant to the club secretary, who says, "There are no gulls in Gullane").

Second, you have to climb that hill. And, rather than provide a graceful "switchback" climb of the sort found at Pitlochry, for example, the golfer is given a straight-away chute up a wind tunnel at #2 ("Windygate"), then a ski-slope ride back down to sea level at #17 ("Hilltop"). In between, you'll find fourteen holes routed around and through the crevices and flats of Gullane hill. The great views come at the aforementioned #7 "Queen's Head"—a hole that shoots practically straight downward for 400 yards. With a tailwind, a strong driver can reach the green, but I'm not sure that qualifies as great design.

On the other hand, this is a tough, highly-regarded qualifying course when the British Open is held at Muirfield and golf has been played on these grounds for over three hundred years, so it can't be all bad. In fact, everything else about Gullane is great. The public clubhouse, opened in 1993, is comfortable, modern, and efficiently run (the private Gullane Golf Club located alongside the first fairway of Gullane #1 is open only to the #1 combatants). The village of Gullane is attractive and is stocked with good restaurants and quality lodging, including *The Golf Inn* (01620-843-259; *www.golfinn.co.uk)*, *Faussetthill House* (01620-842-396), and Hopefield House (01620-842-191; *www.hopefieldhouse.co.uk)*—all on Main Street. Out in the countryside, nicely situated in Direlton between Gullane and North Berwick, you'll find the four-star *Open Arms Hotel* (01620-850-241). Just behind the public clubhouse is a nine-hole layout for kids (adults are not allowed unless accompanied by a child). The presence of this little gem serves as a reminder of how completely integral golf is to Scottish life. And near the children's nine sits the "Old Clubhouse," now a bar/restaurant not to be missed by any visitor to Gullane.

For the 36-holers out there, Gullane #1 is complemented by the more benign Gullane #2, a 6200-yard track that flanks #1 on the slopes of Gullane Hill and sweeps down toward Aberlady Bay before turning back toward the clubhouse. The management offers a day ticket on #s 1 and 2 for £85 weekdays and £95 weekends. In Scottish golf these days that's a good deal. There's still another eighteen-hole course to play (you guessed it, Gullane #3) and some locals think that's the most enjoyable of the trio. Adjacent to the courses at Gullane, toward Aberlady, is the Tom Morris course at Luffness New. In short, plenty of golf to be played in this little village.

Finally, I've saved the best until last: that is the small golf museum located next to the pro shop just off the first tee at Gullane #1. Here you can commune with the now legendary Archie Baird, perhaps the most avid living collector and interpreter of Scottish golf history and memorabilia. But you can't just walk in on Mr. Baird. Tours of his museum are by appointment only. Phone him in advance at 01875-870-277. Make an appointment before or after your round and, if available, he'll meet you for a personalized tour. Archie Baird will give you an experience to remember. Nothing is behind glass. Archie will let you feel the weight and texture of old clubs, feathery balls, gutta percha balls, and Gene Sarazen's original sand wedge. He'll take you on a memorable tour through the history of golf.

23. Honourable Company of Edinburgh Golfers (1744) - at Muirfield, Gullane *

Region #: 3   **Category:** seaside links
Architect(s): Tom Morris (1891), Tom Simpson, Henry Colt
Length: 6601 yds   **SSS:** 73   **Par:** 70

Address: Muirfield, Gullane, E Lothian EH31 2EG
Directions: through Gullane, left on road signposted "Greywalls Hotel" at edge of town

Reservations phone: 01620-842-123   **Fax:** 01620-842-977
Email: hceg@btinternet.com   **Website:** no
Booking Contact(s): Secretary's Office/Anne McCarthy
Secretary: Group Captain J A Prideaux
Fee(s) (2003): £100, day tkt £130; credit cards not accepted
Deposit (2003): 50% prepayment by bank draft in pounds sterling within 2 wks after booking approved
Visitor Policies: Tues & Thurs, 8:50 - 9:30 am; four-ball play only in am; two-ball foursomes in pm; Mon & Fri - some times for residents of Greywalls Hotel; maximum of 12 in visiting groups;
Buggies: no

Other: hdcps - men 18, women 24; no cell phones on course or in club-house; jackets/ties in dining room; women may not lunch in clubhouse and must be accompanied by a man on the course

One of the most difficult tee times to secure in Scottish golf is a tee time at The Honourable Company's course at Muirfield. This is the oldest golf club in the world (1744) and a certain exclusivity comes with the territory. Yet, to the club's credit, visitors are allowed to play at this historic course on Tuesdays and Thursdays. In addition, from April to September, about ten tee times per month, for play on Mondays and Fridays, are granted to residents of Greywalls Hotel adjacent to the golf course (01620-842-1444; *www.greywalls.co.uk*). A comparison of this policy to the members-only approach at private clubs in the United States makes Scotland's most exclusive clubs look warmly welcoming.

To apply for a tee time at Muirfield, the magic date to circle on your calendar is May 1. That's when the "diary" opens for the following year (e.g., May 2003 for dates in 2004). The times go fast and are usually gone by August. You'll get a relatively quick reply from Muirfield because the volume of applications is not so great as at St. Andrews and fewer slots are available. Your request should be made to the secretary in writing (fax is ok) and should include the following information: a lead golfer, names of other golfers, handicaps, club affiliations, and a requested date of play.

If you do get a tee time at Muirfield you will encounter a course quite unlike any other in Scottish golf. Though the turf is links turf and the sea is in sight, the course is set away from the sea in a vast field of billowing rough and gently rolling terrain. No strip of linksland here. Old Tom Morris had a lot of ground to work with at Muirfield. Applying his talent and imagination to that ground in 1891, Morris developed a uniquely creative layout in which the first nine, moving clockwise, encircles the second nine holes that run counter-clockwise. The result: constant shifts of direction and—unusual in links golf—a pattern that placed the #1 and #10 teeing grounds near the clubhouse. Given the relatively flat ground at Muirfield, all targets are in view. There are no blind shots. Challenge is provided by length; large, undulating greens; narrow fairways, unforgiving rough; and over 160 bunkers—most of them severely penal, with sides so steep the only play is up and out but not far forward. Most holes present at least eight bunkers for the golfer to avoid.

Golfers great and not-so-great have applauded this design for over one hundred years. James Braid was so taken by the course that he gave the name Muirfield to one of his sons. This was Harry Colt's favorite course and, in the mid-1920s, he and Tom Simpson re-shaped the Morris original to achieve the course we have today. More recently, Jack Nicklaus named his most famous early project Muirfield Village. Tom Watson is another devotee of Muirfield. Among the rest of us mere mortals, when readers of the UK's *Golf World* were polled a few years back, they named Muirfield the best course in Scotland and third most difficult. One measure of the greatness of Muirfield is to simply note the winners of the British Open tournaments held at Muirfield since 1959. They are: Gary Player, Jack Nicklaus, Lee Trevino, Tom Watson, Nick Faldo, and Ernie Els. The British Open played here in 2002, when Tiger Woods fell away in the third round and Els triumphed in a four-way playoff, provided a level of drama only seen on the truly great courses—and, among those, Muirfield must be counted at the top rung with St. Andrews and Turnberry.

Accommodations: See *Gullane Golf Club* and *North Berwick Golf Club - West Links*

24. Irvine Golf Club (1887) - "Bogside"

Region #: 2   **Category:** links-parkland hybrid - no view
Architect(s): James Braid
Length: 6408   **SSS:** 73   **Par:** 71

Address: Bogside, Irvine KA12 8SN
Directions: N of Irvine toward Kilwinning (A737), left at Ravenspark Academy

Reservations phone: 01294-275-979   **Fax:** 1292-278-209
Email: no   **Website:** no
Booking Contact(s): secretary (a.m. hours)
Secretary: WJ McMahon   **Professional:** James McKinnon
Phone - Starter/Pro shop: 01294-275-626
Fee(s) (2003): wkday £40, day tkt £50; wkend £50

Deposit (2003): £5
Visitor Policies: M-F anytime; wkend after 3 pm   **Buggies:** no

One might best think of Irvine in league with the nearby courses at Gailes and Barassie. While these courses all lie a few miles south of Irvine, "Bogside", as it is popularly known, is situated a few miles north of town. Together, they offer alternatives to the more famous Ayrshire courses at Troon, Prestwick, and Turnberry.

Understandably, most first-time visitors to the Ayrshire coast want to play the area's fabled trio. The returning veteran may well be looking for the next tier of courses and, in that tier, Irvine's Bogside should be on everyone's must-play list.

At Bogside we experience another James Braid classic—perhaps most similar to Ayr's Belleisle in its expansiveness, changes of direction, and position relative to the sea (close but not at seaside). Here, Mr. Braid—Scotland's caped crusader for the unforgiving two-shotter—showed his ultimate disdain for the stroke-saving par 5 and the pushover par 3. Bogside sports only two par 3s (not much to challenge at 165 yards and 156 yards) and one par 5 (476 yards). The remaining fifteen holes are two-shotters! Thus, what at first glance seems a course of average length, in typical Braidian style, turns out to be a bearcat where most golfers will not play to their handicap.

Those who have played Bogside applaud the remarkable variety of holes that Braid created on this fairly flat expanse of links turf. Another striking feature: the silky-smooth, well-tended greens. This is a characteristic not only of Bogside but of all the courses along the Ayrshire coast. For whatever reason—probably the mild temperatures and wet weather—I think it's fair to say these are the best greens in all of Scotland, from Irvine right on down to Turnberry and beyond. Irvine also offers an excellent clubhouse, practice facilities, and a friendly, welcoming staff.

Nongolf: Only twenty-six miles from Glasgow, near the mouth of the Firth of Clyde, Irvine reminds us that Scotland is a land of seafaring folk. We get that reminder at the Scottish Maritime Museum and at the impressive "Harbourside" Development, an attractive urban renewal project that lends a modern interpretation to Scotland's coastal past. This is Burns country, so Irvine boasts a Robert Burns Museum. A few miles south of town, between Troon and Irvine, you'll find the ruins of Dundonald Castle, first home of Scotland's Stuart kings and, in the scheme of things historic, Scotland's third most important castle after the better-known structures at Edinburgh and Stirling.

See also: Belleisle, Glasgow Gailes, Kilmarnock Golf Club, Western Gailes.

25. Kilmarnock Golf Club (1887) – Barassie +

Region #: 2   **Category:** seaside-heathland hybrid
Architect(s): various
Length: 6484-6817   **SS:** 73   **Par:** 71-72

Address: 29 Hillhouse Rd, Barassie, Troon KA10 6SY
Directions: follow signs at corner near oceanside where B746 (Kilmarnock Rd) turns into/out of Troon

Reservations phone: 01292-313-920   **Fax:** 01292-313-824
Email: barassiegc@lineone.net   **Website:** kbgc.co.uk
Booking Contact(s): secretary
Secretary: Donald Wilson   **Professional:** Gregor Howie
Phone - Starter/Pro shop: 01292-311-322
Fee(s) (2003): day tkt M-F £50, wkend £60; jrs (under 18) £35 & £45
Deposit (2003): £10 nonrefundable
Visitor Policies: M, T, Th; Fri & wkend pm only
Buggies: 4 - general hire
Other: relief course 2788 yds - Hillhouse Course

Now, let's get this straight: if you want to play "Kilmarnock," *don't* go to Kilmarnock. You need to go to Barassie about ten miles westward. That's because this is a coastal course built in the late 1880s at Barassie by inland Kilmarnock merchants for their sporting pleasure. That was the time of the first big "boom" in golf—a time when outstanding golf courses were built along the railway running out of Glasgow down the Ayrshire coast. And these courses at Irvine, Gailes, Barassie, Troon, Prestwick, Ayr, and Turnberry have stood the test of time. They're just as good today as they were then (or better).

The Kilmarnock course at Barassie is among the courses that lie within fifteen minutes north of Troon town center and appeal primarily to the seasoned traveler who, having played the "rota" courses, is now looking for golf on new ground. It's interesting how the reputations within this second tier of courses seep through the international golf community. In this case, even though Barassie is practically within the proverbial stone's throw of Royal Troon, it is Western Gailes, a little farther northward along the coast, that has captured the attention of visitors. No denying the greatness of Western Gailes, but neither are Barassie, Glasgow Gailes, and Irvine far behind. I can only think the lack of notoriety of the latter three is a result primarily of their members' relative lack of interest in marketing the club to visitors. It's not that the members are unwelcoming. They just have their priorities set on member play. In the case of the Kilmarnock club, visitor restrictions can be off-putting to tour operators, but they're actually a bonus to the independent traveler. Since Barassie sees so few tourists, access to the course is relatively easy.

Once you're on the course, you'll find a compact layout on rather flat ground wedged between two rail lines that converge at Barassie. This course has everything you're looking for in a links layout—heather-lined fairways, pot bunkers, gorse, and those wonderful Ayrshire greens. All this, including the rail lines, might make you think you're playing Prestwick for half the price. Three par 5s, three par 3s, and twelve par 4s typify the Scottish approach to a "traditional" round with par at 72. In other words, this is tougher than your average par 72 track and, with a head wind off the water, Barassie can be severely challenging. With member tees stretching to 6800 yards, it's easy to understand why Barassie is used as a qualifying course when the Open is held at Royal Troon. Most golfers will be quite adequately challenged from the visitors' yellow tees set at 6408 yards.

In sum, I'd like to pass on the comment of a visitor who registered his observations on Barassie to the Scottish Travel Forum at the fine web site *www.uk-golfguide.com*: "Forget some of the 'name' courses and try this one." That advice could apply to about forty-five of the sixty courses in this directory. And I'll say it again: to the extent a golf visitor to Scotland can disengage from the grip of the "name" courses, that visitor will have a less expensive, more interesting trip.

See also: Belleisle, Glasgow Gailes, Irvine (Bogside), Royal Troon, Western Gailes.

26. Kingsbarns Golf Links (2000)

Region #: 1 **Category:** seaside links
Architect(s): Kyle Phillips, Mark Parsinen
Length: 6174-7126 **SSS:** 73 **Par:** 72

Address: Kingsbarns, nr St. Andrews, Fife K16 8QD
Directions: 8 mi S of St. Andrews off A917 just past village of Kingsbarns

Reservations phone: 01334-460-861 **Fax:** 01334-460-877
Email: info@kingsbarns.com **Website:** kingsbarns.com
Booking Contact(s): Donna Clark, Teresa Stewart, Wendy Low
Manager: Stuart McColm **Professional:** David Scott
Phone - Starter/Pro shop: reservations
Fee(s) (2003): £125 wkday, £185 day tkt Apr-May; £135 wkday, £200 day tkt - June onward
Deposit (2003): 50%; balance 1st day of month preceding month of play
Visitor Policies: all wk **Buggies:** no
Other: closed Dec through March

From its entrance, straight through to the nineteenth hole, Kingsbarns Golf Links (not club) has the look and feel of a daily fee course where the owners are on site and really care about the product they are selling. For, make no mistake, there's a lot of selling going on here and the product is golf—not club memberships or horseback riding or tennis, but pure, unadulterated links golf.

And, while the American owners, Mark Parsinen and Art Dunkley, are not, in fact, always on site these days, they once were and they still spend a lot of time here. In any case, their presence is felt in the businesslike attention to detail at Kingsbarns. First-rate staff carry out every wish of Messrs. Parsinen and Dunkley and the result is a golf experience designed and determined to be "world class" without the snobbery typical of many golf clubs in that category.

Kingsbarns and golf course architect Kevin Phillips fairly exploded onto the international golf scene in 2000—so completely that, within two seasons, the course had gathered up virtually every "Best New . . ." award there was to be had and had leaped to the upper tier of *Golf Magazine's* rankings of "World's Best Courses." In 2001 Kingsbarns joined the ranks of Carnoustie and St. Andrews' Old

Course in hosting the annual Dunhill Cup, now played as a pro-am event—all pretty heady stuff for the new kid on the block.

Was all this hoopla and hype justified? In a few words: well, yes, probably. Kingsbarns is, indeed, a world-class course and, given four sets of teeing grounds, players of all levels can enjoy the challenge. The terrain at Kingsbarns has a wonderful rolling quality about it and sea views abound from every corner of the course. Six holes skirt the rocky shore, offering a scene reminiscent of Pebble Beach, particularly at the 566-yard, doglegged par 5 twelfth hole that sweeps the shoreline *à la* Pebble, as well as the "signature" par 3 fifteenth hole playing from elevated tee to elevated green across a roiling inlet from the sea. There's not a weak sister in the bunch and modern routing returns the golfer to the clubhouse between nines. All this and more can be seen at Kingsbarns' excellent web site.

Now for the bit of reservation you may have sensed in the previous paragraph. Kingsbarns came upon Scotland's golf stage at precisely the right moment—when the golf travel industry and Scots were starving for something new and bold and different, yet at the same time traditional. Scotland really had not turned out a new world-class venue since Mackenzie Ross reworked the Ailsa at Turnberry. Oh, there was the stray and underappreciated course like Craighead down the road at Crail. But Kingsbarns was something special and the world responded. This, we were told, might be the last and greatest seaside course ever built in Scotland. Praises and hosannas were fulsome and continuous.

A very few years later, we have two new courses practically next door to Kingsbarns—the Torrance and Devlin courses at St. Andrews Bay, plus the newly-announced championship course to be located just south of St. Andrews and slated for play by 2007. Add to these the new course by Kevin Phillips at Southern Gailes and, in the context of all these new courses, Kingsbarns' newness does not shine quite so brightly as it did in 2000. I guess if Alan Greenspan were a golfer (and he may be, for all I know), he might suggest that the golf world reacted to Kingsbarns' arrival with a mild case of "irrational exuberance."

The other part of my reservation about Kingsbarns is about cost. There's no doubt a new course has startup costs that older clubs have put behind them—land costs, course construction, a clubhouse, etc.— and these costs justify above-average green fees. But, somehow,

Kingsbarns has seen fit to raise the high-season visitor fee from £85 in 2000 to £135 in 2003—a tad under sixty percent in three years!

To my mind, a cost increase like this has a deadening effect in several ways on all of Scottish golf: first, by economic definition, it discourages untold numbers of golfers from playing a great course course because it's just too darned expensive; second, by suggestion, it encourages other courses to raise their rates to "keep up with Kingsbarns"; third, it ensures that few visitors will ever play the course more than once ("been there, done that, bought the tee shirt"). Seems to me that's just the opposite of what Scottish golf should be doing.

Already I have seen increasing numbers of golfers passing on Kingsbarns because of the cost, and that is unfortunate because this is a great golf course. But, if I can play *four* historic courses in Fife for the price of one Kingsbarns, you know what I'm going to do—and I think I'm pretty representative of a whole lot of golfers.

27. Kingussie Golf Club (1890)

Region #: 5   **Category:** parkland
Architect(s): Harry Vardon - extended existing nine (1908)
Length: 5411-5615   **SSS:** 68   **Par:** 66

Address: Gynack Rd, Kingussie, Inverness-shire PH21 1LR
Directions: 1/2 mi N of town center off A78, turn at Duke of Garten

Reservations phone: 01540-661-600   **Fax:** 01540-662-066
Email: sec@kingussie-golf.co.uk   **Website:** kingussie-golf.co.uk
Booking Contact(s): secretary
Secretary: Norman MacWilliam   **Professional:** no
Phone - Starter/Pro shop: 01540-661-374
Fee(s) (2003): wkday £20, day tkt £25; wkend £22, day tkt £28
Deposit (2003): no
Visitor Policies: all wk   **Buggies:** phys/med

The course at Kingussie (pronounced king-YEWsie) is included in this directory for two reasons: First, it was designed largely by the great Harry Vardon and that, alone, is cause for inclusion. Second, it is representative of the many "wee" courses found in the resort towns strung out along the A9 south of Inverness. In addition to the excellent course at Boat of Garten, you'll find eighteen-hole delights at

Newtonmore (Kingussie's twin town just a few miles away on the A86), Aviemore, and Grantown-on-Spey. And little Carrbridge has its own charmer—a nine-hole track where, if you stop, you'll probably be the only foreign visitor on that day and thus receive a warm welcome from the locals. The common denominator here is not championship golf, but holiday golf in the Highlands—relaxed, scenic, and invigorating.

Like the Boat of Garten, Kingussie is something more than a pleasant walk in pretty surroundings. Though quite short, there are no par 5s here. Thus, five of the twelve two-shotters extend well over 400 yards. Hilly terrain adds to the challenge. The Vardon emphasis is on shotmaking rather than length—and one could say, the "Scots emphasis" just as well, for this is a characteristic of most Scottish courses. Nevertheless, most golfers will come away from Kingussie remembering the scenery as much as the individual holes. From high points on the course, once you catch your breath, you'll see the Monadhliath Mountains out to the west and the Cairngorms to the east. In between you'll marvel at the melange of soft colors and the crisp Highlands air. Ah, a piece of heaven on earth!

Nongolf: The nongolf reasons for lingering in this lovely part of Scotland are perhaps more compelling than the golf. Kingussie itself is widely known as the location of one of Scotland's most interesting "living museums;" that's the Highland Folk Museum located on Duke St. near town center. Here is assembled a collection of relics and reconstructed buildings, including a thatch-roofed "Black House" modeled after those common on the Isle of Lewis ("black" because it was a smoky, windowless home to both animals and people). In the summer you'll find "citizens" of the village out tending the gardens and working at spinning wheels, all quite happy to welcome you into their homes and talk about their way of life.

Before arriving at Kingussie, many people stop at the Dalwhinnie Distillery just a mile along where the A889 meets the A9. After Kingussie, one can spend hours or days exploring the forests and moors around Aviemore and Garten. Here, on the Rothiemurchas Estate and in the Glenmore and Abernethy forests you can walk quite literally for hundreds of miles on groomed trails. Rothiemurchas is known especially for its protection of Scotland's largest stand of native Caledonian or "Scotch" Pine. A particularly fine   display of this remarkable tree can be seen on the easy hike around Loch an Eileen. The visitor center for Rothiemurchas is on Ski Road, one mile from Aviemore. Railroad buffs will delight in the steam train that runs between Aviemore and the Boat Hotel in Garten. In short, lots to see and do in this territory twenty to forty miles south of Inverness.

See also: Boat of Garten.

28. Ladybank Golf Club (1879) +
Region #: 1   **Category:** heathland
Architect(s): Tom Morris and others
Length: 6300-6601   **SSS:** 72   **Par:** 71

Address: Annsmuir, Ladybank, Fife KY7 7RA
Directions: From St. Andrews, 1/2 mi from Melville Lodges Roundabout off A92; driving toward St. Andrews, 1/2 mi on rt past town sign

Reservations phone: 01337-830-814   **Fax:** 01337-831-505
Email: ladybankgc@aol.com   **Website:** no
Key Contact(s): admin. secretary
Admin. Secretary: David Allan   **Professional:** Martin Gray
Phone - Starter/Pro shop: 01337-830-725
Fee(s) (2003): wkday £40, day tkt £50; wkend £40, no day tkt
Deposit (2003): £10
Visitor policies: wkdays 9:30 - 4 pm; phone wkends
Buggies: 2 - general hire
Other: fairway mats in use Nov-Mar

Ladybank is a busy course with lots of club play and lots of visitors. And for good reason: it's a beautiful course in the heart of Fife—easy to get to and a joy to play. This flat, tranquil heathland course offers respite from the rigors of Fife's seaside links, yet brings its own unique challenge. Ladybank is a thinking golfer's course, requiring accuracy off the tee to stay clear of thick growths of heather, broom, and pine and birch forest. But beyond accuracy, it requires every shot in the bag.

Ladybank is all positive. The course and clubhouse are well managed and manicured. There's a good practice area. Secretary David Allan and staff are helpful and friendly. It's an Open Qualifying Course and, though many changes have been made since its conception in 1879, Ladybank traces its pedigree to six original holes laid out by Tom Morris.

So, given its popularity and polish, why, on a gut level, does Ladybank disappoint ever so slightly? I can only think it's because Ladybank is so much like a very good American municipal course. No single hole is truly memorable, yet none is entirely pedestrian either. The best measure I can suggest is against other great Scottish inland courses and, when I contemplate a comparison between Ladybank and Blairgowrie Rosemount, Belleisle, the Boat of Garten, or the courses at Gleneagles, Ladybank finishes second every time. That's not to say it's not a great course; I just don't think it's as great as a lot of people do.

I often include Ladybank in an itinerary for my clients (a) because they've heard about it and want to play it; (b) to give them a break from the links courses and get them into the interior of Fife; or (c) because it is the best inland course in Fife. And, though it certainly is *Fife's* finest inland course, I don't think it is *Scotland's* finest inland course. As I've said elsewhere, "I could be wrong." Go experience Ladybank for yourself. You won't be sorry.

29. Letham Grange Resort (1985) - Old Course

Region #: 4   **Category:** parkland
Architect(s): Kenneth Green, Donald Steel, G K Smith (1985)
Length: 6348-6968   **SSS:** 73   **Par:** 73

Address: Colliston, by Arbroath DD11 4RL
Directions: 1 mi E of Colliston (NW of Arbroath) off A933

Reservations phone: 01241-890-377   **Fax:** 01241-890-725
Email: letham-grange@sol.co.uk   **Website:** letham-grange.co.uk
Booking Contact(s): administrator or main desk (890-373)
Administrator: Ben Greenhill   **Professional:** no
Phone - Starter/Pro shop: 01241-890-377
Fee(s) (2003): wkday £35, day tkt £50; wkend £40, day tkt £55
Deposit (2003): 20 percent
Visitor Policies: any time   **Buggies:** yes - plenty
Other: hotel residents - half-price fees; relief course, The Glens, 5800 yds

Letham Grange is a small, four-star resort on the order of Gleneagles—though, at one-third the cost. Let's call it a "poor man's"

162

Gleneagles. It's a product of the 1980s and, specifically, of private developer Kenneth Green's ambition to bring a touch of Augusta to the rolling hills of Angus just twelve miles north of Carnoustie. Apart from two golf courses—questionably named the "Old" and the "New"—the focal point of the resort is a twenty-room Victorian mansion that serves as hotel, restaurant, and clubhouse. Though residents have priority at the course, Letham Grange is open to the public and welcoming to all.

After securing the estate and launching his dream project in the early 1980s, Mr. Green encountered financial difficulties and soon had to bail out, but not before laying out a golf course (the "Old") and hiring famed golf architect Donald Steel to design the greens. The course opened to considerable fanfare in 1985. And a good job they did of it too. Letham Grange is a delight to play. With four sets of tees, broad fairways, undulating greens, and plenty of water, it's a thoroughly modern venue that will remind Americans of courses at home—especially when they see the bevy of buggies lined up near the first tee. Five par 5s, with the customary modern component of four par 3s, extend par to 73. But only one of the par 5s exceeds 500 yards. The tradeoff: lots of hills, some blind shots, and water hazards at #s 8, 9, 10, and 15. Yet none of this will send you away foaming at the mouth, rending your clothes, or swearing at the Scots as you might on a links course. You'll shoot your usual American game here—and enjoy the well-behaved beauty.

In sum, Letham Grange is a good course to play when you're in Angus and ready for a break from the rigors of seaside golf. In particular, Letham Grange makes an excellent 36-hole combination with Carnoustie or Montrose, providing a modern, parkland counterpoint to those ancient and traditional links.

Nongolf notes: With population of about 25,000, Arbroath, near Letham Grange, is the largest town in Angus. Scotland's "Declaration of Independence" from England, proclaimed by Robert the Bruce in 1320, was signed in Arbroath Abbey where visitors can see a replica of the revered document. Twenty miles to the west of Letham Grange stands Glamis Castle, childhood home of the Queen Mother and one of Scotland's major tourist attractions—and for good reason. At nearby Glamis Village, in a row of modest seventeenth-century cottages, the Angus Folk Museum stands in contrast to its opulent neighbor.

30. Leven Links Golf Club (1820) +

Region #: 1   **Category:** seaside links
Architect(s): Tom Morris, others
Length: 6436 yds   **SSS:** 70   **Par:** 71

Address: The Promenade, Leven, Fife KY8 4HS
Directions: off A915 from Leven town center; left on Church Rd, rt on Links Rd

Reservations phone: 01333-428-859   **Fax:** same
Email: secretary@leven-links.com   **Website:** leven-links.com
Booking Contact(s): secretary
Secretary: Sandy Herd   **Professional:** no
Phone - Starter/Pro shop: 01333-421-390
Fee(s) (2003): wkday £30, day tkt £40; wkend £35, day tkt £50; jrs £10
Deposit (2003): no
Visitor Policies: all wk; call on Sat   **Buggies:** no

Literally cheek by jowl with Lundin Links Golf Club, Leven Links occupies the ground to the west of a stone fence ("Mile Dyke") separating the two courses. In many respects these courses are something like Siamese twins and, if you're playing one, it's easy enough to play the other. Leven Links and Lundin Links make for a great day of 36-hole golf with a leisurely lunch break in either one of the handsome clubhouses.

Not surprisingly, the two clubs are joined (and were separated) by history. Leven is the older of the two, tracing its roots to the early 1800s and beyond. In the early 1800s golfers played eastward from Leven on nine holes. Then in 1868 Tom Morris came down from St. Andrews (just twenty minutes away by car today) to lay out a new nine holes on the Lundin side of Mile Dyke. Until 1909, golfers played eighteen holes starting from opposite ends of the two nine-hole layouts! By that time, cries of "Fore!" were probably more common than the screeching of gulls over the Firth of Forth. Thankfully, before anyone was killed, the nines were split equally between the two clubs at the Mile Dyke and each went its merry way.

In terms of course design, what follows is the most interesting part of the history. The original Leven and Lundin nines played along a strand, just two fairways wide, between a rail line and the sea. When the nines were split, there was nowhere to go but inland to the north side of the railway. Eventually the railroad went out of business leaving the rail embankment as an out-of-bounds waste area running the length of both courses. Lundin has left its rail embankment largely intact, while Leven has rather leveled its embankment. But this is the sort of history that makes golf in Scotland—and these courses in particular—unique and fun.

Apart from the terrain, other similarities abound between the two courses. From each direction, the first four holes play parallel to the Firth of Forth as they approach Mile Dyke where each course takes a ninety-degree turn to the north. Classic linksland flows into parkland terrain as the courses move inland and, in the case of Lundin, to a high bluff for several holes. Gorse and stiff rough await errant drives throughout. And, finally, these courses present two of the most difficult finishing holes in Scottish golf—450-yard two-shotters to narrow targets. Leven tops Lundin here, with a little more length and a "wee burn" fronting its eighteenth. Golfers will be watching from the clubhouse windows as you   approach the home hole with either an heroic effort or conservative (probably wise) lay-up shot. Great stuff!
See also: Lundin Links.

31. Longniddry Golf Club, Ltd. (1893)

Region #: 3   **Category:** links-parkland hybrid
Architect(s): Henry Colt (1922), James Braid (1936), Phillip Mackenzie Ross (1945), Donald Steel (1998)
Length: 5969-6230   **SSS:** 70   **Par:** 68

Address: Links Rd, Longniddry EH32 ONL
Directions: from A1, exit B6363 to town; off A198 (Main St), W of town

Reservations phone: 01875-852-141   **Fax:** 01875-853-371
Email: secretary@longniddrygolfclub.co.uk
Website: longniddrygolfclub.co.uk
Secretary: Neil Robertson   **Professional:** John Gray
Phone - Starter/Pro shop: 01875-852-228
Fee(s) (2003): wkday £35, day tkt £50; wkend £45, no day tkt
Deposit (2003): £20
Visitor Policies: wkday, 9:30-4:30; wkend - call
Buggies: 2 - general hire

In choosing to include Longniddry in this directory, I might have deferred to nearby Luffness New or the historic Bruntsfield course in Edinburgh. But I particularly like Longniddry for its picturesque beauty and its design characteristics crafted by four great golf architects. Personally, I would rather play this course than any of the courses at Gullane.

Like Royal Musselburgh, Longniddry is near the Firth of Forth but presents distinct parkland characteristics—Longniddry less so than Musselburgh. Forested ground approaches the sea on this stretch along the south coast of the firth, giving the golf courses from Gullane to Musselburgh a lushness uncharacteristic of the courses from Gullane eastward (Muirfield, North Berwick, Dunbar). This makes for a visual treat with water in view but framed by woodlands. In this case, Longniddry is blessed with deciduous trees and stands of Scotch Pine scarcely represented in the Scottish lowlands.

The design of Longniddry is, at once, traditional and modern. Flanking the firth, the course is essentially two fairways wide—out-and-back in classic links fashion—with a three-fairway bulge in the middle. But, instead of linking one hole to another in a relatively straight line, the primary designers, Henry Colt and James Braid, concocted exhilarating changes of direction on virtually every one of the outgoing nine holes. On return, along the shore, the course straightens but, even so, there's a twist at the end—for, just as at Western Gailes, the clubhouse here sits at the "finish line" of a racetrack routing. Thus, the "out-and-back" tradition is really (1) off to the turn, (2) down the backstretch, (3) round the turn, and (4) heading for home. This simple but effective variation on a traditional theme came from Colt and Braid's determination to break from nineteenth-century conventions.

Braid's influence on course design is seen also in the absence of par 5s at Longniddry. Naturally, this phenomenon was often dictated by available land. But that never stopped him from designing an interesting course. The result at Longniddry? You guessed it, no less than seven two-shotters of 400+ yards and an SSS of 70 against par 68. At 432 and 430 yards respectively, the home holes (#17 "Arthur's Seat" and #18 "Hame") will test your mettle. In other words, this is one tough little course you'll be glad you found. What's more, when you get back to the clubhouse you'll arrive at a handsome building filled with friendly staff. They don't get a lot of visitors here, so you will be appreciated. Longniddry is one of the real "hidden gems."

32. Lundin Golf Club - Lundin Links (1868) +

Region #: 1   **Category:** seaside-parkland hybrid
Architect(s): James Braid (1908)
Length: 6394 yds   **SSS:** 71   **Par:** 71

Address: Golf Rd, Lundin Links, Leven KY8 6BA
Directions: From St. Andrews, on the A915; sharp left turn 3/4 mi W of Largo town center just past Old Manor Country House Hotel

Reservations phone: 01333-320-202   **Fax:** 01333-329-743
Email: secretary@lundingolfclub.co.uk   **Website:** lundingolfclub.co.uk
Key Contact(s): secretary
Secretary: D R Thomson   **Professional:** D K Webster
Phone - Starter/Pro shop: 01333-320-051
Fee(s) (2003): wkday £37; day tkt £47; wkend £47
Deposit (2003): £5
Visitor Policies: wkday 9 am - 3:30 pm; Sat after 2:30
Buggies: no
Other: £180 weekly tkt; £90 3-day tkt

If I were playing golf in Fife on a regular basis, I would sooner play at Lundin Links than on any course in St. Andrews. Why? First, the price is right. Next, looking over the Firth of Forth to North Berwick and Musselburgh, the setting is dramatic. Third, the course combines elements of seaside links and parkland terrain. And, finally, not a single hole disappoints and several will stay forever in your memory even if played only once: there's the stunning first hole that plays down to a broad fairway then back up to a tabletop green; farther along the sea front, moving away from the clubhouse, before the course makes a turn to the north, there's an impossibly difficult (often copied) 452-yarder to another elevated green set behind a burn and a steep embankment; the par 3, #12, takes you straight uphill to another tabletop green; then #14, advisedly named "Perfection," plunges back down Lundin's bluff to a green far below. Then it's on toward the clubhouse as each of the finishing holes becomes more demanding. "Home," at 442 yards into a prevailing wind, finishes the test with fittingly stiff character. No wonder Lundin Links is used as a qualifying course when St. Andrews hosts the Open.

But Lundin Links is a lot more than a test. It has *character*. True, Jack Nicklaus thought it pretty strange, but where else do you find out-of-bounds running through the middle of the entire course?! This phenomenon is due to club history: the original nine holes, laid out by Tom Morris in 1868, utilized the linksland between the sea and a rail line; the course, like many in Scotland, was only two fairways wide. Later, the course was redesigned and extended to the other (north) side of the rail line, thus creating the parkland component of the course. When the railroad went out of business, the rail embankment was left alone. Consequently, the possibility of "OB" follows the golfer around Lundin Links, first on one side, then on the other, even in the middle of the course! Other qualities of Lundin Links: shared fairways, lots of bunkers, a few wee burns, and a high-ground view (#13 and the teeing ground of #14) overlooking the entire course set against the Firth of Forth. All in all, simply grand.

Lundin Links is a great place to base while playing courses in St. Andrews and Fife. Several choice accommodations deserve special mention: at the upper end, the *Old Manor Country House Hotel* (01333-320-368; *www.oldmanorhotel.co.uk*) overlooking Lundin Golf Club; in the middle, *Lundin Links Hotel* (01333-320-207; *www.lundin-links-hotel.co.uk*); and, in the budget category, *Sandilands B & B* (01333-329-881) at 20 Leven Rd. Incidentally, Sandilands is one of the best deals I've found in Scotland. It backs up on the town's "relief" nine-hole course and its rooms are the equal of hotels twice as expensive .

33. Machrie Hotel and Golf Club

Region #: 8   **Category:** seaside links
Architect(s): Willie Campbell (1891), Donald Steel (1978)
Length: 5964-6226   **SSS:** 70   **Par:** 71

Address: Port Ellen, Islay PA42 7AN
Directions: From Port Ellen ferry dock, 3 mi toward airport, left off A846; from Port Askaig, about 15 mi, rt past airport

Reservations phone: 01496-302-310   **Fax:** 01496-302-404
Email: machrie@machrie.com   **Website:** machrie.com

Booking Contact(s): hotel staff
Professional: none   **Phone - Starter/Pro shop:** n/a
Fee(s) (2003): hotel residents £30, day tkt £40; non-res £35, day tkt £50
Deposit (2003): no
Visitor Policies: any time   **Buggies:** 2 - general hire

Though it is possible to make a day-trip from Glasgow into and out of Islay (pronounced EYE-*la*) by air, the best way to schedule golf at Machrie is within the context of a trip encompassing the Isle of Arran and the Kintyre Peninsula (to play Machrihanish). Starting by ferry from Ardrossan to the Isle of Arran, allow at least five days to do justice to this wild and wonderful part of Scotland. On Arran (visible from the Ayrshire coast) you'll have an opportunity to play Shiskine, a twelve-hole throwback to the nineteenth century. Ancient standing stones and magnificent gardens await your exploration on a day of sightseeing. Kintyre deserves two days before pushing on to Islay, where vacationers are drawn to the golf, the whisky distilleries, and the open spaces. Jura—home of one famous whisky distillery (The Isle of Jura) and about 200 permanent population—lies just northeast of Islay. Finished with this island-hopping and ready to return to the mainland, you will have passed through a total population of perhaps 15,000 souls. So, if you're looking to get off the beaten path, this is the way to do it.

Whether such an island journey begins or ends at Islay, you will need to get familiar with the Caledonian MacBrayne ferry schedules available at their excellent web site *www.calmac.co.uk*. Reservations can also be made by phone at 08705-650-000. The connection to Islay is at Kennacraig, a few miles south of Tarbert at the isthmus of the Kintyre Peninsula. Two ferries cover the distance daily—one at 7:50 a.m. to Port Ellen, the other at 12:50 p.m. to Port Askaig. Travel time: about two hours. If taking a car, plan to reserve space well in advance during the busy summer months. General information about Islay can be had at *www.visit-islay.com*, and *www.isle-of-islay.com*. The Islay Whisky Society has its own site, *www.islaywhiskysociety.com*.

As at Turnberry, Gleneagles, and Letham Grange, the golf course at Machrie belongs to a hotel—in this case, the *Machrie Hotel and Golf Club* (*www. machrie.com*). Once in sad disrepair, the hotel was purchased by Malcolm King in 1995 and since has been restored to a level of comfort befitting its history and location. Mr. King, indeed, has been something of a savior to Machrie. In addition to pumping money into the hotel buildings and grounds, he has hired a permanent greenkeeper and, according to Tom Dunn, secretary of the Islay Golf Club, the greens are now in "top nick" and the course is as finely tuned as it has been anytime in his memory (a long time).

With improvement comes increased cost. The Machrie Hotel is no longer a rundown "bargain." Double rooms cost £47 per-person, per-night, (about $140 for two people). On the other hand, newly-refurbished "chalets" accommodating up to six people go for £85 per night in high season. Off-peak and golf-package rates can reduce the cost of staying at the course.

But you don't have to stay at the Machrie Hotel to play the course. Near the golf course, there's the 4-star *Glenmachrie B & B* where, for £60, you can do bed, breakfast, and dinner with one of the best cook's in the land, Mrs. Rachel Whyte (01496-302-560; *www.glenmachrie.com*). At Bridgend you'll find the classic, ten-room *Bridgend Hotel* ((01496-810-212; *www.bridgend-hotel.com*) and the *Fairlie B & B* hosted by David and Emily Boyd (01496-810-464). I particularly like this Bridgend location because, from here, you can proceed in either direction on the forked main highways of Islay— either toward Port Ellen or toward Port Charlotte. For more ideas see the web sites mentioned above. Jazz Fans!—for a special treat, plan to be on Islay in late August/early September for some of the best main-stream jazz available in the UK in memorable settings, including several of the local distilleries. Book well in advance.

Now for the course: Machrie is cut from the same cloth as Cruden Bay, Western Gailes, North Berwick, and Machrihanish. Here you'll find, as Jim Finegan puts it, "a bona fide relic . . . a priceless example of the way golf courses were once brought into being." And, as you might imagine, Machrie and those mentioned above are on a short list of my favorite courses in Scotland. Natural ground defines them all, with minimal sculpting from the hand of man; each presents a fair share of blind shots over dunes and hillocks to big, undulating greens; each is a bit quirky, carrying with it a piece of the nineteenth century and golf history into our time; each brings sheer fun to the golfer on a scale no modern course can approach; each is in a magnificent location relatively removed from the most heavily-traveled tourist trails.

"Brought into being"—that nicely-turned Finegan phrase—says a lot about the old process of coaxing a golf course out of the natural landscape; of giving life to a golf course already there, just waiting to be born; of finding the best green sites, then working back through the landscape to the most arresting teeing grounds. The gem at Machrie was brought into being in this way in 1891 by one Willie Campbell of Musselburgh. Campbell was a young and leading light in Scottish golf when he came to Machrie to lay out a championship course. He left for America soon after completion of his work at Machrie and became head professional at The Country Club in Brookline, Massachusetts, where he died way before his time in 1900. His wife, Geraldine, lived on to become a pioneering female golf professional.

Willie Campbell's purpose was to create a long and difficult course, challenging enough to bring golfers from the mainland to visit the Machrie Hotel and Golf Club. At more than 6000 yards, with no hole less than 200 yards, and with blind shots on virtually every hole, he succeeded. Within ten years, Machrie was attracting Scotland's finest golfers to compete for the Kildalton Cross Trophy and a prize of £100—at that time the highest stake in the world of golf. With such riches to be won in such a fine setting, Harry Vardon, James Braid, and J.H. Taylor came here to compete in 1901. Today the Kildalton Cross Trophy Tournament continues as an amateur open event held the first full week of August—the highlight of the season at Machrie. Incidentally, the Kildalton Cross is Islay's prized historic relic: the only remaining Celtic "High Cross" in Scotland. It dates from the late eighth century and can be seen at the Kildalton Chapel five miles northeast of Port Ellen.

To bring the story of the golf course design up to date, in 1978 Donald Steel was asked to eliminate at least *some* of the blind shots imposed by Machrie's terrain and Campbell's brain. He did that mainly by shortening the par 3s and thereby lengthening the remaining two and three-shotters (only two of those). In common consensus, the result was an improved course—one more suited to the modern game while retentive of the spirit and character of Campbell's creation.

See also: Machrihanish.

34. Machrihanish Golf Club

Region #: 8   **Category:** seaside links
Architect(s): Tom Morris (1879); J.H. Taylor (1915); Sir Guy Campbell
Length: 5960-6228 yds   **SSS:** 71   **Par:** 70

Address: by Campbeltown, Argyll PA28 6PT
Directions: 5 mi W of Campbeltown on B843

Reservations phone: 01586-810-277   **Fax:** 01586-810-221
Email: kenneth.m.campbell@talk21.com
Website: machrihanishgolfclub.co.uk
Booking Contact(s): professional
Secretary: Mrs. Anna Anderson   **Professional:** Kenneth Campbell
Phone - Starter/Pro shop: 01586-810-277
Fee(s) (2003): wkday & Sun £30, day tkt £50; Sat £40, day tkt £60;
jrs 50%
Deposit (2003): 50%
Visitor Policies: all wk   **Buggies:** no

Machrihanish. Machrihanish. Mock-ri-hon-ish. The syllables roll off the tongue, conjuring visions of Celtic clans, pipers, and warrior kings in some mythical medieval kingdom. Out on the golf course you encounter "Balaclava" (#6), "Bruach Mor" (#7), "Gigha" (#8), "Ranachan" (#9), "Nocmoy" (#10), and Kilvian (#13)—and, at this point, you're likely to wonder, "Where am I? And what language is this anyway?".

In this peninsular part of Scotland—not so far away from Glasgow as the crow flies, but poles apart in spirit—Scotland's kinship to Ireland is more apparent than in other parts of the country. Indeed, from the southernmost tip of the peninsula—the Mull of Kintyre—the Emerald Isle is clearly visible (on most days), no more than twelve miles away. After being closed since 2000, a ferry connecting Campbeltown to Ballycastle in Northern Ireland will resume service in the fall of 2003. Thus, golfers on an expedition encompassing the two Celtic homelands might consider Campbeltown a crossing point to or from Ireland.

The pastoral beauty of Kintyre, the romance of Celtic history, and the reputation of the golf course at Machrihanish, have combined to make a trip to this place something of a pilgrimage. Americans are starting to show up in increasing numbers. Machrihanish is no longer a secret known only to the *cognoscenti* of Scottish golf.

Actually, it's not so hard to get to Kintyre but, due to its location, getting to and from will take a full day or, more likely, a two-day bite out of any itinerary. Loganair (0845-773-3377), a franchisee of British Airways, runs two daily flights in and out of Kintyre from Glasgow. But that's not the best way to get to Machrihanish because, remember, *getting there is half the fun.* That means by automobile on the A82 from Glasgow, up along the west side of lovely Loch Lomond, then down the west side of Loch Fyne to Tarbert at the isthmus of Kintyre. From Tarbert, forty miles southward on the A83 through stirring coastal countryside will get you to the promised land. Alternatively, one can ferry across from Ardrossan to Brodick (on the Isle of Arran), then on to Kintyre from Lochranza to Claonaig. Either way, plan on three to four hours from Glasgow.

To my mind, the most satisfying way to make the pilgrimage to Machrihanish is within the context of an "island-hopping" trip through what I've designated as Region #8—encompassing the Isle of Arran, the Kintyre Peninsula, and Islay (*see Machrie Hotel and Golf Club*). This approach allows one to linger, to sink into the pace and pleasure of a magical landscape. At the course, it encourages one to *play more than one round.* For at both Machrihanish and Machrie, the golfer will encounter a host of "blind shots"—shots from tee and fairway to unseen landing areas. It's true, "The shots are only blind once," but to realize that truism, more than one round is required. I firmly believe the *only* way to play Machrihanish and Machrie is to leave time for multiple rounds.

Is the course at Machrihanish as good as its reputation? Is it worth the effort required to get here? How much of the allure of Machrihanish lies in its setting? All I can say, to paraphrase Julius Caesar, is that I came, I saw, and I went away convinced. There's magic in the air of Kintyre and, as with all great golf courses, the setting of the course is part of a total experience. Not only playing at Machrihanish, but *getting* there and *being* there, are among the most treasured memories of my trips to Scotland.

Kintyre and Machrihanish have had the same effect on others. Beatle Paul McCartney came here to vacation and ended up buying a farm, writing a song ("The Mull of Kintyre"), and recording that song with the Campbeltown Pipe Band. Golf writer Malcolm Campbell has concluded, "If there is a golfing heaven somewhere, then it is a safe bet that Machrihanish will have to be passed to get there." Not to be outdone, Michael Bamberger, in his modern classic *To the Linksland*, sought the mystery of the Scottish game and found it at Machrihanish, waxing rhapsodic with words like, "ambrosial," "Nirvana," and "exquisite" to describe the course and his experience. Bamberger finished, "If I were allowed to play only one course for the rest of my life, Machrihanish would be the place." That's a pretty strong endorsement.

So, what is it about this course that turns grown men to mush? The romance starts right at the first hole ("Battery")—universally regarded as one of the great experiences in Scottish golf. James Finegan calls it, "my favorite first shot in all the world." Battery is a 423-yarder requiring a drive over Machrihanish Beach to a fairway aslant to the line of play. It's a risk-reward setup—the more beach you risk, the shorter your second shot. Four bunkers are set to capture any ball hit through the fairway from 230 yards to 290 yards. This is a Tom Morris course, so, once in the vicinity of the green, the golfer will find broad undulations and devilish green-fronting swales.

Now it's on to the second and third holes and the first two of Mac's blind shots. The first one, from the #2 fairway, takes you across the Machrihanish Water (a burn running through the course to the sea) to another rolling green high up on a grassy knoll. The second, from the #3 tee, now changing direction toward the sea, requires a 200-yard carry over and through dunes to a sloping landing area. A good drive here is a must and is rewarded with a bird's-eye view of a green shaped like a jelly-bean set in a hollow below the fairway.

The fourth and fifth holes offer more exquisite links golf—first a short par 3 across a grassy swale, then a dogleg-left requiring two perfect shots to negotiate another route through dunesland. From here, the string of four two-shotters with the Celtic names begins: varying yardage at 315, 432, 337, and 354 likely will have you using every club in the bag. Thus ends what, in my view, is the most interesting "front nine" in Scottish golf.

Notice that the outward nine presents no par 5s and only one par 3. Now, on the inward nine, moving away from the sea to less dramatic ground, the pattern changes: here we have two 5s, three 3s, and four

4s—an entirely different arrangement lending spice to what must be described as the more bland of the two nines. Two holes are particularly memorable to me: first, #14, a 442-yard straightaway two-shotter over billowing ground; then, the extremely difficult 233-yard, par 3, #16 over wasteland to a smallish green protected by mounds and a deep bunker. Mac's two closing holes play over relatively plain ground and often are disparaged but, with OB lurking all the way down the left side, a good card can be easily ruined on "The Burn" and "Lossit" before the clubhouse door is reached.

When the clubhouse door *is* reached, you'll find a convivial place to while away a few hours with a good book, a pint or two, and an occasional glance through large windows to watch the golfers teeing off on Battery. Bamberger was right: this is Nirvana.

Accommodations and nongolf notes: Good B & B choices—small, but clean and comfortable—can be found near the clubhouse at tiny Machrihanish village. These are *Ardell House* (01586-810-235) run by David Baxter and *The Warren* (01586-810-310) run by Judy and Bryan McClement. With golf the focus, this is the logical place to be if room is available. If not, Campbeltown offers lodging, though the old hotels in town center are marginal at best. I'm not aware of anything approaching luxury lodging on Kintyre, though *Craigard House* (01586-554-242; *www.craigard-house.co.uk*), one mile north of Campbeltown on the bay, comes closest. It's an eight-room guest house with singles starting at £40 and doubles at £60. I'm pleased to report that in 2002 the former Putechan Lodge on the A83 nine miles north of Campbeltown was acquired by one Stiubhard Kerr-Lidell, a dyed-in-the-wool Scotsman with the finest whisky collection on the peninsula. This fine property facing the sea is now called *The Hunting Lodge* and offers the best full-service hotel accommodation on the peninsula (01583-421-323; *www.thehuntinglodge.com*).

For some of the most dramatic scenery on Kintyre, take time to drive down to Southend, then westward along the coast on a single track as far as you can go. When the road dead-ends, you can walk another mile onward—sharply downward, then sharply upward—to a high point with views to a lighthouse on the coast far below and westward to Ireland and Islay. At the end of the trail is a memorial to servicemen killed in a Chinook helicopter crash that occurred off the coast in 1994.

Here at the bottom of Kintyre, you'll also find ancient ruins, cemeteries, standing stones, and the short but challenging Dunaverty Golf Course (4800 yards) where a sign suggests that you deposit your fee in an "honesty box" before starting play. On the course you will be joined mainly by four-legged creatures chewing the cud—another memorable experience available only in the remote regions of Scotland.

See also: Machrie Hotel and Golf Club.

35. Monifieth Golf Links - Medal Course +

Region #: 4 **Category:** links - heathland hybrid - no view
Architect(s): Allan Robertson, Alexander Pirie
Length: 6459-6655 **SSS:** 72 **Par:** 71

Address: Princes St, Monifieth DD5 4AW
Directions: N side of town off A930

Reservations phone: 01382-535-553 **Fax:** same as reservations #
Email: monifiethgolf@freeuk.com **Website:** monifieth.co.uk
Secretary: Sandy Fyffe **Professional:** Ian McLeod
Phone - Starter/Pro shop: 01382-532-767
Fee(s) (2003): wkday £35, wkend £45; no day tkt
Deposit (2003): 25%
Visitor Policies: M-F after 9:32 am; Sat after 2:00 pm; Sun after 11 am
Buggies: no

Monifieth is a brawny course usually paired with a main event at the even brawnier Carnoustie Golf Links. In between the two, Panmure sits as a relatively delicate gem. These three, strung out along the A930 northeast of Dundee, encourage a prolonged stay probably based in Carnoustie. Less than an hour from St. Andrews, Monifieth also can fit into an itinerary based in that fair city.

The impression made at Monifieth—both around the course and on the course—is unique in Scottish golf. At bottom, the most important aspect of this part of Scotland is its working-class character. To me, Monifieth represents "lunch bucket" golf. There's absolutely nothing pretentious or ritzy here. This is a municipal course, flanked by another municipal course (the Ashludie). Situated between the coastal railway and the town in a remarkably plain neighborhood of solid stone flats and commercial buildings, the links are played mostly by common folk. And that's the way it has always been at Monifieth, where one of Scotland's oldest clubs was organized by artisans and foundry workers in the mid-1800s. Lining the eighteenth fairway are no less than five golf clubhouses and assorted stone row houses, all equally stolid and nondescript. In short, you'll see nothing graceful or light or scenic at Monifieth.

On the course, you arrive with knowledge that this is ancient golf ground. Public records show golf being played here for at least 450 years! Thus, at a course like Monifieth, the golfer sensitive to history can actually see and feel the evolution of a game. After several centuries of haphazard play along the links, nine holes were laid out in 1856 by Alexander Pirie and the legendary Allan Robertson of St. Andrews. In 1880, after institutionalization of the idea of eighteen holes for a "round" of golf, nine more holes were added. The course underwent other major changes in 1912, 1930, and 1968. Along the line, especially during the 1950s, long groves of pine trees were installed, creating a links course with lots of trees! Unfortunately, the trees look as if they were planted in rows all on the same day. So they stand like Wellingtonian brigades of soldiers lined up along one or another side of the fairways, particularly on the outgoing nine. Design modifications are not always positive. On the other hand, Monifieth boasts plenty of good holes. On balance, as golf writer Jim Finegan notes, "Monifieth has neither the weaknesses nor the strengths of Panmure." It's a straightforward, no-nonsense course with several long two-shotters, excellent one-shotters, and at least one great par 5 (#9). All said and done, you may not remember individual holes, but you *will* remember Monifieth's unique working-class setting and the long stands of pine trees lining the fairways.

See also: Panmure, Carnoustie.

36. Montrose Links Trust (1810) - Medal Course +

Region #: 4   **Category:** seaside links
Architect(s): evolution; Willie Park, Jr.; Tom Morris (1901)
Length: 6229-6495   **SSS:** 70-72   **Par:** 71

Address: Traill Dr, Montrose DD10 85W
Directions: N of town center off A92

Reservations phone: 01674-672-932   **Fax:** 01674-671-800
Email: secretary@montroselinks.co.uk
Website: montroselinks.co.uk
Key Contact(s): secretary
Secretary: Margaret Stewart   **Professional:** Jason Boyd
Phone - Starter/Pro shop: 01674-672-634
Fee(s) (2003): wkday £36, day tkt £46; wkend £40, day tkt £54
Deposit (2003): £10
Visitor Policies: all wk; Sat after 2:30 pm; Sun after 10 am
Buggies: 1 - med/phys

On the east coast, situated halfway between Dundee and Aberdeen, about thirty-five minutes north of Carnoustie, Montrose Medal is in a bit of a no-man's land for the golf tourist. On a two-day stay in Carnoustie, it makes a good pairing with that great course—superior, in my opinion, to both Panmure and Monifieth. It's just a little farther away.

Montrose fits in well with any itinerary prepared to turn its back on the golf Meccas of Fife, Ayrshire, and East Lothian. For example, on a second or third trip to Scotland, the now-seasoned aficionado of Scottish golf, might focus on the east coast northward from the Firth of Tay. This focus would take you from the wealth of courses at Dundee and Carnoustie, to Montrose and nearby Edzell, then on to Stonehaven, Aberdeen and Cruden Bay. Montrose also fits well with any itinerary combining the Highlands and the east coast.

In any event, the reward is great when you get to Montrose. Golf history books will tell you about the ancient pedigree of this linksland that rivals all the better-known "homes" of golf. Records show golf being played here in the middle of the sixteenth century. The course is usually described as the fifth oldest in the world and its oldest associated golf club dates its articles of incorporation to 1810 with records of informal activity stretching much farther back into the eighteenth century. Until the idea of a golf round finally settled on eighteen holes during the 1870s, Montrose was famous for playing the game on twenty-five holes. While Prestwick was hosting the Open with twelve holes during the 1860s, in 1866 Montrose hosted its own Open played to all twenty-five holes! The winning score was 112 (quick math: that's about 81 for eighteen holes).

I like the Montrose course. It's a bit of a patchwork. On one hand, it's everything you expect from a seaside links—towering sandhills; long wispy beach grass; rumpled fairways; and deep, revetted bunkers. On the other hand, when the course veers off on the bias toward town for six holes, you get the distinct feeling you're on an entirely different course. That's not all bad (see my remarks about Panmure near Carnoustie). But, at Montrose, the change seems rather abrupt and you think there might be a story behind this routing. There is. I don't know it all, but I do know the Montrose golf clubs have had to fight more than once for their linksland and some compromises have been made along the way.

The important fact is that a lot of good golf awaits you at Montrose. In my view, the aptly named one-shotter, "Table" (par 3, #3), is as good as the famous "Redan" hole at North Berwick. From the teeing grounds at #s 2, 3, and 6, you have views of beach and sea equal in wild flavor to anything in Scottish golf. The holes, themselves, happen to be very good too, especially #6, "Sandy Braes," where I once finished with a "snowman" after landing in an innocent-looking bunker next to the green. The redeeming moment in that round was my par on the superb two-shotter, "Rashie's" (#17), where, it is said, "it takes three good shots to reach the green in two." Holes ten through fifteen are the ones that jut inland in a loop before the course resumes its more traditional links routing back to the clubhouse. You'll decide for yourself whether you like this configuration. Personally, I rather like the change in direction and character. Montrose should be on anyone's list of Top Twenty links courses in Scotland. It might creep into my Top Ten because I like to visit historic courses a bit off the beaten path.

See also: Edzell.

37. Moray Golf Club (1887) - Old Moray

Region #: 6   **Category:** seaside links
Architect(s): Tom Morris (1889), Henry Cotton (1970)
Length: 6004-6643   **SSS:** 72   **Par:** 69-71

Address: Stotfield Rd, Lossiemouth, Morayshire IV31 6QS
Directions: well signposted from center of town

Reservations phone: 01343-812-018   **Fax:** 01343-815-102
Email: secretary@moraygolf.co.uk   **Website:** moraygolf.co.uk
Booking Contact(s): Mrs. McPherson
Secretary: SM Crane   **Professional:** A Thomson
Phone - Starter/Pro shop: 01343-813-330
Fee(s) (2003): wkday £40, day tkt £55; wkend £50, day tkt £70
Deposit (2003): £10
Visitor Policies: Sat after 2pm; Sun after 10am - call
Buggies: 4 - general hire
Other information: adjacent Royal Air Force base is quiet on wkends; New Moray, a companion course - 6258 yds

Traveling out of Cruden Bay, along northeast Scotland's "Coastal Trail," the golfer will find a remarkable array of courses laid out along the coast like pearls on a strand. Though only two of these courses are featured in this directory (Moray Old and Duff House Royal), good eighteen-hole courses can be played (in order, south to north, east to west) at Peterhead, St. Combs, Fraserburgh, Portknockie, and Buckie.

A little farther along we come to Moray Old at Lossiemouth—a classic links course by Tom Morris (1889) and probably the finest pearl in the strand. Situated twenty-five miles east of Nairn and six miles north of Elgin, Lossiemouth is about the last westward stop before the northeast coast becomes the western Highlands. This makes Moray Old a great course to combine with the championship course at Nairn and/or inland courses to the south (e.g., Boat of Garten, Grantown-on-Spey). This is also an excellent base for making a foray along Scotland's "Whisky Trail," a seventy-mile, signposted jaunt encompassing most of the country's best-known, single-malt distilleries (including Glen Grant, Glenfiddich, Glenlivet, and Strathisla).

Moray Old is among those most classic of Scottish courses that begin in town (in this case, one block off the main street), proceed outward, then return to a handsome stone clubhouse overlooking a dramatic home hole. Thus, Moray Old stands in atmospheric league with St. Andrews' Old, Montrose, North Berwick, and Prestwick. Moray, in fact, is best known for its challenging 423-yard, par-4 finishing hole. Scots golf writer David Hamilton calls it "the noblest finishing hole in Scotland." With the Moray Firth and dunes to the left, and the clubhouse beckoning from behind a plateaued green (*à la* St. Andrews), golfers will return to town where, as Hamilton puts it, "a small, well-informed audience is usually present to watch futile attempts at the difficult second shot."

In some respects this is my favorite among the courses by Tom Morris. I know part of that judgment comes from Moray's northern location in a small town that sees relatively few visiting golfers. But there's more to it: there's a beguiling, straightforward purity here that contrasts with Morris's work at Dornoch. All the usual links features abound—deep rough, dunes, ocean views—but there are no blind shots, no severely-convoluted greens, no deep swales fronting greens. In fact, there's much to remind here of a course that came six years later in Morris's *oeuvre*—namely, the New Course at St. Andrews: seven holes out, then a collection of holes featuring directional changes before the return to the clubhouse. Straightforward, no nonsense. I just love this northern setting on the relatively dry Moray Firth. And, excepting the noise from the jets flying in and out of the Royal Air Force base at Lossiemouth, you'll love it too. And what about that funny name "Lossiemouth"? Well, Moray and Lossiemouth are at the *mouth* of the River Lossie. This is literal Scotland.

See also: Nairn, Boat of Garten, Duff House Royal.

Muirfield - *see Honourable Company of Edinburgh Golfers*

38. The Nairn Golf Club (1887)

Region #: 5   **Category:** seaside links
Architect(s): Archie Simpson, Tom Morris (1890), James Braid (1910-26)
Length: 6472-6722   **SSS:** 73-74   **Par:** 72

Address: Seabank Rd, Nairn IV12 4HB
Directions: 16 mi E of Inverness; W side of town off A96

Reservations phone: 01667-453-208   **Fax:** 01667-456-328
Email: secretary@nairngolfclub.prestel.co.uk
Website: nairngolfclub.co.uk
Booking Contact(s): Wilma Kerr
Secretary: David Corstiphine   **Professional:** Robin Fyfe
Phone - Starter/Pro shop: 01667-452-787
Fee(s) (2003): £70 all wk May-Sept; April & Oct £50; jrs (17 & under) £22
Deposit (2003): £25   **Buggies:** no
Visitor policies: all wk; hdcp - men 28, women 36

Most golf visitors to Scotland's northern Highlands have Nairn and Royal Dornoch at the top of a short list of priority courses. Invariably, Nairn is *second* on the list. In my view, that puts the two in the right order. The courses have a lot in common, including the long hand of Tom Morris. Both are attractive, out-and-back, seaside courses featuring difficult greens and dense banks of gorse and heather. But Nairn has neither the dramatic elevations of Dornoch nor Dornoch's spectacular setting on a crescent bay. Nevertheless, the Moray Firth is quite nice and it's visible from virtually every hole. The course is impressive in its own way and Nairn deserves to be on everyone's Top Twenty list.

This is a course where most golfers will lose a lot of balls and thus gain a lot of penalty strokes. Tight fairways lined with gorse await the errant drive. More than one hundred bunkers dot the fairways and surround the greens. Once on the firm, silky greens, the average golfer can expect an unusual number of three-putt experiences. The greens are huge and, just as at Dornoch, there's nary a straight line to be found. In short, getting *on* the green here is one thing; getting on the *right part* of the green is quite another. Bottom line: your normal stroke index won't mean much at Nairn; anything under 90 is a good score for most mortals.

Nairn's design pedigree is about as good as it gets. The course was conceived by Archie Simpson of the famous Carnoustie Simpson family. In 1890 Tom Morris was called in to extend and modify the course. Between 1910 and 1926, James Braid tinkered with the course, first, in minor ways, then in major ways, until essentially the present design was achieved. Since then, to accommodate the longer modern game, championship tees have extended the course to 6700+ yards.

Most golfers will remember Nairn for its graceful three-hole loop in the otherwise straightforward, out-and-back design. In the middle of the inward nine, #s 13, 14, and 15 make a jog inland, then back out again. Apart from that feature, there's a raft of memorable holes starting with all the first seven along the seashore and the closing three holes that follow the inland loop. My favorite among the closers is the par 4, #16. It's 418 yards of pure challenge first across a waste area to a rolling fairway, then across a burn fronting an elevated green surrounded by five bunkers. The next hole crosses another burn, then a brawny par 5 at 516 yards takes you to the clubhouse—incidentally, one of the newest and finest in Scottish golf. Nairn also sports a nine-hole "relief" course (The Newton) designed by James Braid. A little farther down the road, on the east side of town, is Nairn Dunbar, another eighteen-hole challenge, though on less attractive ground than its more famous neighbor.

Accommodations and nongolf activities: Nairn is no fishing village transformed for the modern age. It's a Victorian-era seaside resort town and, in that respect, resembles North Berwick in East Lothian. The town is thus well stocked with vacation lodgings. A first-rate golf hotel—close to the course, a good bargain, and appropriately named—is the *Links Hotel* (01667-453-321; *www.linkshotel.co.uk)* run by serious golfers, Carol and Ian Cooper. Similar golf-nut management (Rosemary and Andy Machan-Young) can be found at the *Claymore House Hotel,* a small hotel popular on many mid-price golf tours (01667-453-731; *www.claymorehousehotel.com).* Another couple of steps up in price are the "Morton Hotels"—the *Newton* (01667-453-144) and the *Golf View Hotel and Leisure Club* (01667-452-301; *www.morton-hotels.com).*

Many golfers playing at Nairn will base in Inverness for good reason: it's the acknowledged capitol of the Highlands—a small city (population about 45,000) in a lovely setting. All major northern highways and rail lines converge at Inverness and it's loaded with accommodations in every price category. At last count, Inverness had more than two hundred B & Bs and at least fifty more hotels and guest houses. Tourism drives the local economy and, accordingly, lodging values abound in an atmosphere of fierce competition. Given such a plethora of accommodations, I am loathe to cite specific hostelries. Good ones will be left out. Yet, as a starting point, I would mention the following where I can make a personal recommendation: at the upper end, Culloden House (*www.cullodenhouse.co.uk)* and The Dunain Park Hotel (*www.dunainparkhotel.co.uk)* are in the country on opposite sides of town. Another popular choice away from town centre is the Bunchrew House (*www.bunchrew-inverness.co.uk).* First-rate guest-houses and B & Bs are Ballifeary House (*www.ballifeary.com),* Moyness House (*www.moyness.co.uk),* and the Lyndale Guest House (*www. guesthouseinverness.com);* all are centrally located and offer good value. Budget accommodations can be found clustered along Kenneth Street, Old Edinburgh Road, and many other locations. An

Inverness lodging can be found at *www.scotland-*
».uk. The Inverness Bed and Breakfast Association has its
e, *www.invernessbedandbreakfast.co.uk*.

Since this is not a general travel book, I am also somewhat loathe
to even open the subject of nongolf activities in this part of Scotland.
Suffice to say Inverness is a logical jumping off point for compelling
and uniquely Scottish tourist experiences—the beauty and mystery of
Loch Ness, the Speyside whisky trail, the northern coastal fishing
villages, the amazing sub-tropical gardens of the west coast, the barren
reaches of the far north and the wild and lonely island chains of the
Outer Hebrides and the Orkneys. Closer to home base, most tourists
visit historic Culloden Battlefield where Bonnie Prince Charlie and
Scotland's Jacobite supporters were defeated in 1746 in the last battle
fought on British soil. Not far from Culloden, Cawdor Castle draws
thousands of tourists annually to walk the beautiful grounds and re-
visit the history and legend of MacBeth. In town, Inverness offers the
best shopping and range of services to be found in the Highlands. The
attractive High Street is restricted to foot traffic. There's a castle to
tour on a high bluff overlooking the downtown, and the lovely Ness
River flows through the heart of the city on its way to the Moray Firth
and the open sea. In short, Inverness is one of Scotland's enchanted
places and you'll soon realize why so many people come up here to
start their vacations in the country's northern Highlands.

North Berwick - East Links - See: The Glen.

39. North Berwick Golf Club (1832) - West Links

Region #: 3   **Category:** seaside links
Architect(s): evolution
Length: 6033-6420   **SSS:** 71   **Par:** 71

Address: Beach Rd, North Berwick, E Lothian EH39 4BB
Directions: W end of town center, 1 blk off A198

Reservations phone: 01620-892-135   **Fax:** 01620-893-274
Email: bookingsnbgc@aol.com   **Website:** no
Booking Contact(s): Mrs. Norma Ogg
Secretary: Norman Wilson   **Professional:** David Huish

Phone – Starter: 01620-892-666
Fee(s) (2003): wkday £45, day tkt £70; wkend £70; jrs (12-17) - 50%
Deposit (2003): £10 non-refundable   **Buggies:** no
Visitor Policies: all wk after 10 am; Sat after 3:30; Sun after noon

For North Berwick I'll go out on a limb: If I *had* to choose my favorite golf course in Scotland—a course to play day in and day out—it would be the West Links at North Berwick. Part of the reason for this choice is the golf course itself. North Berwick offers pure links golf on a beautiful stretch of emerald green ground bordered by the town on the south, grand homes and the Marine Hotel on the west, and broad ocean vistas to the north and east—if you will, a bit of St. Andrews with a view and the crowds long gone.

Another part of the reason is North Berwick's ambience and location. It's a small, attractive seaside town, rural and secluded, yet only thirty minutes by train from Edinburgh. And, since I like small towns *and* big cities, this combination means North Berwick is among my favorite spots in Scotland. The golf course cements the deal and its location puts it at the top of the list.

In the interest of persuasion, a few more details: First is the West Links' extraordinary setting one block off the town's main street. Just as at St. Andrews, golfers start at the first tee in town, play down the strand to the ninth, then return to town on the back nine. You'll find the eighteenth green no more than seventy-five yards from a road tracing the beach to the East Links (The Glen) about one mile away. There's a "connectedness" in this setting that, at once, exudes the history of golf and its central place in the social and cultural life of Scotland. Among Scotland's most venerable courses, only St. Andrews, Prestwick, Moray Old, and Montrose so clearly transmit this sense of history and unity with their town surroundings.

North Berwick is thirteenth or fourteenth on the list of Scotland's oldest golf clubs (depending upon who's counting). And the course is one of those designed more by "evolution" than by any individual. Historians indicate that, after several centuries of play along the links, club members settled on the current layout by about 1895—with little change since. Thus, there's an historic unity about the West Links surpassed only by that at the Old Course in St. Andrews.

As for individual holes on the West Links, there's not a weak link to be found. In fact, several are so striking as to be unforgettable—

185

more than one can say about most of the holes at St. Andrews. Start with "Point Garry (Out)," where a second shot must be made to a black and white target perched behind an elevated green adjacent to rocks and beach below and to the right. Then come two long, difficult par 4s where, on the #3 "Trap," the first of North Berwick's famous stone walls makes its appearance. Next follows a 175-yard one-shotter called "Carlekemp" that should be called, "Precision" ("Perfection" comes later—that's #14). If all that weren't enough to announce a round of joyful challenge, bumps and humps and hollows follow over more exhilarating ground to close out the first nine.

Not to be outdone, the inward nine, if anything, exceeds the outward half in eccentric appeal. Here one finds, from the thirteenth to the eighteenth, a string of holes among the most famous in Scottish golf. Number thirteen, "Pit," is one of those you'll never forget—a 365-yarder whose sunken green is separated to the left side of the fairway by a low stone wall. Only a perfect second shot can find the green; more likely, you'll be laying up with the hope of getting close in three. Next comes the aforementioned "Perfection," where a second shot toward the beach to a blind green requires just that. After ringing a bell to announce a clear green at Perfection, it's on to the par 3 "Redan"— one of the most copied holes in golf, sitting at an angle to the line of play across a grassy divide and pitched front to back. Par is a good score at the Redan. With no pause in the action, #16 ("The Gate") plays to the most unusual green in Scottish golf—a raised tri-partite tabletop with two large flats separated by a trough about three feet deep by nine feet wide! Number seventeen—"Point Garry (In)"—is another long two-shotter that once shared a green with Point Garry (Out). Finally, as at St. Andrews, the short home hole (274 yards) presents opportunity for heroics in front of onlookers ranged along the road and at the clubhouse windows. But wait! The green here, flat as a proverbial pancake, sits on a sharply-cut tabletop, surrounded by a moat of short-cut grass. After a strong drive, even a short pitch shot requires a deft touch to enable a closing birdie or par.

Does this sound like fun? Indeed, it is. I first played North Berwick in a driving rain storm only briefly interrupted by relative calm and glimpses of sunshine—yet, it was among the most enjoyable rounds of golf in my experience. Since then I've played the West Links when it was possible to relax, look around, and savor the setting. In both cases, North Berwick delivered the best of what Scotland has to offer on a golf course. Silver-tongued Jim Finegan sums it up best: "For sheer golfing pleasure—a pleasure bred of variety, unpredictability, challenge, and proximity to the sea—few courses surpass North Berwick's West Links. Admittedly, it is old fashioned and, on occasion, even odd. But it is irresistibly old fashioned and irresistibly odd."

Back at the handsome stone clubhouse behind the eighteenth green, you can relax in the visitors' lounge and look out over the red-roofed town through a powerful old telescope to the landmark Bass Rock—now a bird sanctuary but once home to political prisoners—and on to Dunbar on the eastern shore. It's a perfect end to a perfect round of golf.

Accommodations and nongolf activities: Given its history as a Victorian resort, North Berwick offers choice lodging for such a small town. This is a place where the rich and famous mingle with common folk and have done so for more than a century (making the reasonable green fee at the West Links all the more surprising). On the gentle hills fronting the westerly flank of the links, handsome and even palatial homes look over the linksland to the water beyond. But, back in town, the beach front is lined by surprisingly modest flats, private homes, and a few public accommodations. Not among the modest, but worthy of mention, is the imposing *Marine Hotel* (01620-892-406; *www.macdonaldhotels.co.uk*), sitting as if at anchor above the seventeenth fairway. This has long been the town's "golf hotel," and it still draws a lion's share of visitors. But, frankly, it's a bit of a tattered old dowager. My advice: use the public rooms at the Marine—the woody bar, the billiard room, and the lounge overlooking the golf course—but stay elsewhere. Better values can be had. Among these is John and Maggie Free's *Belhaven Hotel* (01620-893-009; *www.belhavenhotel.co.uk*). The Belhaven is really a guest house (no bar or restaurant). It's a two-star bargain in a five-star location within one hundred yards of the eighteenth green at one of Scotland's finest courses. Along Beach Road to the east, closer to The Glen (East Links) than to the West Links, Colin and Karen Chalmers operate the *Tantallon Inn* (01620-892-238), a small hotel with an excellent restaurant popular with locals. Mid-town, two blocks south of the main street on Law Road, Gwen and Jake Scott preside over a walled

Georgian mansion once attached to the church land in town center. Here, at *The Glebe House,* amidst an astonishing collection of fine furniture, prints, and paintings, you'll feel like you've been served visual champagne. It's North Berwick's classiest B & B (01620-892-608; *www.aboutscotland.com/glebe/house).*

When not on a golf course or at your lodgings in North Berwick, the interesting streets of this attractive town beckon and, if the legs can tolerate another workout, you can climb nearby "North Berwick Law," an extinct volcano that rises to 613 feet and visually dominates the relatively flat Lothian coastal plain for miles around. Two enticing castle ruins—Tantallon to the east and Dirleton to the west—offer historic ramblings. With Dunbar only twenty miles farther east along the coast and vibrant Edinburgh only thirty minutes away by train, North Berwick has it all without the hoopla of St. Andrews.

40. Panmure Golf Club (1899) +

Region #: 4   **Category:** links - parkland hybrid - no sea view
Architect(s): members
Length: 6085-6317   **SSS:** 70   **Par:** 70

Address: Burnside Rd, Barry by Carnoustie DD7 7RT
Directions: first village SW of Carnoustie on A930; turn left after crossing bridge over Barry Burn

Reservations phone: 01241-855-120   **Fax:** 01241-859-737
Email: secretary@panmuregolfclub.co.uk
Website: panmuregolfclub.co.uk
Key Contact(s): secretary
Secretary: Major (ret) GW Paton   **Professional:** Neil Mackintosh
Phone - Starter/Pro shop: 01241-852-460
Fee(s) (2003): £45 all wk, day tkt £60; no day tkt Sat
Deposit (2003): £10   **Buggies:** 2 - general hire
Visitor Policies: Sat - call; Sun after 10:30

After playing the championship course at Carnoustie, if one is inclined to linger awhile, Panmure is a logical first choice for the next round of golf. For less than half the price of its prestigious neighbor, Panmure offers a superb round of golf on a delightful, challenging course. In fact, at a more reasonable length of 6085 yards from the visitor tees, the game here may be more enjoyable to the average golfer than the test of strength at Carnoustie.

Panmure has been characterized by some golf writers as twelve great holes surrounded by six holes of sheer banality. Personally, I think it's more like fourteen and four. Nevertheless, the critique bears some truth. Panmure's opening three holes and closing three holes play over flat, uninteresting pastureland. Yet this presumed weakness adds variety and symmetry to the layout. The flat holes at each end bracket the hillocky, gorse-laden interior. To me, that composition makes the course memorable; I like the rhythm of the course.

Club historians like to remind everyone this is where Ben Hogan practiced in secret before winning the British Open in 1954 at Carnoustie—and that Hogan went away trumpeting the #6 hole at Panmure (now called "Hogan's Hole") as one of the best two-shotters in the world. As usual, he was right. Other memorable holes include #8, where a flat green is guarded by a large, conical sandhill; #12, a long par 4 requiring a precise second shot over the Buddon Burn to an elevated green; and the 234-yard par 3 fifteenth hole.

Panmure Golf Club has a long and proud history. Organized in 1845, the club shared playing time at neighboring Monifieth until its own clubhouse and course were finished in 1899. Panmure boasts one of Scotland's most attractive golf clubhouses with its turrets and gables and filigreed latticework. Lovers of historic architecture can only hope the clubhouse will be forever maintained.

41. Pitlochry Golf Club (1908)

Region #: 7   **Category:** parkland
Architect(s): Willie Fernie (1909)
Length: 5811   **SSS:** 69   **Par:** 69

Address: Golf Course Rd, Pitlochry PH16 5Q7
Directions: well signposted N of town off the A924 (Atholl Rd)
Reservations phone: 01796-472-792   **Fax:** 01796-473-599
Email: no   **Website:** no
Booking Contact(s): professional
Secretary: DM McKenzie   **Professional:** Mark Pirie
Phone - Starter/Pro shop: 01796-472-792
Fee(s) (2003): wkday £22, day tkt £32; wkend £28, day tkt £40
Deposit (2003): none

Visitor Policies: all wk; members only until 9:30
Buggies: no

I think I fell in love with Scotland at Pitlochry—the golf course and the town. It was the first course I encountered in Scotland and quite unlike anything I had seen in my part of the world. From the opening shot to a fairway split by a gully; then up a great hill for #s 2 and 3; then on to the blind shot at "Queen Mary's Rest" (#5); and the dramatically elevated tee shot at #6 "Druid's Stone," here we have one of Scotland's most scenic courses, with spectacular views westward across the Tummel Valley and the Rivers Tay and Tummel. After playing holes #4 through #17 back and forth, round and about, on the top of Pitlochry's graceful hill, the golfer descends to an attractive and welcoming clubhouse situated next to the #18 "Home" green. Not incidentally, among these eighteen holes, I would rank four as highly as any in Scottish golf for design brilliance and challenge (#s 1, 5, 10, and 16). As for the rest, they're all enjoyable, though, as a whole, they add up to only mildly challenging golf. As golf writer Malcolm Campbell puts it, "Pitlochry is not the most testing golf course in the wide world of golf—and who is to say it is not the better for it—but it certainly is one of the most delightful to play."

Accommodations and nongolf activities: Equally delightful as the golf course is the town itself. About thirty miles north of Perth on the A9 (Scotland's main artery northward), Pitlochry bills itself as "The Gateway to the Highlands." Pitlochry is a destination resort and has been since Victorian times. In summer the streets can be positively crawling with visitors perusing the shops of the main street (Atholl Road). But don't let that scene get you down on Pitlochry. Off the main street, there's much to see and do here and the crowds can be avoided. This is an excellent base for making day trips throughout Perthshire and central Scotland. It's ideal for golfers playing the courses at Gleneagles, Blairgowrie, Crieff, and Kingussie. Stirring, scenic drives meander westward from the A9 on narrow roads along Loch Rannoch, Glen Lyon, and Loch Tay. To the east, one of Scotland's most scenic highways, the short A924 connecting the A9 to the equally-scenic A93, starts from Pitlochry in the middle of town. Just a few miles along the A924, at a leftward bend, as the narrowing road starts to climb, you'll find the entrance to Edradour Distillery, renowned as Scotland's smallest distiller of single-malt whisky (tours are free). A few miles to the north on the A9 lies Blair Castle, one of Scotland's most popular castle parks, and just a bit farther along is the House of Bruar, a prodigious gift emporium.

But you don't have to leave town to have a good time. Pitlochry's winding streets are fun tó walk. Hiking and nature trails are close by (some surrounding the golf course). And the River Tummel awaits just below town where you'll also find the Pitlochry Dam and Fish Ladder and the famous Pitlochry Festival Theatre that draws visitors from miles around throughout the summer season (ph: 01796-484-626).

Pitlochry is loaded with bargain accommodations. Typical of these is the *Dunmurray Lodge* operated by Ian and Isabel Tait (01796-473-624; *www.dunmurray.co.uk*). In Pitlochry's heated competition among B & Bs, this is a four-star home where you can rest and relax for less than £30 per night. Moreover, you'll meet two of the nicest people in all of bonnie Scotland. Pricier lodgings line Atholl Road, but that's the "main drag" and I would advise staying away from it. A better choice is the *Moulin Hotel* (01796-472-196; *www.moulin.u-net.com*), three-quarters of a mile up the A924 (Moulin Rd). The Moulin is one of Scotland's best lodging bargains and one of the most colorful small hotels in the country. Proprietors Chris Tomlinson and Heather Reeves preside over an historic coaching inn (1695) with seventeen comfortable rooms and an attached pub with its own microbrewery—all manned by first-rate staff. The Moulin's pub is a hangout for locals as well as visitors. It's a great place to meet and be met. To learn more about this enchanted and enchanting place called Pitlochry, visit the web site *www.pitlochryhospitality.co.uk*.

42. Portpatrick Golf Club - Dunskey Course (1903)

Region #: 9   **Category:** seaside links
Architect(s): C W Hunter
Length: 5538-5908   **SSS:** 68   **Par:** 70

Address: Golf Course Rd, Portpatrick D69 8TB
Directions: well signposted NW of village

Reservations phone: 01776-810-273   **Fax:** 01776-810-811
Email: enquiries@portpatrickgolfclub.com

Website: portpatrickgolfclub.com
Booking Contact(s): secretary
Secretary: John McPhail   **Professional:** no
Phone - Starter/Pro shop: 01776-810-273
Fee(s) (2003): wkday £25, day tkt £30; wkend £30, day tkt £40
Deposit (2003): £5 for groups of 8+
Visitor Policies: all wk   **Buggies:** 5 - general hire

Tucked away as it is in the southwest corner of the country, few golf tourists set foot in the Dumfries-Galloway region of Scotland. To my mind, that's the best reason to consider a trip to this beautiful area. Beginning just fifty miles south of Turnberry, that trip might include golf at Stranraer, Portpatrick, Southerness, and Powfoot with an admixture of inland courses at Newton Stewart, Selkirk, Roxburghe, and other "Borders" towns—all set in a paradise of rolling green hills and picturebook villages and towns perched beside sparkling rivers. Different from the rugged beauty found in the Highlands, the Galloway-Dumfries beauty is of the soft, green sort found in England's Lake District and in Ireland. And, if it sounds like I'm a fan of the "Southern Uplands," I am.

Among the southern courses mentioned above, Portpatrick is perhaps the most dramatically situated on the rocky coast of an anvil-shaped piece of land dead across the water from Belfast, Northern Ireland, just twenty miles away. On a clear day you can see Ireland (#10 is "Erin View"), the Mull of Kintyre to the northwest, and the Isle of Man off to the southwest.

Wind, rain, and long, grassy rough are the main determinants of a golf score at Portpatrick. With few bunkers and no two-shotters over 400 yards, there's not much else to contend with. Given a day of benign weather, in fact, most will find this short course a lovely pushover and, in either case—blustery or calm—this is one place I would ask for permission to play from the member tees at 5908 yards.

See also: Powfoot, Southerness, Stranraer.

43. Powfoot Golf Club (1903)

Region #: 9   **Category:** seaside links-parkland hybrid
Architect(s): James Braid (1903)
Length: 6010-6238   **SSS:** 70   **Par:** 71

Address: Annan, Dumfries-shire DG12 5QE
Directions: B724 off A75 at Annan, then 1/2 mi S of Cummertrees

Reservations phone: 01461-700-276   **Fax:** same
Email: briansutherland@powfootgolfclub.ssnet.co.uk
Website: under construction
Booking Contact(s): mgr
Manager: Brian Sutherland MBE   **Professional:** Stuart Smith
Phone - Starter/Pro shop: 01461-700-327
Fee(s) (2003): wkday £26, day tkt £33; wkend £27, day tkt £35; jrs £10
Deposit (2003): £5
Visitor Policies: Sat 11-11:30 and after 1 pm; Sun 10:30-11:15
and after 1 pm
Buggies: 4 - phys/med

Like Southerness Golf Club, Powfoot lies near the border between England and Scotland and, therefore, might be played most often by golfers traveling from England to one of Scotland's golf Meccas farther north. For all the reasons cited in my descriptions of Portpatrick, Stranraer, and Southerness, these courses and the beautiful Dumfries-Galloway countryside deserve more than a drive-through. Powfoot is another James Braid course. This one came early in Braid's design career, before the full development of characteristics typical of his later work. For that reason, alone, Powfoot is interesting. Another point of interest: due to the configuration of available land (101 acres), Powfoot is not the typical out-and-back links layout but, rather, a *series* of out-back patterns with several holes near the attractive clubhouse looking out over the course and the Solway Firth. Though no pushover, Powfoot is considerably more manageable than Southerness. And I think all golfers will like the variety and changes of direction Braid drew out of the available terrain.

Like most of the golf courses on Scotland's southern coast, Powfoot was used as a military camp during World War II. The war left its mark quite literally on this course—in one dramatic way and one less obvious way. You'll find the dramatic residue of the war at the #9 "Crater" hole where a mammoth depression created by a German bomb has been left as an "unnatural hazard" about eighty yards short of the green. The less obvious legacy is the rather flat second nine played over ground leveled for military purposes. The last five holes, playing largely over parkland terrain, were reconstructed after the war. So, yes, this is Braid, but it's a bit of Braid put through a blender—an unfortunate accident of history, yet well worth a visit.

See also: Portpatrick, Southerness, Stranraer.

44. Prestwick Golf Club (1851) *

Region #: 2   **Category:** seaside links
Architect(s): Tom Morris (12 holes, 1851; others)
Length: 6544-6700 yds   **SSS:** 73   **Par:** 71

Address: 2 Links Rd, Prestwick, Ayshire KA9 1QC
Directions: From N on A79, 1 mi S of Prestwick Airport; rt at Station Rd (light); under rail overpass 400 yds toward beach. From S, left at Station Rd in Prestwick town center off A79 (Main St)

Reservations phone: 01292-671-020   **Fax:** 01292-477-255
Email: bookings@prestwickgc.co.uk   **Website:** prestwickgc.co.uk
Booking Contacts: Margaret Campbell, Morven English
Secretary: I T Bunch   **Professional:** Frank Rennie
Phone - Starter/Pro shop: 01292-477-404
Fee(s) (2003): wkday £90, day tkt £130; Sun £105; jrs - 50%
Deposit (2003): £40
Visitor Policies: wkdays except Th pm; no Saturdays or bank holidays; limited play on Sundays in summer
Buggies: no
Other: hdcps - men 24, women 28

"You would like to gather up several holes from Prestwick and mail them to your top ten enemies." —Dan Jenkins

When my clients include the Ayrshire coast on an itinerary, I like to start them out at Prestwick Golf Club if possible. This is where you return to an older age of golf—to the nineteenth century and the historic days of the first Open championships. At Prestwick, on the course and in the clubhouse, you can soak in the aura and origins of professional tournament golf in an atmosphere little changed by the passage of time. And though its time has come and gone as a venue for the British Open, Prestwick remains among the most challenging courses in Scottish golf. And the word "challenging" really doesn't get to the heart of the matter. The course is also vexing, devilish, and entertaining in ways unique among the classic courses, past and present, on the Open "rota."

Between 1860 and 1925 Prestwick was the main venue for the Open Championship (now called the British Open). No less than twenty-four of the first sixty-five Opens were held here. And, as testimony to the quality of Prestwick's course, those twenty-four tournaments were dominated by all the great names in the first two generations of Scottish golf: the Morrises from St. Andrews, the Parks from Musselburgh, the Simpsons from Carnoustie, and, later, Harry Vardon and James Braid. Tom Morris, Jr., considered the finest golfer of his day, won the Open at Prestwick three years in a row between 1868 and 1870 and thus was allowed to keep the original Open prize: a red Moroccan leather belt with silver buckle. Subsequently, a new prize was produced—the now famous "claret jug" engraved with the name of each winner of the Open since 1871.

Prestwick is another course where you will find the living presence of golf's nineteenth-century father figure, Tom Morris. Morris moved from St. Andrews to Prestwick in 1851 as a young man to lay out twelve holes, assume a position as Keeper of the Green, and, incidentally, raise a family. Today, much of that early layout remains, including seven of Morris's green sites. Morris returned to St. Andrews in 1864. Prestwick's clubhouse was constructed in 1868, and in 1883 the course was extended to eighteen holes. By that time the club was firmly established as one of the preeminent clubs in Scottish golf.

When you step to the first tee at Prestwick you will be immediately struck by the vexing, devilish side of the place. A pusher or slicer of the ball will cringe, for tight up against the right side of the entire first fairway is a railroad embankment (OB). But, compensate too far leftward and you're into the gorse and rubble. The second shot isn't any easier. Prestwick's first lesson: accuracy will beat distance every time. The first hole, a mere 369 yards, will remind you, as Jim Finegan puts it, "this course may be a monument to the era of the gutta percha ball. But it is no tombstone. The golf here continues to be gloriously vital."

Now on to the attractively deceiving par 3 second hole before tackling the famous "Cardinal" par 5 with its strategically-placed, mammoth bunkers stretching the width of the fairway and lined with railroad ties. If this sight brings Pete Dye to mind, it's no coincidence. Pete came here to play in 1963 and went away a changed man. You can read about his Scottish epiphany in the book, *Bury Me in a Pot Bunker*.

Cardinal and Bridge (#4) play alongside the Pow Burn—a critical natural feature of Prestwick that cuts into the course behind the second green and then runs the full length of the layout. Thirteen of Prestwick's holes are crammed into the west side of the burn, while only five holes (#s 5-9) lie on the more expansive east side of the burn. This configuration gives the course a certain rhythm I like: tight at the beginning and end; open in the middle.

With all this excellent terrain covered in the first four holes, you can hardly expect it to get better—and, yet, it does—for now we approach the equally famous "Himalayas," a blind one-shotter (206 yards) over a 25-foot-high sandhill to a green surrounded by five bunkers. This is antique Scottish golf at its best.

Well, I could go on and on, hole after hole. Just two more: First, "Arran" (#10), is one of my favorite holes in Scottish golf. It's a 454-yard, par 4, dogleg right across the Pow Burn and then straight down a bunkered fairway aimed at the Isle of Arran off in the distance. Par is a good score, but the setting is so spectacular you don't care that much if you don't meet the test. Prestwick's most famous hole is the #17 "Alps" (one of the Morris originals). It's a 391-yarder with a drive up a hill, then a blind shot to a green fronted by a bunker so cavernous you need steps to get in and out (more Pete Dye material).

With the course largely unchanged in one hundred years, Prestwick stands as a living link between the past and present of golf course design. The line between Tom Morris, the most influential designer of the nineteenth century, and Pete Dye, the most influential designer of the twentieth century, cuts right through Prestwick Golf Club. And that's why I like to have my clients start at this historic course if they can.

Back at the clubhouse you won't be surprised to find the place loaded with priceless golf memorabilia, including a replica of Young Tom Morris's red Moroccan leather belt (the original is in possession of the Royal and Ancient Golf Club). Lunch is available 10 a.m. to 3:30 p.m. in the casual Cardinal Room. The more formal Long Room requires coat and tie and advance reservation (men only).

Accommodations: Just south of Troon, Prestwick makes base for golf along the Ayrshire coast. There's a lot of lodging just off Prestwick's Main Street (Monkton Rd, Ayr Rd). But that's the A79—a busy thoroughfare choked by a constant flow of traffic. The better choices are right at the golf course on Links Road. These are the "golf hotels," all suited up in row house fashion. There's the *North Beach* at #7 Links Rd (01292-479-069), the *Prestwick Old Course Hotel* at #13 (01292-477-446), the *Golf View* at #17 (01292-671-234), and the *Fairways Private Hotel* at #19 (01292-470-396). None of these converted Victorians has more than twelve rooms, but they all have plenty of character and the personal attention of on-site owners. A little farther along, facing the sea, is the *Parkstone Hotel* (01292-477-286; *www.parkstonehotel.co.uk*), a larger, more modern hotel. These hotels are all comparable and are reasonably priced considering their location. It doesn't get any easier than walking out your front door, then across the street to the first tee.

45. Royal Aberdeen Golf Club (1780) - Balgownie Course
Region #: 6   **Category:** seaside links
Architect(s): Willie Park, Sr., Robert Simpson, others
Length: 6104-6415   **SSS:** 70   **Par:** 71

Address: Balgownie, Bridge of Don, Aberdeen AB23 8AT
Directions: N of Aberdeen on A92; first rt at Links Rd N of Bridge of Don
Reservations phone: 01224-702-571   **Fax:** 01224-826-591
Email: admin@royalaberdeengolf.com   **Website:** royalaberdeengolf.com
Booking Contacts: Nina Mackie, Sandra Nicholson
Secretary: Fraser Webster   **Dir of Golf:** Ronnie MacAskill
Phone - Starter/Pro shop: 01224-702-221
Fee(s) (2003): wkday £65, day tkt £90; wkend £75; Apr & Oct - £50 per round; jrs - 50%
Deposit (2003): 25%   **Buggies:** no
Visitor Policies: wkday 10-11:30 am, 2-3:30 pm; wkend after 3:30
Other: limited caddie pool - limited # of pullcarts; hdcp - men/women 24

If Royal Aberdeen's Balgownie Course were located *anywhere* in the lowlands of Scotland, undoubtedly it would be as well known as

Muirfield and Troon and Scotland's other "rota" courses, and it would probably host the British Open as well. The course is that good.

So it's just a matter of location, location, location. Most golf tourists are so fixated on the courses in central Scotland that they don't consider traveling a little farther northward to play not only Royal Aberdeen and Cruden Bay, but the other great courses that dot Scotland's Northeast Coastal Trail and the interior of Aberdeenshire. And it's really not that hard: all you have to do is get on a plane that flies to Aberdeen, Scotland's third largest city. Voila! You're in another golf Mecca—and one far more relaxed and affordable than the tourist magnets to the south.

The venturesome traveler who finds the northeast corner of Scotland will uncover all the best the country has to offer: castles, country house hotels, whisky distilleries, fishing villages, mountains, rich pastureland, and a variety of outstanding golf courses. It's no accident that this is the part of Scotland where England's royal family likes to hang out (i.e., at Balmoral Castle). They know a great locale when they see one.

Nor is it an accident that Royal Aberdeen and the great course at Cruden Bay are often considered in tandem. Only thirty miles apart, their moonscape terrains are cut of the same coastal cloth patterned by towering dunes and rumpled fairways in such extreme that they form a pair nearly unique in Scottish golf. Readers of *Golf World* ranked these two courses sixth (Cruden Bay) and seventh (Royal Aberdeen) in a "Best Courses" poll a few years ago. My guess is that they would rank even closer to the top if more people made the trek northward.

Despite its relatively short yardage (the championship tees can be stretched to 6600), the Balgownie is one tough customer. Golf writers, in virtual unanimity, acclaim the first nine among the finest in the country. Part of this acclaim derives from the first three holes that combine a 410-yard opener with a 530-yard par 5 and a 223-yard par 3. No "warm-up" typical of Scottish golf here! These are monsters that can wreck a scorecard before you know what hit you. A little farther along, the brutal 453-yard ninth hole, doglegging to the right as it falls off to the left, achieves star status: David Hamilton (*Scottish Golf Guide*) places it among the best eighteen holes in Scotland. In comparison, the inward nine may disappoint a bit but, played into the customary wind off the North Sea, it's no pushover even though 300 yards shorter.

A little history: One of the seven "royal" clubs of Scotland, the Aberdeen Golf Club received its designation in 1903 when King Edward VII agreed to become Patron of the Club. Such was the momentary culmination of a proud history that began officially in 1780 but clearly stretched back to the middle of the sixteenth century when some form of golf developed along Scotland's eastern seaboard. In short, when the Society of Aberdeen Golfers formed in 1780 it became Scotland's fifth oldest golf club, joining the distinguished and defining company of clubs that played in Leith, Edinburgh, Musselburgh, and St. Andrews.

In 1903, the Royal Aberdeen Golf Club had been at its current Balgownie location, about a mile north of Aberdeen, only since 1888. Prior to golf's explosion of popularity and standardization in the late 1800s, the club had played its golf along the linksland nearer town between the Rivers Don and Dee. Balgownie was just a suburban jump away to the north side of the Don and, there, several golf architects from Carnoustie's Simpson family (also involved at Cruden Bay) had the principal hand in creating one of Scotland's finest. Though Willie Park, Sr., was involved early on, it is Robert Simpson who is generally given credit for the Balgownie Course. More recently, Donald Steel was engaged to revamp Royal Aberdeen's 18-hole relief course (4021 yards), the "Silverburn."

Finally, I would be remiss if I didn't mention the Royal's splendid clubhouse—one of the finest in Scottish golf. It's another one of those that overlook the first tee and eighteenth green, thus providing continual entertainment for the members and guests within. And, not surprisingly, it's loaded with a priceless collection of golf memorabilia.

Accommodations and nongolf activities: As in all large cities, the traveler will find a wealth of accommodations. Popular on high-end golf tours are the baronial *Ardoe House* (01224-860-600; *www.macdonaldhotels.co.uk*) and the more understated *Marcliffe at Pitfodels* (01224-861-000; *www.marcliffe.com*). For more information, see *www.granite-city.com*. Most golf travelers choose to stay outside Aberdeen; for them, in my profile of *Cruden Bay* I have cited two outstanding small hotels that cater to golfers.

Aberdeen, population about 225,000, is often called "the Granite City." Massive, gray stone buildings dominate the central part of town and give the place a stoic façade. But, beneath the gray aesthetics of Aberdeen, lies Scotland's most contemporary, prosperous city, driven by North Sea Oil and its related industries. Take a look at downtown Aberdeen just about anytime and you'll see the High Street crawling with shoppers on a mission. Moreover, this is a university town—so, you'll sense all the modernity, promise, and energy of youth. If Edinburgh is Scotland's history book and Glasgow is its warehouse, then Aberdeen is Scotland's "E-commerce" window on the future. It's an exciting little city with a personality all its own.

Historically speaking, you'll be reminded of Aberdeen's fishing-port past at the Maritime Museum near the harbor. Various distilleries and castles (including the royal family's Balmoral) are within striking distance of Aberdeen. And the usual array of fine homes, gardens, and woodland walks abound. For anyone who really wants to get off the beaten path in Scotland, this is the starting line for a memorable visit.

See also: Cruden Bay

46. Royal Dornoch Golf Club (1877)

Region #: 5   **Category:** seaside links
Architect(s): Tom Morris (1891); Donald Ross (1900); John Sutherland & J.H.Taylor - various; George Duncan (holes 7-11)
Length: 6229-6514   **SSS:** 71   **Par:** 70

Address: Golf Rd, Dornoch IV25 3LW
Directions: 45 mi N of Inverness on A9; well signposted, rt at town square, left to clubhouse

Reservations phone: 01862-810-219   **Fax:** 01862-810-792
Email: rdgc@royaldornoch.com   **Website:** royaldornoch.com
Booking Contact(s): Donna Sutherland, Claire Riddell
Secretary: John S Duncan   **Professional:** Andrew Skinner
Phone - Starter/Pro shop: 01862-810-902
Fee(s) (2003): M-F, £66, wkend £76; day tkt w/ Struie £76 wkday & £86 wkend; jrs (up to 15) - 50%; no day tkt on championship course
Deposit (2003): £30
Visitor Policies: all wk; Sat after 2 pm   **Buggies:** 1- med/phys
Other: relief course (Struie - 5438 yds designed by Donald Steel); hdcps - men 24, women 39

In 1886, when Old Tom Morris came up to Dornoch to help John Sutherland and friends lay out "nine proper golf holes" and plan nine more, he is said to have remarked, "The a'mighty had gowf in his eye when he made this ground." Of course, Tom Morris—not only the father of modern golf, but golf's greatest diplomat—said something like that about every course he planned. At Dornoch, there's every reason to think Morris meant exactly what he said. I am personally convinced that, when Morris saw this ground, he saw an opportunity to create the most difficult classic links course in his repertoire—classic in its "out and back" setup, two fairways wide; difficult in its elevation changes, its natural sitings for greens, and its susceptibility to every trick in the Morris bag.

Despite a host of alterations in ensuing years—first by Donald Ross in 1900, by John Sutherland over a long stretch of years, then by George Duncan in the 1940s—Dornoch is through and through a Morrisonian course, for its successive architects were decided disciples of Morris. Dornoch native Donald Ross even went to St. Andrews to work with Tom Morris before returning to Dornoch to serve for a few years as its first professional and greenkeeper. Ultimately, of course, he emigrated to the United States where he became the most prolific golf course architect of the twentieth century. He returned to Dornoch in 1900 only to lengthen the course in response to introduction of the rubber-cored golf ball.

Thus, the hallmarks of Dornoch stand as a collective monument to Tom Morris and his disciples: large, severely-contoured, shaved greens sitting on plateaus; bunkers by the dozens; green-fronting swales; elevated teeing grounds; a few blind shots (but not many); tight driving areas often to aslant fairways. Natural phenomena add further difficulty to Dornoch: first, the wind, then the acres of whins (gorse) bushes that eat golf balls. The net result: stroke for stroke, in my view, one of the two or three most difficult courses in Scotland. Also, one of the most beautiful. Indeed, in May and early June, at the elevated third, fourth, and fifth tees, set amidst thick banks of gorse in full yellow bloom stretching down the entire left side of the course, this is among the most breathtaking seaside vistas in all of Scotland.

Golf was played at Dornoch long before Tom Morris and his disciples came upon the scene. Public records dating to 1616 give Dornoch status as the third oldest locus of golf after St. Andrews and Leith

(Edinburgh). True or not, the historical record is significant as an indicator that, by the seventeenth century, golf had secured a certain hold on Scotland over the entire length of the eastern seaboard—even in the most remote parts of the country.

After organizing as a club in 1877, Dornoch came into its own at the turn of the century, partly as a result of the area's association with Andrew Carnegie—CEO of U.S. Steel and library-builder *nonpareil*. Born in Dumfermline in Fife, Carnegie never left his Scottish roots entirely behind. He built Skibo Castle in the northern Highlands outside of Dornoch, and he learned to play golf on a course built for him there. In 1901 he presented the Dornoch Golf Club with a silver shield as reward to the winner of a tournament held annually ever since during early August (2001 was the centennial year). In 1903, the railway reached Dornoch, enabling vacationers to make an overnight from London to the far reaches of the northern Highlands. In 1906, Dornoch received its "royal" designation from King Edward VII via the patronage of the Duchess of Sutherland. In 1909, Carnegie paid for a clubhouse at the newly-christened "Royal Dornoch."

Despite this flurry of attention, until recent years Royal Dornoch remained largely unvisited by the international community of golf travelers. It was simply too far north—at least until 1985. That was the year new bridges spanning the Cromarty Firth and Dornoch Firth cut driving time from Inverness by about one hour. Suddenly, Dornoch became more accessible. Tom Watson and Ben Crenshaw came to Dornoch and went away raving (having left behind quotable tidbits). Then, adding fuel to the fire, golf writer Lorne Rubenstein's hymn to Dornoch, *A Season in Dornoch*, published in 2001, brought still more pilgrims to catch a glimpse of what Rubenstein and his wife experienced over a summer in this magical place. The upshot: these days Dornoch is one popular place to play golf. Book early.

I've expended more ink here on the history of Dornoch than on the course itself. But here's the bottom line: if you can play good golf at Dornoch, you can play good golf anywhere. Leave some extra time. It's a course to play more than once.

Accommodations: If Royal Dornoch is the only northern golf course on your itinerary and your time is short, your preferred base may be Inverness or Nairn (see *Nairn Golf Club* for my notes on Inverness/Nairn lodging). On the other hand, if one can linger awhile in the northern Highlands above Inverness, a logical base is the Dornoch/Tain area. There's plenty of golf to be played (see *www.golfhighland.com*) and, from here, one can explore the interior of Sutherland, Caithness, and Easter Ross. A stirring coastal route either by automobile or train will take you to Wick and Thurso and then on to John O' Groats—Scotland's "land's end" and northernmost ferry point to the Orkney and Shetland Islands.

A popular lodging choice in Dornoch is right at the golf course at the *Royal Golf Hotel* (01862-810-283; *www.morton-hotels.com*). In town there's the historic *Dornoch Castle Hotel* (01862-810-216; *www.dornochcastlehotel.com*). But the best choice is the *Eagle Hotel* on Castle St (01862-810-008; *www.eagledornoch.co.uk)*. The key here is to ask for rooms in the "Bank House." A couple of years ago, across the street from the main hotel, owners Paul and Irene Hart acquired the Clydesdale Bank property, including the sumptuous director's quarters above and behind the bank. After refurbishing of the quarters, Paul and Irene moved in and had three rooms left over to let. The rooms are spacious and well appointed—quite simply four-star quality at a three-star price and one of the best lodging bargains I have found in Scotland. Now, for those (like Madonna) who want to indulge in Scotland's most extravagant splurge, I would be remiss not to mention *Skibo Castle* (01862-894-600; *www.carnegieclub.co.uk)*. Skibo is a few miles outside Dornoch and, for a mere £800 (double occupancy 2003), visitors to the Carnegie Club can stay for one night, play golf on the newly-minted Carnegie Links (Donald Steel, 1995), and eat and drink all you want without seeing another tab. Such a deal!

Nearby Tain is home to the world-famous Glenmorangie Distillery and it also boasts two exceptional hotels. Perhaps the most popular hotel in the region, both for golfers and nongolfers, is the *Morangie House Hotel* (01862-892-281; *www.morangiehotel.com*) where room rates start at £95 double occupancy. Competing with the Morangie House is the *Mansfield House Hotel* (01862-892-052; *www.mansfield-house.co.uk*). My favorite B & B in Tain is Ian and Ray Ross's four-star *Golf View House* (01862-892-856; *www.golf-view.co.uk*). Set on two acres of land on a bluff overlooking Tain Golf Club, it's the best deal in town.

See also: Brora, Fortrose & Rosemarkie, Golspie, Nairn, Tain.

47. Royal Musselburgh Golf Club (1774)

Region #: 3   **Category:** parkland
Architect(s): James Braid (1924)
Length: 6284   **SSS:** 70   **Par:** 70

Address: Preston Grange House, Prestonpans EH32 9RP
Directions: W of Prestonpans off A198

Reservations phone: 01875-810-276   **Fax:** same as ph
Email: royalmusselburgh@btinternet.com
Website: royalmusselburgh.co.uk
Booking Contact(s): secretary
Secretary: Thomas Hardie   **Professional:** John Henderson
Phone - Starter/Pro shop: 01875-810-139
Fee(s) (2003): wkday £25, day tkt £35; wkend £35, no day tkt; jrs £15
Deposit (2003): £7
Visitor Policies: wkdays except Fri pm   **Buggies:** 3 - general hire
Other: no credit cards

The courses at Musselburgh (pronounced *muscle-burra*) are situated between Musselburgh and Prestonpans on the estate of the Barons of Prestoungrange. In point of fact, the clubhouse of the RMGC—one of the finest in Scottish golf—is housed in a mansion the barons called home from the sixteenth century to the early twentieth century.

In the preceding paragraph, I have referred to "the courses" at Musselburgh because Royal Musselburgh is closely associated with the *Old Links at Musselburgh*, one mile *east* of Musselburgh town center. It was here, at the Old Links, that some kind of golf took root in Scotland—verifiably so by 1672 and probably as early as the 1400s. During the eighteenth century, four of Scotland's five oldest golf clubs played on the nine holes of the Old Links (in addition to the RMGC, this included the Honourable Company of Edinburgh Golfers, Royal Burgess Golf Club, and the Bruntsfield Golfing Society). Between 1868 and 1889 this ground was the site of *six* British Opens. And, when the last Open was played at Musselburgh in 1889, a chapter in the history of golf closed.

The Royal Musselburgh Golf Club was the last major club to vacate the Old Links in favor of newer, more expansive digs—in this case, the club's current parkland site designed by James Braid in the early 1920s. Subsequently, the Old Links suffered from neglect but, today, efforts are being made to resurrect the old lady as a living museum of golf history. To enhance the time-machine experience, you can even rent a set of hickory sticks for your round. Since 1816, the course has been surrounded by a mile-long racetrack, making it not only the most historic but the most unusual layout in the country. For more information about the Old Links at Musselburgh, see *www. musselburgholdlinks.co.uk* (ph/fax: 0131-665-5438).

So, when discussing Royal Musselburgh, golf fans, we are talking *history.* We're talking about a golf club formed two years before the issuance of the Declaration of Independence, housed in a sixteenth-century mansion, with a history of play on ground dedicated to golf since the time of Columbus. For all these reasons, I encourage my clients to make a day of *the courses at Musselburgh* with a nine-holer on the Old Links in the morning, followed by lunch at the Royal Musselburgh clubhouse, before an afternoon round on Braid's twentieth-century creation. This combination makes for an unforgettable day of Scottish golf.

As for the course at Royal Musselburgh, this is a tree-lined beauty with heavy rough and a collection of imaginative holes designed by James Braid, with his usual emphasis on long, difficult par 4s, a mix of par 3s, and a de-emphasis on round-saving par 5s. Even though near the sea (and with occasional views out to the Firth), Royal Musselburgh sports parkland turf at a seaside setting reminiscent of Belleisle at Ayr (another Braid course). When in Edinburgh or East Lothian, don't miss it.

48. Royal Troon (1878) – Old Course *

Region #: 2   **Category:** seaside links
Architect(s): Willie Fernie (1888)
Length: 6201-6640-7097   **SSS:** 73   **Par:** 71

Address: Craigend Rd., Troon, Ayrshire KA10 6EP
Directions: terminus of B749 at corner of Craigend and Bentinck Dr

Reservations phone: 01292-311-555   **Fax:** 01292-318-204
Email: bookings@royaltroon.com   **Website:** royaltroon.com
Booking Contact(s): Michael McCallum, Hamish Harkness, Douglas Bull
Secretary: JW Chandler   **Professional:** R Brian Anderson

Phone - Starter/Pro shop: 01292-313-281
Fee(s) (2003): £170 (includes play on the Portland Course & lunch)
Deposit (2003): £50; balance taken 60 days before play
Visitor Policies: May 1 thru 4th wk of Oct: M, T, Th only, 9:30-11 am & 2:30-4 pm; no jrs (under 18) on Old Course
Buggies: no
Other: Portland Course, 6289 yds, SSS 71; hdcp - men 20, women 30

With the British Open scheduled for Royal Troon in 2004, I have a feeling that club members here looked into their crystal ball and caught a glimpse of Hootie Johnson and Martha Burk. They weren't about to play the UK version of Augusta's *Sturm und Drang*. Thus, the big news out of Troon in 2003 was a change of policy vis-à-vis the ladies. Women with a handicap of 30 or below can now play the Old Course. End of discussion. Case closed.

There's another policy that needs changing, but it may take a little longer: The only option at Troon is a "day ticket" for play on the Old Course and the neighboring Portland Course (in other words, you *pay* for both courses regardless of whether you *play* both courses). For golfers who want to spend an entire day playing golf, this arrangement can lead to a certain kind of Nirvana—a perfect day in a perfect place. The setting is superb; the championship course is excellent; the Portland, across the road and a bit inland, is good. The clubhouse is grand and the staff is first-rate. No complaints from the 36-holers.

The problem is that most people don't want to play two rounds of golf in one day. And, if they do, they might rather play the second round at Western Gailes or Glasgow Gailes or Barassie. *In practice, nearly half of those who book at Troon play only the championship course.* The net result: lots of open times on the Portland and lots of disappointed golfers who end up paying the highest fee in Scottish golf for lunch and one round on a championship course—£170 (about $255) in 2003.

I say "disappointed" simply because that's the way a lot of golfers feel after visiting Troon. Troon, by itself, is simply not worth $255. It's a good and historic golf course. But it's not £65 better than St. Andrews' Old Course, Muirfield, Turnberry or Carnoustie. Indeed, I would put Troon at the tail-end of the "rota" list. The Old Course is more historic and structurally unique; Muirfield is more creatively unique; Turnberry is more uniquely beautiful; and Carnoustie is a tougher track. Even neighboring Prestwick has a certain quirky character lacking at Troon. In short, the visiting golfer is likely to feel gouged by Troon's two-course policy. Perhaps at one time the management committee found friendly logic in the policy but, today, the only logic seems to be aimed at the pocketbooks of visiting golfers.

Despite all the carping, Royal Troon is a great golf experience. Demand is strong and, because visitors are accepted on only three weekdays, a tee time at Troon can be difficult to get in high season. In this regard, two important notes: First, Troon is welcoming to single golfers. You *can* pre-book as a single; also, since the daily "waitlist" is not so long as at St. Andrews, even without a reservation, you can often get onto the course just by showing up and joining a two-ball or three-ball game. Second, speaking of Troon's "waitlist," if the course is booked up on your first call, it's a good idea to go onto Troon's waitlist with the hope of filling a cancellation. Troon is the target of a lot of speculative booking by tour operators; thus, cancellations are common as deadlines for payment come and go.

Once on the course, the golf pilgrim, if poorer in pocket, certainly will be richer for the experience. Royal Troon is a classic links course—out and back, counter-clockwise, first along a gently-curving bay; then, after meandering a bit at the turn, back to the clubhouse on an inland track. In this respect, among Scotland's Open courses, Troon is most similar to St. Andrews' Old Course, though with superior sea views. The course is essentially the work of Open champion Willie Fernie (1883) who came here in 1888 to serve as Troon's club professional and to extend an existing small course to eighteen holes. The main changes since then have largely involved lengthening the course to a 7,000-yard championship stretch. Visitors normally will play the course at a considerably easier 6200 yards.

In general, Royal Troon lacks the dune-filled drama found on the linksland at places like Cruden Bay, Royal Dornoch, and Western Gailes. Requisite humps and bumps and wispy beach grasses are ever-present, but the terrain is relatively flat. Troon's six opening holes and six closing holes march in a rather straight line to and from the clubhouse. It's the inside six holes (#7 through #12) that give Troon its character and reputation. These holes feature constant changes of direction, doglegs to left and right (four of the six), a straightaway par 4 at 438 yards (#10, "Sandhills"), and one of the most famous par 3s in the world ("Postage Stamp," #8)—all in all, six of the best holes you will play on your trip to Scotland. The homeward nine is nearly three hundred yards longer than the first nine and, into the wind, can make for a rather trying experience. Most golfers are tired when finished with Troon and are quite happy to reach the clubhouse where a buffet lunch awaits in the handsome lounge.

Troon is the youngest of Scotland's "royals" but not the youngest of its Open venues (that honor goes to Turnberry). The royal designation was granted by Queen Elizabeth II on the occasion of Troon's centenary celebration in 1978. Open championships have been held here since 1923—testimony to the high regard given Troon by Scotland's "East Coast Establishment." Troon was the logical west coast heir to Prestwick's place in the Open rota. Indeed, as at all the Open venues, the quality of Royal Troon's challenge is reflected in its parade of champions. South African Bobby Locke won here in 1950. Since then, it's been an all-American parade. The winners have been Palmer ('63), Weiskopf ('73), Watson ('82), Calcavecchia ('89), and Leonard ('97).

The town and accommodations: Troon is an ideal base for enjoying golf along the Ayrshire coast. The courses at Irvine, Gailes, and Barassie all lie a few miles to the north. Prestwick and Ayr are the next towns south. Troon, itself, boasts five municipal golf courses, two of them of championship quality (the Darley and Lochgreen). Most important, there's a relaxed, inviting air about Troon that you don't find on the busy streets of its larger neighbors. The town is big enough to be served by a variety of shops and restaurants. There's easy access to the beaches and to a harbor where in season a SeaCat ferry makes two daily runs between Troon and Belfast, Northern Ireland. Thus, Troon can be a base for golf combining Scotland and Ireland.

Troon is short on B & Bs but is well served by hotels of varying size and distinction. A popular B & B about three hundred yards from the first tee at Troon is George and Norma McLardy's *Copper Beech* at 116 Bentinck Dr. (01292-314-100). The setting here is Tudor elegance; George, alone, with his repartee and extraordinary breakfast presentation, is worth the price of admission. A little farther along Bentinck Dr. at Darley Place is the *Glenside Hotel* (01292-313-677) operated by Stewart and Lynne Watt. This is one of Scotland's best lodging bargains in proximity to championship golf. With only four bedrooms and no restaurant, the Glenside is really a guest house— comfortable, cozy, and ideal for a golf party of four to eight people. One long block away, the Watt family owns and operates a larger inn, the *South Beach Hotel* (01292-312-033, *www.southbeach.co.uk*), one of the most popular full-service hotels on the Ayrshire coast. Rooms are generally spacious and the dining/bar facilities are popular with local residents—always a good sign. On the harbor is the classic Anchorage Hotel (01292-317-448; *www.theanchorage-hotel.com*).

Moving up the price scale, the massive *Marine Hotel* (01292-314-444; *www.paramount-hotels.co.uk*) overlooking the eighteenth fairway at Royal Troon is a famous golf hotel comparable in vintage to Rusacks in St. Andrews and the Marine at North Berwick. Catty-corner from the Marine is the popular *Piersland House Hotel* (01292-314-747; *www.piersland.co.uk*), the ancestral manse of the Johnny Walker (whisky) estate. Two establishments in the country-house category are *Lochgreen House* (01292-313-343) and *Highgrove House* (01292-312-511). These two properties are owned and operated by master chef Bill Costley (*www.costley-hotels.co.uk*). The Lochgreen House is on the B749 about one-half mile from Royal Troon Golf Club. Highgrove House is a few miles east on the A759 at the "Loans" crossroads. Both hotels feature luxury in small-scale surroundings, personal attention, and "Four Rosette" dining (the best).

See also: Glasgow Gailes, Irvine, Kilmarnock, Prestwick, Western Gailes.

The Courses at St. Andrews
49. The Old Course *

Region #: 1   **Category:** seaside links
Architect(s): evolution, Tom Morris
Length: 6566   **SSS:** 72   **Par:** 72

Address: St. Andrews Links Trust, Pilmour House, St. Andrews KY16 9SF
Directions: A91 to St. Andrews; 2nd left at Golf Pl

Reservations phone: 01334-466-666   **Fax:** 01334-477-036
Email: reservations@standrews.org.uk   **Website:** standrews.org.uk
Booking Contact(s): Pamela Pollock/Advance Reservations Office; Old Course application ok by mail, fax, or Email
General Manager: Ewan MacGregor

Fee(s) (2003): £105; 17.5% VAT on 3rd-party bookings
Deposit (2003): 100% nonrefundable prepay
Visitor Policies: closed Sun (see *Part II, Chapter Three* for more detail)
Buggies: none
Other: no trolleys until after 12 noon; hdcps - men 24, women 36; host to British Amateur in June 2004 and the British Open in July 2005

So many thousands of descriptive words have been written about this storied, historic course there is absolutely no reason for me to add to the word count. Most of what I have to say of a practical nature is in *Part II, Chapter Three*. All I want to add here is that, when people ask me, "Allan, what are your favorite courses?", I always start by saying, "First, the Old Course is in a class by itself." I really believe that. The moonscape setting, the huge double greens, the monstrous bunkers, and the grand scale of the Old Course are enough to distinguish it from all others. Layered on top of all that is the weight of history. And there's still another factor I find equally compelling about the Old Course: On no other course do I get such a clear appreciation for the interplay of skill and fate. Lady Luck plays a huge role here— for good and ill, just as in life. And, to me, that's why every golfer should play the Old Course at least once. It will keep you humble and appreciative of life (and of Tiger Woods).

Bogies: Getting up at 5:30 a.m. to stand in the "walk-on" queue with twenty-five other golf nuts. Far worse is paying the price for a guaranteed tee time through a tour operator or the Old Course Experience. I'd rather plan a year ahead or not plan on playing the Old Course at all.

50, 51. The New Course and The Jubilee
Region #: 1   **Category:** seaside links
Architect(s): New - Tom Morris (1895); Jubilee - various, Donald Steel (1988-9)
Length: New 5992-6604; Jubilee 6043-6805   **SSS:** New 72; Jubilee 73
Par: New 71; Jubilee 72

Address: St. Andrews Links Trust, Pilmour House, St. Andrews KY16 9SF
Directions: A91 to St. Andrews; 2nd left at Golf Pl

Reservations phone: 01334-466-666   **Fax:** 01334-477-036

Directions: A91 to St. Andrews; 2nd left at Golf Pl

Reservations phone: 01334-466-666   **Fax:** 01334-477-036
Email: reservations@standrews.org.uk   **Website:** standrews.org.uk
Key Contact(s): Pamela Pollock/Advance Reservations Office
Secretary: Ewan MacGregor
Fee(s) (2003): New £50; Jubilee £45; 17.5% VAT on 3rd-party bookings
Deposit (2003): 100% prepayment
Visitor Policies: all wk   **Buggies:** a few - med/phys and seniors

I'm treating these two courses under one subject heading because the courses sit side by side and are often considered in tandem. The New and Jubilee are the options most golfers weigh when looking for play on another St. Andrews course. Then the question arises, "Which course is better, the New or the Jubilee?". Ask that question of any twelve experienced St. Andrews golfers and you'll most likely get "six of one, half dozen of the other." It's usually a split decision. At 6800 yards, the Jubilee is the longer of the two and is often cited as, "the toughest course in St. Andrews." Yet the New Course, not much changed since it was laid out by Tom Morris in 1895, is considered the natural heir to Old Course tradition. Appropriately enough, the New Course is positioned next to the Old Course, while the Jubilee occupies a narrower strip of land between the New Course and the sea.

Play on the New and Jubilee begins at the attractive Links Clubhouse overlooking the second fairway of the Old Course. This is where visiting golfers will find plenty of parking and all the information and service they are looking for: a reception desk, changing rooms, bar, restaurant, gift shops, practice putting greens, plus the starter office and first tees for both the New and Jubilee. An observation deck atop the clubhouse is an excellent place to get photographs and a panoramic view of the links layout.

In comparing the courses, one can only conclude that the similarities are more important than the differences. Obviously, they play over similar terrain. Given its position, the Jubilee offers more ocean view but, since there is really no high ground on the links at St. Andrews, this factor is negligible. Both courses are out-and-back classics. And, even in length, the 200-yard difference (New, 6600; Jubilee, 6800) is insignificant when spread over eighteen holes. Both courses feature great banks of gorse that line the fairways and frame

St. Andrews sand. Both have large, undulating greens and one double green. Indeed, the similarities indicate a toss-up.

That much said, my own preference is for the New Course. Why? First, the New Course carries the indelible stamp of Old Tom Morris and thus sports a certain pedigree and integrity of design. The Jubilee, first opened as a twelve-hole course for women and children in 1897, has gone through several incarnations and, though Donald Steel brought championship length and wholesale redesign to the course in 1988-89, the course has a more layered history than the New. More important, land available to the two courses has had its affect. While the Jubilee is shaped like the sheath of a dagger, the New Course resembles the more graceful shape of a spoon. Five opening holes traverse the "handle" of the New Course, while three return to the clubhouse—all in a straight line. In the "bowl" of the spoon, Tom Morris exercised his imagination, creating ten varied holes with frequent changes of direction. In contrast, the Jubilee rather resembles a forced march out (seven holes straight out), with a brief respite (six holes back and forth), before the return to the clubhouse (six holes straight back in). Admittedly, some figure-eight routing increases the angles, but, overall, I much prefer the greater variety and grace of the New Course.

A closing word in behalf of the Jubilee (and golf at St. Andrews): For high handicappers the Jubilee offers a set of Bronze Tees, shortening the course to 5674 yards. In other words, even a marginal golfer can enjoy St. Andrews linksland in proximity to the Old Course. St. Andrews provides golf for all ages and all levels of ability and, in the process, reminds us of the democratic roots of the game. In this respect, the town of St. Andrews is a model citizen—indeed, the First Citizen—in the world of golf.

See also: Part II, Chapter Three, for more detail on the courses at St. Andrews and Links Management policies.

52. St. Andrews - Old Course Hotel - The Duke's Course (1995)

Region #: 1   **Category:** parkland
Architect(s): Peter Thomson (1995)
Length: 6264-6749   **SSS:** 73   **Par:** 72

Length: 6264-6749 **SSS:** 73 **Par:** 72

Address: Craigton, St. Andrews, Fife KY16 8NS
Directions: from town, Hepburn Gardens Rd 2 mi SW to Craigton Pk

Reservations phone: 01334-468-001 (Old Course Hotel)
Fax: 01334-477-668 **Email:** reservations@oldcoursehotel.co.uk
Website: oldcoursehotel.co.uk
Secretary: S Toon **Professional:** Ron Walker
Phone - Starter/Pro shop: 01334-470-214
Fee(s) (2003): hotel residents - £50 or incl in package rates - call hotel;
visitors M-Th £65, F-Sun £75; jrs (16 and under) - £20
Deposit (2003): no
Visitor Policies: all wk **Buggies:** 30

As if St. Andrews did not already offer an embarrassment of golf riches, in 1995 the Old Course Hotel unveiled this gem by Peter Thomson, the celebrated Aussie who won the British Open five times between 1952 and 1965.

Just two miles southwest of town (Hepburn Gardens road to Craigton Park), the Duke's occupies high ground affording excellent views over St. Andrews to the waters beyond and, on a clear day, off to Angus in the far distance. Usually billed as an alternative to links golf, the real beauty of the Duke's Course is that it is such a fine inland course in *proximity* to links golf. It's a rare combination. So, yes, the Duke's serves as an alternative to the St. Andrews links, but it happens to be an outstanding golf course worthy of play in its own right.

In expansiveness and length, as well as name and vintage, the Duke's may remind one of Jack Nicklaus's PGA Centenary (formerly Monarch's) Course at Gleneagles. But that's about as far as the comparison goes, for Peter Thomson's idea of course design contrasts sharply with that of the Golden Bear. While Nicklaus never met a water hazard or forced carry he didn't like, Thomson eschews both, giving the golfer every opportunity to play the game along the ground as well as in the air. While both designers offer big greens, Thomson opts for relatively flat spaces in contrast to Nicklaus's approach that announces, "no straight putts here." This is not to say the Duke's is without challenge. With eighty bunkers scattered about and several "wee burns" to negotiate, along with punishing rough, there's plenty here to keep one's attention. Moreover, at 7110 yards from the championship tees, this is Scotland's longest inland course. Most male visitors will play the course at 6749 yards or even the next step down at 6264 yards. As with most modern courses, there's a track here for every level of ability and strength.

To reiterate, the Duke's Course is owned and operated by the Old Course Hotel and is entirely independent of the Links Trust Management. Hotel residents receive priority treatment, but the course is rarely full up, so a visitor normally can secure a tee time with no problem. Another practical tip: this is a good course to play on Sunday when the Old Course is closed. As a daily fee course, it is easier to get on than many other courses in Fife.

53. Scotscraig Golf Club (1817) +

Region #: 1   **Category:** seaside links
Architect(s): Robert Simpson, James Braid (1904)
Length: 6303-6550   **SSS:** 72   **Par:** 71

Address: Golf Rd, Tayport, Fife DD6 9D2
Directions: E at Tay Bridge roundabout; to Tayport town centre; lft at signposted "golf course"

Reservations phone: 01382-552-515   **Fax:** 01382-553-130
Email: scotscraig@scottishgolf.com   **Website:** no
Booking Contact(s): Alison Harvey
Secretary: B D Liddle   **Professional:** S J Campbell
Phone - Starter/Pro shop: 01382-552-855
Fee(s) (2003): wkday £38, wkend £44 - up to 36 holes; jrs (18 & under) £8
Deposit (2003): £10
Visitor Policies: M-F 9:30-11:28; 2:30-4:00; Sat 10-11 am and Sun after 2:30 pm; Sunday - call
Buggies: 4 - general hire

For such a great golf course to be so ignored, the only conclusion one can reach about Scotscraig is that the club either does a poor job of marketing or they rather like being overlooked in Fife's flurry of golf flak. When looking for a course outside St. Andrews, visitors think automatically of Kingsbarns, Crail, Elie, Lundin Links, and Leven— all to the south. Rarely do they consider driving ten miles north to

Tayport, just off the A919, on the Fife side of the Tay Bridge. That's their mistake. This is one of the best in Fife or anywhere else.

Admittedly, Tayport is not one of Scotland's beauty spots. It's a working man's bedroom community for Dundee and a bit on the "other side of the tracks"—though in this case we're talking about the other side of the firth. Well, so be it. Once there, you'll experience the challenge of an Open Qualifying Course some people judge as demanding as Carnoustie. It's a seaside links with views of the firth, though the water does not come into play. This is the home of one of Scotland's oldest golf clubs (1817) and a friendly place it is. An original nine holes were laid out by Carnoustie professional Robert Simpson. The course was extended to eighteen holes by James Braid in 1904—plenty of pedigree here and plenty of good golf. If not on my list of Scotland's top twenty seaside courses, it's close—in a group with the likes of Leven Links, Elie, Tain, The Glen, Powfoot, and Gullane #1. Scotscraig is a relatively good bargain, and its low deposit requirement makes it a good choice for booking as an optional course when trying to get on St. Andrews' Old Course in the daily ballot.

54. Southerness Golf Club (1947)

Region #: 9   **Category:** seaside links
Architect(s): Mackenzie Ross (1947)
Length: 6105-6564   **SSS:** 70-73   **Par:** 69

Address: Southerness, Dumfries DG2 8AZ
Directions: 3 mi S of Kirkbean off A710

Reservations phone: 01387-880-677   **Fax:** 01387-880-644
Email: bookings@southernessgc.sol.co.uk
Website: southernessgolfclub.com
Booking Contact(s): secretary
Secretary: I A Robin   **Professional:** none
Fee(s) (2003): wkday £38; wkend £48 - unlimited play
Deposit (2003): £10 UK residents; foreign visitors, none
Visitor Policies: M-F 10-12, 2-4, wkend 10-11:30, 2:30-4
Buggies: no

Travelers heading northward out of England on their way to the Ayrshire coast have a unique opportunity to stop along the way to play one of Scotland's finest linksland courses. For a combination of bargain golf and links challenge, there is none better.

But let's back up to get our bearings. On its approach to Scotland, England's M6 becomes the A74. Just inside the Scottish border at Gretna, the A75 branches westward twenty-five miles to Dumfries. Dumfries is a large town of considerable interest and good accommodations. That's the place to stop for a rendezvous with Southerness, situated on the coast of the Solway Firth just fifteen miles south of town.

In this location, quite remote from the centers of Scottish golf, you'll find a course consistently ranked among the top twenty in Scotland. Some put Southerness comfortably in their top ten. Case in point: in the fall of 1999 I had the pleasure of playing a round of golf at Royal Dornoch with Neil Stott, a Southerness club member making his annual pilgrimage to that great course in the far north. Somewhere mid-round, in response to my complaints about Dornoch's "tricks" and tortuous greens, Neil said, "You ought to come down and play Southerness. It's tougher than this course but it's more fair. I think it's a better course."

So I did. And I can testify that Neil was right on at least one count; Southerness is even tougher than Dornoch. Whether it's better or not is in the eye of the beholder. At about 6600 yards, Southerness plays more like 7000 due to the absence of par 5s (only two) and the presence of five par 3s. That leaves eleven two-shotters—virtually all 400+ yards. Note that SSS here is 73 against a par of 69. That's about as big a gap as you are likely to find in Scottish golf, rivaling Carnoustie's gap from the championship "Tiger" tees. And, yet, I found Southerness eminently fair. All the elements of links golf are present, but nothing is hidden from view. It's all in front of you and— surrounded by pastureland, the Solway Firth, and distant hills—it's all a visual treat. The only problem: average golfers will be hitting drivers and fairway woods most of the day on the long two-shotters and that gets a bit old.

The architect responsible for this southern gem was Mackenzie Ross, who resurrected Turnberry from its role as an air landing strip after World War II. Ross came to Southerness in 1947 to create what Malcolm Campbell has called, "arguably the only truly championship-standard seaside links to have been built on the British mainland since the Second World War." Though we may now need to make room for Kingsbarns and The Devlin in that assessment, Campbell's words are an extraordinary endorsement of a great golf course.

Nongolf activities: This is a pretty town where Robert Burns died in 1796 and his wife, Jean Amour, lived until 1834. Burns and his wife are buried in St. Michael's churchyard in central Dumfries. Arbigland Gardens can be found at nearby Kippford and only one mile from Southerness you can see the birthplace of John Paul Jones—an American revolutionary war hero widely regarded as a traitor in Britain. Lockerbie, site of the infamous Pan Am bombing, is just twelve miles northeast of Dumfries and well worth a visit. A moving memorial, "Garden of Remembrance," is located in a cemetery on the A709 at the edge of town.

55. Stonehaven Golf Club (1888)

Region #: 6   **Category:** seaside links
Architect(s): Artie Simpson (1897)
Length: 4804-5103   **SSS:** 65   **Par:** 67

Address: Cowie, Stonehaven AB39 3RH
Directions: 1 mi N of Stonehaven off A92

Reservations phone: 01569-762-124   **Fax:** 01569-765-973
Email: stonehaven.golfclub@virgin.net
Website: stonehavengolfclub.co.uk
Secretary: W A Donald   **Professional:** no
Fee(s) (2003): wkday £15, day tkt £20; Sun £22, day tkt £25
Deposit (2003): no
Visitor Policies: M-F anytime; wkend - call   **Buggies:** no

Located about fifty miles north of Carnoustie and fifteen miles south of Aberdeen, the golf course at Stonehaven, by any measure (4800-5100 yards), is not much more than an "executive" course. It is the shortest course included in this directory. Yet, Stonehaven is here because those 5100 yards pack quite a wallop perched atop perhaps the most dramatic seascape in Scottish golf.

Sited between the scenic coastal rail line and the sea, on steep cliffs above the North Sea, Stonehaven is also among the most exposed of courses to occasionally brutal winds and weather. A nasty day of wind and rain can make this course virtually unplayable. But a calm day will leave the golfer with nothing less than a golden memory of golf in an unforgettable location. In either case you'll be surprised to discover how challenging a short course can be.

Stonehaven town is an historic fishing village boasting population of about 10,000 hardy souls. It's a good place to poke around a bit after a stop for lunch in the attractive town centre. Another reason to put Stonehaven on the itinerary: a mile or so south of town are the ruins and remains of Dunnotter Castle—like the golf course, perched dramatically atop a broad escarpment overlooking the sea. Dunnotter was used as the setting in Franco Zefferelli's treatment of *Hamlet* starring Mel Gibson.

My advice on Stonehaven: Make it a half-day stopover between points south and points north. With a ticket price of £15 in 2003, as golf writer Bob Kroeger says, "Stonehaven is one of the most overlooked scenic bargains in Scotland."

56. Stranraer Golf Club (1905)

Region #: 9   **Category:** parkland (seaside)
Architect(s): James Braid (1950)
Length: 6056-6308   **SSS:** 72   **Par:** 70

Address: Creachmore, Leswalt, Stranraer DG9 0LF
Directions: 3 mi NW of Stranraer on A718

Reservations phone: 01776-870-245   **Fax:** 01776-870-445
Email: no   **Website:** stranraergolfclub.net
Booking Contact(s): secretary
Secretary: Bryce C Kelly   **Professional:** no
Fee(s) (2003): wkday £24, day tkt £34; wkend £28, day tkt £40
Deposit (2003): £5
Visitor Policies: all wk; members only to 9:30 am & b/w 12:30 - 1:30
Buggies: 3 - general hire

Among the quartet of southern courses featured in this book—Stranraer, Portpatrick, Southerness, and Powfoot—Stranraer is the first in line along the coastal route southward from Turnberry (just 40 miles on the A77). Stranraer is a ferry town (to Belfast and Larne, Northern Ireland) and is also on the rail line from Glasgow.

Stranraer sits near the shores of Loch Ryan, an inlet from the North Channel, at the neck of the anvil-shaped peninsula called the "Rhinns of Galloway." In this location, far from the golf Meccas to the north, James Braid created another fine golf course with a typically unusual combination of holes—this time only one par 5 and three par 3s. At 6308 yards, you can imagine the length and difficulty of the remaining fourteen two-shotters! It was James Braid's last creation before he died in 1950 (Stranraer Golf Club was formed in 1905, but the original course was abandoned when it became a military post during World War II). Though seaside, Stranraer is a parkland course. Several holes skirt the shoreline, but the rest of the course is inland.

So, why visit Stranraer? First, it's an excellent course. Second, at £24 weekday it's one of the relatively few bargains left in top-tier Scottish golf. Third, getting there is half the fun. Fourth, if you're coming to Scotland from England, heading for the Ayrshire coast, it's not much out of the way at all. Fifth, at the new clubhouse you'll experience a particularly warm Scottish welcome; they don't see a lot of North American visitors here, so your presence will be noticed and appreciated. Need more reasons? I would add the attractions of southern Scotland. This is Clan Kennedy country and near Stranraer you'll find the magnificent 75-acre Kennedy Castle Gardens—among the most famous in Scotland and a great nongolf combination with a round at Stranraer.

See also: Portpatrick, Powfoot, and Southerness.

57. Tain Golf Club (1890)

Region #: 5   **Category:** seaside links, no views
Architect(s): Tom Morris
Length: 6109-6404   **SSS:** 71   **Par:** 70

Address: Tain, Ross-shire IV19 1PA
Directions: well signposted from ctr of town
Reservations phone: 01862-892-314   **Fax:** 01862-892-099
Email: tgc@cali.co.uk   **Website:** mywebaddress.net/taingolfclub
Booking Contact(s): admin secretary
Admin Secretary: Mrs. Kathleen D Ross   **Professional:** none
Phone - Starter/Pro shop: 01862-892-314
Fee(s) (2003): wkday £33, day tkt £40; wkend £40, day tkt £50
Deposit (2003): 20%

Visitor Policies: wkend after 11:30 am
Buggies: 4 - general hire

Golf writer Jim Finegan describes Tain as "golf in a minor key," and that says it about as well as it can be said. Tain simply lacks the grandeur of setting that belongs to its near neighbor Royal Dornoch. Thus it will always be played in the shadow of that magnificent course.

Having said that, let me quickly go on to say that for many reasons Tain, in its minor key, is one of the most unusual and enjoyable courses in the entire country. It's a Tom Morris layout, so it comes replete with penal bunkers, green-fronting swales, a few blind shots, and several difficult and imaginative one-shotters. The first hole alone is worth the price of admission: from the first tee it looks straightforward enough, but, out in the fairway, you realize you are about to make a blind second shot over a public byway *and* a fence to a tucked away, smallish green. Welcome to quirky Tain! Most of the front nine humps and bumps along *in extremis* before the ground smoothes out a bit on the inward nine. "Alps," a two-shotter (#11), is reminiscent of Carnoustie's "Spectacles" and two superb par 3s over a burn at #16 and #17 bring the round to an unusual and interesting close. The home hole is plain vanilla made venturesome only by the proximity of the green to the plate-glass windows of the attractive clubhouse built in 1998. Inside the clubhouse, the food is good and the staff is friendly and welcoming to visitors.

For some reason, a lot of pesky black flies inhabit Tain. In calm weather they can be annoying. You can hope for a stiff Scottish breeze. And one final note on the setting of Tain Golf Club: Tain is a small town so you'll have no problem finding the golf course (as usual, just drive toward the sea). On Golf Road, a one-lane track leading to the clubhouse, you'll drive the length of a striking gothic cemetery and, if you're a golfer, you can't help but think, "Here lies the ultimate 19th hole." I guarantee the setting of Tain Golf Club will leave an indelible imprint on your mind.

58. Turnberry Hotel – Ailsa Course *

Region #: 2   **Category:** seaside links
Architect(s): Mackenzie Ross (1946-51)
Length: 6440-6976   **SSS:** 72   **Par:** 69-70

Address: Turnberry, Ayrshire KA26 9LT
Directions: 5 mi N of Girvan on A77

Reservations phone: 01655-334-135; main desk #01655-331-000
Fax: 01655-331-152
Email: turnberry.reservations@westin.com   **Website:** turnberry.co.uk
Booking Contact(s): reservations office for hotel and courses
Director of Golf: Paul Burley; 01655-334-300
Phone - Starter/Pro shop: 01655-334-043
Fee(s) (2003): hotel res £105 all wk; non-res £130 wkday; £175 wkend
Deposit (2003): none
Visitor Policies: all wk; hotel residents have priority; non-res may book 2 wks prior to date of play;
Buggies: no; caddies only; no pullcarts (carry or be caddied)
Other: companion course, the Kintyre (formerly Arran), redesigned by Donald Steel, opened 2001

I'd love to wax poetic about Turnberry's incomparable location in South Ayrshire, for this is Robert Burns's romantic countryside where the Ayrshire coastal plain gives way to the rolling, green hills of Galloway. Above it all, the Turnberry Hotel sits on a majestic bluff overlooking an expansive seascape encompassing two golf courses and views to the Isle of Arran, the Kintyre Peninsula, and, on a clear day, Ireland on the far-off southwest horizon. Ten miles offshore, the Ailsa Craig—a tortoise-shaped volcanic rock (1208 feet high)—anchors the scene with primeval certitude. Here we have Scotland's premier seaside resort—indeed, one of the world's premier seaside resorts.

But this is a practical book. Travelers want to have less poetic information—like, "Do you have to stay at the hotel to play the golf course?" and, "If you stay at the hotel, how much does it cost?".

OK. *Do you have to stay at the hotel to play the golf course?* Technically, NO. A single golfer or even a twosome can usually get onto the Ailsa Course, even in high season, without staying at the hotel. The way to do that is to request a tee time with the Director of Golf two weeks prior to the desired date of play. Alternatively, one might simply call the course when in the area to determine if a tee time is available. The custom at Turnberry is to put twos and threes off early, the better to speed play and leave the meat of the day to foursomes. Thus, open slots *are* available to free-lancing golfers. For a group of three or more golfers, as a practical matter, the hotel is so "full up" between April and October that, to secure a round of golf, residency at the hotel is advisable. Nevertheless, even a foursome can sometimes get lucky.

How much does it cost to stay at the hotel? That's the stopper for most people. Frankly, when most of my clients learn what it costs to stay at the hotel, the normal response is, "Well, let's check that one off the list." Here's the damage, circa 2003: £375 ($580) per night, double occupancy, plus £105 for golf on the Ailsa. That's a hotel-golf experience of about $450 per person, per day. Which is not to say there aren't package deals you can buy into. But, is Turnberry worth the cost at whatever price? Only you can decide.

Like the great hotels of the Canadian Rockies, Turnberry Hotel was a product of the golden age of rail transportation. Built in 1907, it was owned and operated by a railroad company as a destination resort. Sitting atop the great bluff overlooking the linksland, with its russet roof and white façade, the building looks as if it might have been transferred wholesale from colonial America—maybe George Washington's Mt. Vernon on steroids. Edwardian or neo-colonial, in either case it's a classic—timeless in its appeal, yet a monument to times gone by. One can only hope it will continue giving visual pleasure and physical comfort for centuries to come.

The history of golf at Turnberry falls into two distinct periods: the War Years and the Post-War Years. Britain's engagement in the twentieth century's two world wars wreaked havoc at Turnberry. Twice within thirty years, the linksland was commandeered as an airstrip by the Royal Air Force. After World War I, James Braid and C.K. Hutchinson were hired to reconstruct the golf courses (Ailsa and Arran). With the coming of World War II, land was bulldozed and runways were built (fortunately, most of the damage was done a bit inland below the hotel, away from the seaside linksland). By 1945, Turnberry was as exhausted as the British nation.

Into this breach stepped a determined hotel director, Frank Hole, who would not allow his parent company to abandon the golf courses at Turnberry. Hole persevered and ultimately contracted with Mackenzie Ross to design a new course. Work began in 1946 and continued over a period of five years. When it was done, Ross had achieved a course widely recognized as a classic of championship quality equal to its setting—the first such course built in Scotland in many years and the first of the post-war period (ultimately, the only twentieth-century course included on the "rota" of the British Open). Tournament golf found its way to Turnberry immediately, culminating, first, in its hosting of the Walker Cup in 1963, then in its designation in 1977 by the Royal and Ancient as the newest venue for the British Open. Turnberry arrived on the international golf scene as the stage for one of the two or three most dramatic tournaments in Open history—the famous "Duel in the Sun" between Tom Watson (the winner by one stroke) and Jack Nicklaus. In a literate introduction to one of the best "stroke savers" in Scottish golf (a hole-by-hole guide to the course), architect Donald Steel tells the Turnberry story:

> Turnberry's graduation to the envied ranks of host to the Open championship was a dream in every sense. When, at last, the ultimate accolade was conferred upon the incomparable Ailsa course in 1977, it inspired one of the most memorable weeks in the long history of championship golf.
>
> It was a week dominated by Tom Watson and Jack Nicklaus, the supreme players at the time; it was a week when the record books were rewritten, a week when the sun shone. As Watson and Nicklaus discovered, there are few more inspiring places to play golf than Turnberry, a true delight with spectacular ocean holes and views not exceeded anywhere.
>
> Polls now regularly acknowledge the Ailsa as one of Britain's top three courses, confirmation that gives it eminence worldwide. Together with a handsome new clubhouse and a magnificent new spa to augment the splendours of the hotel, its facilities are second to none.

Since 1977, Turnberry has hosted two additional Opens—in 1986 (won by Greg Norman) and in 1994 (won by Nick Price). Interesting, isn't it, how these Scottish tracks seem to bring the cream to the top! With the Open at Troon in 2004, my guess is that we'll see Turnberry as the host again in 2007. And how fitting that would be—the centenary of the hotel and the fortieth anniversary of "The Duel in the Sun" and Turnberry's status as an Open venue.

A few notes on the Ailsa course: This is certainly one of the two or three most beautiful seaside courses in Scotland. Turnberry does not have the dramatic, towering dunes of Cruden Bay or the elevation changes of Dornoch. There's some of that, but the feeling here is more similar to Muirfield's in its expansive layout, rolling terrain, and wispy, waving grasses. But it's "Muirfield with a view." Hole #s 4 through 11 play along the water in Scotland's finest stretch of sustained seaside golf—first, tacking leftward along Turnberry Bay to the promontory where the famous #9 tee is perched; then cutting ninety degrees to the right past Turnberry's landmark lighthouse.

These magnificent seaside holes are bracketed by superb inland combinations of (1) three parallel opening holes (par 4s of varying length) and (2) seven closing holes that feature imaginative changes of direction, length, and variety. There is simply no weak link here—all told, some of the most memorable holes in Scottish golf.

Now what do you think about forking over the money for Turnberry? It's not an easy decision, but remember that classic bumper sticker: "We're not extravagant. We're just spending our kids' inheritance."

59. Western Gailes Golf Club (1897) +

Region #: 2   **Category:** seaside links
Architect(s): Willie Parks, Sr. and Jr., Fred Hawtree (1975 - north end)
Length: 6179 - 6639   **SSS:** 73   **Par:** 71

Address: Gailes, Irvine KA11 5AE
Directions: 8 mi N of Troon off A78 (2 mi S of Irvine)

Reservations phone: 01294-311-649   **Fax:** 01294-312-312
Email: enquiries@westerngailes.com   **Website:** westerngailes.com
Booking Contact(s): Lyn Scott
Secretary: David Lithgow   **Professional:** no
Phone - Starter/Pro shop: call reservations #
Fee(s) (2003): £90 wkday, £125 day tkt (includes buffet lunch M, W, F); Sunday £90, no day tkt
Deposit (2003): £45 non-refundable   **Buggies:** no
Visitor Policies: M, W, F only 9-12; 2-3:50; call for Sunday play

With the courses at Kingsbarns, Nairn, Cruden Bay, and Royal Dornoch, Western Gailes in recent years has formed a sort of second tier of elite courses increasingly familiar, at least by reputation, to prospective golf tourists to Scotland. This is due largely to its presence on some package tours and then the word-of-mouth buzz that follows such experiences. Certainly, if price is a measure of self-worth, Western Gailes has put itself in the company of Carnoustie and Prestwick and only a notch below St. Andrews' Old Course.

Is the reputation and price of Western Gailes justified relative to the rest of Scottish golf? In a word, yes. This is among Scotland's finest linkslands. It's in my personal Top Five list along with Cruden Bay, Machrie, Machrihanish, and North Berwick. That's a list that has as much to do with location, cost, accessibility, and clubhouse ambience as with the golf courses themselves. I like this northern part of the Ayrshire coast and, though Western is not in the bargain category, it's a uniquely satisfying place.

The great draw at Western Gailes, as at Cruden Bay, is the extraordinarily convoluted links terrain and the powerful challenge of golf on a characteristically windy venue. Here, a kaleidoscope of sandhills, hillocks, humps, bumps, depressions, marram grass, gorse, and heather present an ever-changing visual treat and persistent challenge to the shotmaker. Holes #5 through #13 play along the coast—one of the longest stretches of seaside play in Scottish golf. And it is here that the gales common to Gailes come so frequently into play, for this is a course fully exposed to the prevailing winds (just as Royal Troon is down the road). And, though the visitor tees play to only about 6200 yards, these middle holes can often make you feel like you're grappling with a 7000-yard monster. Certainly, the average golfer will be adequately challenged from the yellow tees; if you are allowed to play from the white tees (unlikely, but ask), you'll fully understand why Western Gailes is used as a qualifying course when the Open is held at Royal Troon or Turnberry.

Western Gailes sits on a narrow strip of land between the coastal rail line and the sea. The course is two fairways wide—at first glance, a classic out-and-back links. The difference at Western is the position of its elegant whitewashed clubhouse. Rather than residing at one end of an out-and-back chain of holes, this clubhouse sits on high ground nearly at mid-point in the chain. Thus, the routing is a racetrack loop—off to the first turn (#1 to #5), down the backstretch (to #13), then on to the wire (#14 through #18). Just as at a racetrack, the Gailes clubhouse looks out over the finish line. There's no stopping at the ninth hole; that's way off on the other side of the track!

Now, with the opening (in 2003) of Southern Gailes just to the east of Western and adjacent to Glasgow Gailes, there's a powerful attraction to spend a full day playing golf at the Gailes. Certainly, any combination of these three courses makes for one of the strongest one-two punches in Scottish golf

See also: Glasgow Gailes, Irvine, Kilmarnock, and Royal Troon.

60. Whitekirk Golf Club (1995)

Region #: 3   **Category:** parkland
Architect(s): Cameron Sinclair
Length: 6225-6526   **SSS:** 72   **Par:** 72

Address: Whitekirk nr N Berwick, E Lothian EH395PR
Directions: 5 mi SE of N Berwick off A198

Reservations phone: 01620-870-300   **Fax:** 01620-870-330
Email: countryclub@whitekirk.com   **Website:** whitekirk.com
Booking Contact(s): David Brodie, mgr **Professional:** Paul Wardell
Fee(s) (2003): wkday £20, day tkt £30; wkend £30, day tkt £45; jrs (17 and under) - 50%
Deposit (2003): £10
Visitor Policies: all wk   **Buggies:** 10 - general hire

Surrounded by rolling farmland, Whitekirk is perched on and around a high, graceful hill that dominates the terrain near Whitekirk hamlet midway between North Berwick and Dunbar. This place reminds me of the movie *Field of Dreams:* "Build it and they will come." Landowner-developer George Tuer built it in 1995 and they are coming, though not in anything like the numbers Kingsbarns has been able to ring up in Fife.

Americans will feel right at home at Whitekirk. Visitors are welcome at all times. Indeed, the whole idea of Whitekirk is visitor appeal. To that end, the facility features a comfortable, classy club-house where, as the Whitekirk brochure says, you'll find "good food at reasonable prices in a warm and friendly atmosphere." Outside about a dozen golf carts are lined up just like at home (actually this is an up-and-down course where a buggy will be appreciated by many) and a 300-yard, American-style practice range encourages a proper warm-up (a rarity in Scottish golf). Near the parking lot, a large sign announces impending construction of a thirty-room hotel to accommodate golfers. Even a couple of shuttle vans are parked, ready to ferry golfers to and from Edinburgh.

So, the folks at Whitekirk have not missed a beat when it comes to marketing. Furthermore, the course itself happens to be a worthy addition to Scottish golf. A young Scottish designer, Cameron Sinclair, did the work here and he did a good job of it. Four sets of tees accommodate golfers of all abilities. Strong par 3s and several long par 4s put a lot of starch in this golf experience. Elevated teeing grounds provide outstanding views over the rolling Lothian countryside—to nearby Tantallon Castle and out to the sea five miles away. Of course, Whitekirk does not and will not compete with the historic courses of the Lothians for the affections of the visiting golfer. It will be on the "optional play list" for a long time to come. On the other hand, if Mr. Tuer would add about five hundred yards to the course and quadruple his green fee, he might have a "championship course" on his hands. Such are the vagaries of golf snobbery. In the meantime, give me Whitekirk just as it is. It's fine and it's one of the best bargains in Scottish golf.

Most Frequently-Called Reservations Telephone Numbers

From outside the United Kingdom, dial 011-44, then the following:

Brora 1408-621-417
Carnoustie 1241-853-789
Crail Golfing Society 1333-450-686
Cruden Bay 1779-812-285
Dunbar 1368-862-317
Gleneagles 1764-694-469
Golf House Club - Elie 1333-330-301
Kingsbarns 1334-460-861
Leven Links 1333-428-859
Lundin Links 1333-320-202
Montrose 1674-672-932
Nairn 1667-453-208
North Berwick 1620-892-135
Prestwick 1292-671-020
Royal Aberdeen 1224-702-571
Royal Dornoch 1862-810-219
Royal Troon 1292-311-555
St. Andrews Bay 1334-837-412
St. Andrews Links Management 1334-466-666
Scotscraig 1382-552-515
Turnberry 1655-334-135
Western Gailes 1294-311-649

NOTES

NOTES

APPENDICES

APPENDIX A

Golf-Readiness Checklist

☐ A hooded, lightweight bag

☐ Golf balls: at least 3 per round - or buy them there

☐ Tees; divot repair tool; ball markers

☐ Two pairs of shoes (metal spikes are ok)   ☐ or galoshes

☐ Hat (preferably waterproof)   ☐ stocking cap or earmuffs

☐ Umbrella

☐ Waterproof rain suit   ☐ Windbreaker

☐ Sweater(s) (dress in layers)

☐ Two towels and/or washcloths (for cleaning ball, glasses in the rain)

☐ Waterproof gloves (yes, even in summer it can get cold)

☐ Sunscreen

☐ First-aid kit: tape/bandaids/ibuprofen or aspirin/lanolin

☐ Water bottle (there won't be any drinking water on most courses)

☐ Ziploc bags (to keep food, etc., separated/dry)

☐ One or two 2 to 3-foot bungee cords (to secure bag to pull trolley)

☐ USGA handicap card

☐ Allan Ferguson's *Golf in Scotland*

APPENDIX B

Useful Internet Sites

Following is a list of web sites of general interest and of many accommodations mentioned in the text. Sites of individual golf courses can be found in *Part III, The Directory of Courses.*

General Interest
aboutscotland.com - general
activity-scotland.co.uk - hiking, biking, other
bta.org.uk - British Tourist Authority
btb-books.com - British Travel Book & Map Shop
electricscotland.com - general
islaywhiskysociety.com
news.bbc.co.uk - British Broadcasting Co.
nationalgalleries.org - National Galleries of Scotland
nms.ac.uk - National Museums of Scotland
nts.org.uk - National Trust for Scotland
ramblers.org.uk - hiking
scotch-whisky.org.uk - Scotch Whisky Society
scotland-info.co.uk - general
scotsman.com - Edinburgh, national newspaper
visitscotland.net - Scottish Tourist Board (STB)

Transportation and Communication
acfinance.com/rental - Arnold Clark rental cars
ba.com - British Airways *(other airlines - see, p. 74)*
britrail.com - rail transportation
calmac.co.uk - Caledonian-MacBrayne ferries
inter800.com - toll-free telephone numbers
multimap.com - online mapping service
rental-cars-scotland.com - Celtic Legend/Arnold Clark rentals
rental car companies - see p. 79
scotrail.co.uk - rail transportation

Scottish Golf
golfeastlothian.com - regional promotion
golfhighland.com - regional promotion

opengolf.com - official site of the British Open
randa.org - The Royal and Ancient Golf Club
scottishgolf.com - Scottish Golf Union
scottishgolfsociety.com - Scottish Golf Society
teetimescotland.com - internet booking
thebraidsociety.com - James Braid Golfing Society
uk-golfguide.com - course directory; accommodations; links; info bulletin boards

Fife and St. Andrews
eastneukwide.co.uk - East Neuk Promotional Group
eatingoutinfife.co.uk - Fife restaurants
fifeguide.co.uk - Fife Tourist Council
oldcourse-experience.com - The Old Course Experience
st-andrews.ac.uk - University of St. Andrews
standrews.org.uk - St. Andrews Links Management
standrews.co.uk - Royal Burgh of St. Andrews
saint-andrews.co.uk - Town Council

Other Towns and Regions
boatofgarten.com - Boat of Garten
gael-net.co.uk - West Highlands
girvan-online.net - Girvan (nr Turnberry)
granite-city.com - Aberdeen
highlandescape.com - Highlands
host.co.uk - Highlands
isle-of-islay.com - Isle of Islay
north-berwick.co.uk - North Berwick
pitlochry.org.uk - Pitlochry, incl Festival Theatre
pitlochryhospitality.co.uk - Pitlochry
scotland-inverness.co.uk - Inverness
visitdornoch.com - Dornoch
visit-islay.com - Isle of Islay

Lodging - general
2stay.com - private promotional service
hotels-scotland.co.uk - private promotional service
scotlandsbestbandbs.co.uk - B & Bs promotional service
smoothhound.co.uk - private promotional service
theaa.com - UK Automobile Association
uk.hotel.net - private promotional service
visitscotland.net - Scottish Tourist Board

Lodging - Region #1 (Fife)
aboutscotland.com/fife/queensterrace - Jill Hardie B & B, St. Andrews
ardgowanhotel.co.uk - St. Andrews

aslar.com - Aslar House, B & B, St. Andrews
balbirnie.co.uk - nr Glenrothes
balgeddiehouse.co.uk - nr Glenrothes
bestwestern.com - Scores Hotel, St. Andrews
dunvegan-hotel.com - St. Andrews
eden-group.com - Eden House Hotel, Cupar
macdonaldhotels.co.uk - Rusacks, St. Andrews
hazelbank.com - St. Andrews
oldcoursehotel.co.uk - St. Andrews
oldmanorhotel.co.uk - Lundin Links
lundin-links-hotel.co.uk - Largo/Lundin
rufflets.co.uk - St. Andrews
russellhotelstandrews.co.uk - St. Andrews
standrewsbandbs.com - private association of B & Bs
standrewsalbany.co.uk - Albany Hotel, St. Andrews
standrewsbay.com - St. Andrews Bay Resort Hotel
standrews-golf.co.uk - St. Andrews Golf Hotel, St. Andrews
st-andrews-golf-lodge.com - St. Andrews Golfing Lodge, St. Andrews
stayinstandrews.co.uk - local promotional association
thehazelton.co.uk - The Hazelton B & B, Crail
theinn.co.uk - Inn at Lathones, nr St. Andrews
theinnonnorthstreet.com - The Inn on North Street, St. Andrews

Lodging - Region #2 (Ayrshire)
costley-hotels.co.uk - Lochgreen House, Highgrove House, Troon
paramounthotels.co.uk - Marine Hotel, Troon
parkstonehotel.co.uk - Parkstone Hotel, Prestwick
piersland.co.uk - Piersland House Hotel, Troon
southbeach.co.uk - South Beach Hotel, Troon
theanchorage-hotel.com - Anchorage Hotel, Troon
turnberry.co.uk - Turnberry Hotel

Lodging - Region #3 (E. Lothian)
aboutscotland.com/glebe/house - Glebe House, North Berwick
belhavenhotel.co.uk - North Berwick
golfinn.co.uk - Gullane
greywalls.co.uk - Gullane
hopefieldhouse.co.uk - Gullane
macdonaldhotels.co.uk - Marine Hotel, North Berwick

Lodging - Region #4 (Angus)
carnoustie-hotel.com - Carnoustie Golf Course Hotel & Resort
carlogie-house-hotel.com - Carnoustie
letham-grange.co.uk - nr Arbroath

Lodging - Region #5 (Inverness/Dornoch)
ballifhotel.btinternet.co.uk - Ballifeary House B & B, Inverness
carnegieclub.co.uk - Skibo Castle, Dornoch
cullodenhouse.co.uk - nr Inverness
dornochcastlehotel.com - Dornoch
dunainparkhotel.co.uk - nr Inverness
highfieldhouse.co.uk - Dornoch B & B
golf-view.co.uk - Tain
invernessbedandbreakfast.co.uk - Inverness Assoc. of B & Bs
linkshotel.co.uk - Nairn
lyndale.dircon.co.uk/guest - Lyndale Guest House, Inverness
mansfield-house.co.uk - Tain
morangiehotel.com - Tain
morton-hotels.com - Royal Golf Hotel, Dornoch; Newton Hotel, Golf View - Nairn
moyness.co.uk - Moyness House B & B, Inverness

Lodging - Region #6 (North/Northeast)
macdonaldhotels.co.uk - Ardoe House, Aberdeen
marcliffe.com - Marcliffe at Pitfodels, Aberdeen
udny.co.uk - Udny Arms, Newburgh
redhousehotel.com - Cruden Bay

Lodging - Region #7 (Perthshire/Central)
dunmurray.co.uk - Dunmurray B & B, Pitlochry
gleneagles.com - Gleneagles Resort Hotel
moulin.u-net.com - Moulin Hotel, Pitlochry

Lodging - Region #8 (Kintyre/Islay)
bridgend-hotel.com - Bridgend Hotel, Islay
craigard-house.co.uk - Campbeltown
glenmachrie.com - Glenmachrie B & B, Islay
machrie.com - Machrie Hotel & Golf Club nr Port Ellen
thehuntinglodgehotel.com - The Hunting Lodge, nr Machrihanish, Kintyre

APPENDIX C

Tourist Information Offices

Aberdeen
St. Nicholas House
Broad Street
01224-620-415

Arbroath (nr Carnoustie)
Market Place
01241-872-609

Ayr (nr Troon-Prestwick)
Burns Statue Square
01292-288-688

Edinburgh
Waverly Market
Princes Street
0131-557-1700

Girvan (nr Turnberry)
Bridge Street
01465-714-950

Glasgow
35 St. Vincent Place
0141-204-4400

Inverness
23 Church Street
01463-234-353

North Berwick
1 Quality Street
01620-892-197

Pitlochry
22 Atholl Road
01796-472-215

St. Andrews
70 Market Street
01334-472-021

Airport Information
Aberdeen 01224-722-2331
Edinburgh 0131-333-1000
Glasgow 0141-887-1111
Inverness 01667-464-000

APPENDIX D

Daylight Hours, April - October

(All dates 2003 - Glasgow; daylight-saving time observed throughout)

Date	Sunrise	Sunset
April 1	6:49 a.m.	7:54 p.m.
April 15	6:13 a.m.	8:22 p.m.
May 1	5:35 a.m.	8:55 p.m.
May 15	5:06 a.m.	9:22 p.m.
June 1	4:41 a.m.	9:50 p.m.
June 15	4:31 a.m.	10:04 p.m.
July 1	4:36 a.m.	10:05 p.m.
July 15	4:52 a.m.	9:53 p.m.
August 1	5:21 a.m.	9:25 p.m.
August 15	5:47 a.m.	8:54 p.m.
September 1	6:20 a.m.	8:12 p.m.
September 15	6:48 a.m.	7:36 p.m.
October 1	7:19 a.m.	6:54 p.m.
October 15	7:47 a.m.	6:18 p.m.

APPENDIX E

Annotated Bibliography

General

Begley, Eve. *Of Scottish Ways.* Minneapolis: Dillon Press, 1977. A chatty overview of Scots history and socio-political culture for the layman.

Blundell, Nigel. *Scotland.* London: PRC Publishing, Ltd., 1998. A big, beautiful coffee table book with the requisite fabulous pictures, but without fear of substantive history or literature. A chapter on single-malt whiskies is first-rate.

Fisher, Andrew. *A Traveller's History of Scotland.* Gloucestershire UK: The Windrush Press, 1990. Weak on twentieth century, but otherwise thorough review of Scottish history from Roman times.

Fraser, Elisabeth. *An Illustrated History of Scotland.* Norwich UK: Jarrold Publishing, 1997. Lives up to its title; lavishly illustrated and well-written. In a word, excellent.

Herman, Arthur. *How the Scots Invented the Modern World.* New York: Crown Publishers, 2001. The subtitle of this book is "The True Story of How Western Europe's Poorest Nation Created Our World & Everything In It." The publisher may be guilty of hyperbole, but that does not diminish the value of this impressive work. The focus is on the 18th century's vibrant Scottish Enlightenment. A "must" for students of Scotland's intellectual history.

Tranter, Nigel. *The Story of Scotland.* Moffat, Scotland: Lochar Publishing, 1987. The author tries to avoid the catalog approach to history but, frankly, with Scots history that's a tough assignment. Tranter has written dozens of books about Scotland, both fiction and non-fiction.

Fiction: Catherine Coulter, Antonia Fraser, Diana Gabaldon, Margaret George, Neil Gunn, Margot Livesey, Jenifer Roberson, Sir Walter Scott, Jessica Stirling, Nigel Tranter.

243

Guidebooks

Baxter, John, et. al. *Scotland: Highlands and Islands.* Lincolnwood, IL: Passport Books, 1997. Excellent for detailed planning. Divides the Highlands into eight regions and highlights with photographs, maps, and sidebars. A focus on walks will please hikers.

McNeeley, Scott, ed. *Fodor's Scotland.* NY: Random House (Fodor's Travel Publications), revised periodically. The usual Fodor stew including chapters on history and golf. Regional presentation with tour recommendations; two chapters dedicated specifically to Edinburgh and Glasgow. A good index and two dozen stylized maps are helpful. Fodor's is fine, but food/lodging choices are limited in the extreme.

Ramsay, Alex. *Scotland.* London: HarperCollins, 1996. Beautifully-produced paper volume (112pp) features the author's photography. Eleven chapters focus on the regions of Scotland plus Edinburgh and Glasgow. Good maps with evocative text highlight features/attractions of each region.

Smallman, Tom, and Cornwallis, Graeme. *Scotland.* Melbourne, Australia: Lonely Planet Publications, 1999. The best of the general guide-books—packed with useful and esoteric information. Major weakness: Lonely Planet's aggravating habit of citing lodging/restaurants at opposite poles on the expense spectrum. Best combined with a good specialty book on accommodations.

Williams, David. *Scotland's Best-Loved Driving Tours.* NY: Macmillan Travel, 1996. Part of a Frommer series produced by the Automobile Association and updated periodically. Twenty-five itineraries are organized under four broad geographic headings (South, Central, Northeast, & Highlands/Islands). Each tour includes directions, distances between recommended stops/highlights, and an approximation of drive time. Sidebars highlight special attractions to walkers, history buffs, families, etc. Excellent photographs and glossy stock make this a first-class planning guide and travel companion.

Accommodations

Brown, Karen and June. *Karen Brown's England, Wales & Scotland: Charming Hotels & Itineraries.* San Mateo, CA: Karen Brown's Guides, 1999 or latest revision. The subtitle of this volume really should be "Charming and *Unrelentingly Expensive Hotels.*" If your taste runs to the high-end, then these selections are right down your alley; Scotland has some of the most expensive hotels in the world.

Sawday, Alastair. *Alastair Sawday's Special Places to Stay in Britain.* Bristol, UK: Alastair Sawday Publishing, 1998, revised periodically. A selective book that celebrates "variety, individuality, good taste and high standards." The accent is on B & Bs, small hotels, and country inns. Each entry is pictured and described on a half-page, then located with good directions and a flag on regional maps in the front of the book. But watch out! Innkeepers pay to get into this book.

Visit Scotland (Scottish Tourist Board). *Where to Stay: Bed & Breakfast.* Revised annually. This and the following entry for hotels and guest houses combine a wealth of information on accommodations. The books divide the country into eight regions. Introduction explains the tourist board's rating and classification schemes. A location index is organized by town. Double bogie: no size, price, or star-rating indices.

Visit Scotland. *Where to Stay:Hotels and Guest Houses.* Revised annually. Visit Scotland also publishes self-catering and camping guides.

Golf

Bamberger, Michael. *To the Linksland: a Golfing Adventure.* NY: Penguin Books, 1992. Written by a Philadelphia sports reporter who spent a year as a caddie on the European professional tour. This is a hymn to the mystery and romance of golf in Scotland. A contemporary classic.

Browning, Robert. *A History of Golf: The Royal and Ancient Game.* NY: E.P. Dutton & Company, Inc., 1955. A veddy, veddy British (and delightful) look at the history of the great game from the longtime editor of Britain's *Golfing Magazine*, with lavish attention to arcane detail—all of course before the modern era ushered in by Palmer, Nicklaus, et. al.

Callander, Colin (ed.). *Golfing Gems: The Connoisseurs' Guide to Golf Courses in Scotland.* Laddingford, England: Beacon Books, 1997. A selective guide to the editor's favorite sixty courses in five regions of Scotland. Detailed descriptions of courses include color photos, the course card, rates, restrictions, and travel directions.

Campbell, Malcolm. *The Scottish Golf Book.* Edinburgh: Lomond Books, 1999. Probably the best-selling book ever produced on Scottish golf.

You see it everywhere in Scotland at phenomenally low prices for such a lavish production. Photographs by Glyn Satterley. Sketches, drawings, and historic photographs on virtually every page. Seven chapters cover the history of the game and its outstanding players, followed by detailed descriptions of 48 courses organized under three headings—historic courses, classic courses, and hidden gems. A parade of "most fearsome holes," a review of great events and memorable British Opens, and a chronology close out this great contribution to the bookshelf on Scottish golf.

Cornish, Geoffrey S. & Whitten, Ronald E. *The Architects of Golf: A Survey of Golf Course Design from Its Beginnings to the Present, with an Encyclopedic Listing of Golf Course Architects and Their Courses.* Rev. Ed. NY: HarperCollins Publishers, 1993. First published in 1981, the title says it all. The focus is heavy on the American side of the waters, but chapters 1-4 survey the origins of golf in Scotland and, most important, the relationships between the land and the evolution of the game. An encyclopedic listing of architects and their courses allows the traveler to identify the courses of, for example, James Braid and Tom Morris. An index by course name is helpful.

Dodson, James. *Final Rounds: A Father, a Son, the Golf Journey of a Lifetime.* New York: Bantam Books, 1996. This is a moving tribute to the life of a cancer-ridden father with only a few months to live. Someone once said, "Sports writing gets better as the ball gets smaller." Dodson's prose is exhibit #1; he is simply one of the best writers on the planet. This one will bring a tear to the eye, a lump to the throat, and joy to the heart.

Edmund, Nick (ed.) *Following the Fairways.* Northumberland, England: Kensington West Productions, Ltd., 1997. Comprehensive guide to UK golf courses. Informative thumbnail sketches of courses with contact information, fees, restrictions, and directions. Color photographs of signature holes and clubhouses. Schematics of many of the courses. Organized by region. Some inns and hotels in each region are listed in a "Where to Stay" section.

Finegan, James W. *Blasted Heaths and Blessed Greens: A Golfer's Pilgrimage to the Courses of Scotland.* New York: Simon & Schuster, 1996. This charming and informative volume is the result of twenty golf expeditions taken to Scotland since 1971. Finegan reviews some sixty courses in twelve chapters generally organized by proximity.

Careful course descriptions are augmented by the author's evocative portraits of surrounding towns and countryside. Until you go, this is "armchair travel" at its best (unfortunately out of print). Finegan has written a similar review of courses in Ireland.

Golf World (eds.). *Best Courses in Scotland.* London: Aurum Press, 2000. Editors at *Golf World* polled readers and compiled a list of 200 recommended courses and then rated them 1-star to 5-star. Lists on the first few pages feature the Top 20 Courses—"10 Best Values, 10 Most Difficult, 10 Most Efficient, and 10 Most Welcoming" courses. Course data with brief reader comment follows in a directory organized by region. Longer profiles go to the top few in each region.

Hamilton, David. *Golf: Scotland's Game.* Kilmacolm, Scotland: The Partick Press, 1998. A penetrating history from one of the most widely-quoted and respected contemporary students of the game. From primary sources, Hamilton develops a clear and persuasive argument that golf was (a) a winter game; (b) played in a "short" version and a "long" version; and (c) nurtured and organized in Scotland (not imported from Holland). Hamilton's prose is serviceable, if not particularly elegant, and his text is surrounded by oodles of fascinating illustrations and photos. This one's a "must have."

_____. *Scottish Golf Guide.* Edinburgh: Canongate Books, Ltd., 1995. Revised edition of a small book first printed in 1984. Brief descriptions of eighty-four courses are organized alphabetically. A forward by Sean Connery and essays on weather, dress, and the history of golf in Scotland round out the presentation.

Kroeger, Robert. *Complete Guide to the Golf Courses of Scotland.* Cincinnati, Ohio: Heritage Communications, 1992. A unique compilation by an American dentist/golf-nut, this book features useful advice for first-time travelers to Scotland. A listing with brief description of some four hundred courses follows the author's descriptive chapters. Kroeger's love for golf and for Scotland shines throughout, but the contact information is now useless. Order from the publisher at 11469 Lippelman Rd, Cincinnati OH 45242.

McGuire, Brenda and John. *Golf at the Water's Edge: Scotland's Seaside Links.* NY: Abbeville Press, 1997. A small book, lovingly produced, with sketches by John McGuire. Twenty-one courses are profiled. The watercolor renditions of course layouts are helpful and each short essay does a good job of capturing the history and character of the courses treated. An enjoyable if only moderately-useful volume.

Murphy, Michael. *Golf in the Kingdom.* New York: Viking, 1972. After playing a round of golf on a misty Scottish links, imagine yourself sitting in the clubhouse, looking out over the 18th hole, with a bowl of hot soup and a dram of local elixir, reading this cult classic—the top-selling golf book in publishing history. As you commune with Shivas Irons and contemplate the 'mystery of the hole' and the "whiteness of the ball," it just doesn't get any better than this. For literary diversion, this is still the best book to take along on your golf trip.

Pastime Publications. *Scotland: Home of Golf 2000.* Edinburgh: Pastime Publications, 1999. The best available directory of *all* courses in Scotland. After many years of trying, they finally got it right in 2000. The publisher finally created an *index* so that you can find what you're looking for! The publication is underwritten by advertisements from golf clubs, hoteliers, and others in the travel industry. Order from the publisher: 42 Raeburn Pl., Edinburgh EH4 1HL.

Tobert, Michael. *Pilgrims in the Rough: St. Andrews Beyond the 19th Hole.* A delightful perspective on the history of the town by a resident San Andrean. Parallels are drawn between the early pilgrims to St. Andrews and the modern "pilgrims" who flock to the links today.

Whyte, David J. *Golfer's Guide: Scotland - 150 Courses and Facilities.* London: New Holland Publishers, 2001. Part of the Globetrotter series, this book features dozens of stunning pictures taken by Scotland's leading golf photo-journalist. Organized by eight regions, short but informed course descriptions are augmented by an introductory essay on each region and two pages on food, lodging, and nongolf options.

INDEX

The Author

Allan McAllister Ferguson was born in Decatur, Illinois, in 1944. Sometime after that he developed an obsessive personality that led eventually to a fixation on golf in Scotland. He is retired from careers in politics, information science, and business. Mr. Ferguson is an above-average jazz guitarist with several CDs to his credit. During the 1980s, he and his wife, Ruth Wimmer, changed the look of commercial baby toys with their line of black and white developmental products still sold under the trade name, "Wimmer-Ferguson Child Products." Mr. Ferguson lives in Denver, Colorado, with his wife and a dog named Jezebel.